Books by Sara Davidson

Loose Change
Real Property

Published by POCKET BOOKS

REAL PROPERTY

SARA DAVIDSON

PUBLISHED BY POCKET BOOKS NEW YORK

For Kathy Komaroff Goodman,
and for Summer Sara Jennings

Portions of this book have appeared in the following magazines, and I am grateful to the editors: *Esquire, Harper's, Rolling Stone,* the *New York Times Book Review, Ms ,* and the *New York Times Magazine* "Baba Ram Dass" first appeared in *Ramparts,* copyright © 1973 by *Ramparts*

S D

POCKET BOOKS, a Simon & Schuster division of
GULF & WESTERN CORPORATION
1230 Avenue of the Americas, New York, N Y 10020

Published by arrangement with Doubleday and Company, Inc
Library of Congress Catalog Card Number: 79-55371

ISBN: 0-671-41269-8

First Pocket Books printing May, 1981

10 9 8 7 6 5 4 3 2 1

POCKET and colophon are trademarks of Simon & Schuster.

Printed in the U.S.A.

Contents

v

CONTENTS

1

Real Property

"What marijuana was to the Sixties,
Real estate was to the Seventies."
Ron Koslow

"Who is the rich man?" asks the Talmud. The question has never seemed more relevant. The answer of the sages is: "He who is satisfied with what he has."

I live in a house by the ocean with an outdoor Jacuzzi. I owned, until an embarrassing little accident, a pair of roller skates. I still own a volleyball, Frisbee, tennis racket, backpack, hiking boots, running shoes, a Mercedes 240 Diesel and a home burglar alarm system. But I cannot say that I am satisfied.

I live in Venice, California. Venice is the closest place to downtown Los Angeles where it is possible to live by the water. Because of the breezes, it is relatively free of smog. It is also the only place in Los Angeles where there is street life: you are guaranteed to see people outside their cars.

A boardwalk, an asphalt path called Ocean Front Walk, runs the length of the beach. Alongside the boardwalk is a bike path, and beside it, the sand and sea. On the other side of the boardwalk are crumbling houses, new apartments and condominiums packed tightly together. A real estate boom of such proportions has swept through here in the last five years that

3

anyone who bought the most miserable shack for thirty thousand dollars could sell it a few years later for a quarter of a million. And the boom goes on.

Living in Venice is like living in a camp for semi-demented adults. At every hour, day and night, there are people playing volleyball, running, rolling on skates, riding bikes, skateboards, surfboards, flying kites, drinking milk, eating quiche lorraine. Old people sit under umbrellas playing checkers. Body builders work out in a sandy pen, and crowds line up three deep to perform on the paddle tennis courts. When do these people work? I used to wonder.

The residents of Venice fall into two groups: those who work, and those who don't. The latter includes senior citizens, drifters, drug addicts, hopeful movie-makers and aging hippies and surfers who have made a cult of idleness and pleasure. The other group includes lawyers, dentists, real estate brokers, accountants. Many are workaholics, attached to their jobs as they are to nothing else. They work nights and week-ends, eat fast food while driving to and from their work and live alone, longing, in the silence before falling asleep, for connection.

Everyone comes together on the boardwalk. The natives own their own skates and the tourists rent them from places like "Cheapskates" and "United Skates of America." Those who have been at it a while can dance and twirl to music piped in their ears from radio headphones with antennae. The girls are dressed up in costumes like circus performers: sequined tube tops, feathers in their hair and leotards so skimpy that the nipples show and the cheeks of the buttocks hang out. The men wear shorts and vinyl racing jackets unzipped to the waist.

"Hey, that's radical," they call.

"Badass!"

Who are these people? Brown-skinned and lax, they sit around the floors of apartments, eating salads, walking out on balconies to smile and shake their towels. They are waging some kind of sexual competition through T-shirts and bumper stickers:

"I'm ripe—eat me."

"Sit on my face and I'll guess your weight."

"Skin divers do it deeper."

"Body builders pump harder."

"Plumbers have bigger tools."

"Worm fishermen have stiffer rods."

A high school cruising mentality prevails. A girl skates by wearing nothing but a body stocking and a silver g-string, but when two men stop and say, "That's some outfit. Where's the party?" her face turns to ice and she skates away.

Rolling, rolling. The wind is blowing, the palms are blowing and people are blowing every which way. I cannot walk on the boardwalk these days without feeling it in my stomach: something is wrong. There are too many people on wheels. The skaters will fall, the bikers will crash, they will fly out of control and there is nothing to hold onto.

I retreat to my house and remain indoors all weekend. This place is so odd, unique, and yet I see among the crowds on the boardwalk an exaggeration of common symptoms: the worship of wealth; the insatiable partying; the loss of commitment and ideals; the cult of the body; the wanderings of children in a sexual wilderness.

What does it mean, I ask myself, to be dressed as a strip tease artist on skates?

What does it mean to pay half a million dollars for a tacky, two-bedroom condo on the sand?

REAL PROPERTY

What does it mean that everyone I know is looking to make some kind of "killing"?

It means, I think, that we are in far deeper than we know.

In 1904, Abbot Kinney, who had made a fortune on Sweet Caporal cigarettes, traveled to Venice, Italy, and so loved what he saw that he conceived of building a replica in Southern California. Kinney raised the money to build canals, lagoons, bathhouses and bridges with fake Italian design, roller coasters and cottages with docks so people could visit each other by gondola. The idea caught on: "Venice of America" became a fashionable resort. Douglas Fairbanks and Mary Pickford, Charlie Chaplin and Paulette Goddard kept hideaways on Ocean Front Walk.

In time, the novelty wore off and the resort fell to seed. The canals turned stagnant and the unheated cottages became substandard housing for the poor. In the Sixties, Venice was the one place in Los Angeles where numbers of hippies and radicals lived. It was an outlaw gulch, a haven for draft resisters, struggling artists and drug addicts. At the same time, a real estate development was under way that threatened to permanently alter the character of Venice.

The new development was Marina del Rey, which means the King's Boat Basin. The Marina, just to the south of Venice, is a modern reworking of Abbot Kinney's dream. The Marina is the largest harbor for small pleasure boats in the world: a system of manmade channels and piers, on which there are restaurants, bars, discos, shops and acres of condominiums. The twenty-six streets leading to the oceanfront have nautical names from A to Z: Anchorage, Buccaneer, Catamaran, Driftwood, Eastwind, Fleet . . . When I first moved to Venice, I used to put myself to sleep by memorizing the streets in the Marina.

Once completed, the Marina became one of the fastest-appreciating real estate markets in Los Angeles. Everyone wanted to live by the sea and still be close to work. The Marina was especially popular with the newly divorced. It was a playland: almost every condo had a wet bar, a gas barbecue, a waterbed and a fireplace that sprang on at the push of a button. The tenants could use a community sauna, Jacuzzi, pool and gym. People filled their apartments with fish tanks and telescopes and oars and shells and hammocks and in the bathroom, stacks of flying magazines.

Those who could not afford the rents in the Marina began spilling over into Venice. Prices jumped overnight. Speculators bought up shacks, remodeled them and sold them for triple what they had paid. Plans were announced to "clean up the canals," and Venice became a "neighborhood in transition." The poor and the hippies who could not adjust were forced to move east.

I arrived in Venice in 1974, with my own dream. I wanted to do what Don Juan had advised Castaneda to do: erase personal history. I was a refugee from the East, from a tumultuous marriage and the revolutions of the Sixties. I wanted to begin life again in a place with good weather, a place where I could work, and I wanted to find, if such a creature existed, an unscarred man.

It was not long before I met such a person in Venice. His name was Bruce; he was twenty-six, and chief of research at a botanical laboratory. He loved his work but he also loved to be outdoors, to dance and listen to rock 'n' roll. Even his handwriting was happy—he drew little circles over his i's. He cooked and kept his house clean. He had no sexual problems. He had made love with his last girlfriend every day, "at least once," for four years, and he promised to do the same with me, "as long as we love each other."

Being with Bruce was like a happy retrogression to teen-age years. We drove around in his car with the top down, ate hamburgers and milk shakes, watched Kung Fu movies and spent all weekend at the beach. There was a volleyball net by Bruce's house and every weekend the same crowd appeared. The men reminded me of fraternity boys who had never grown up. They had their own businesses now, things like parking lots and vending machines, but they still drank beer and made jokes about fags and big boobs, jokes at which Bruce, to my relief, did not laugh.

The people on the beach played two-man volleyball—a different game entirely from the social volleyball I had played through the years. This volleyball was hard-core stuff. There were two people on a side, they played fast and savagely and were constantly diving in the sand. Bruce showed me the basic hits—bump, set and spike—but as a beginner, I could not keep up with their games. I was walking on the beach by myself one day when I spotted one of the regulars. This man was unforgettable: he had a head shaped like a pineapple. He must have been working out with weights, for the muscles on his arms and legs popped out and he even had small breasts. I told him, hopefully, how much I wanted to learn to play volleyball and how nice it would be if I could find someone who would play with me . . .

"You got a problem," he said in a dunce-like voice. "The good people want to play with other good people. What you should do is take a class."

"A volleyball class?"

"Yeah."

"Where am I supposed to find a volleyball class?"

"At the junior college."

Oh. I found out that Santa Monica College indeed had a volleyball class, and for the rest of the summer, my life had a wonderful rhythm. I would wake up, put on a pair of orange shorts that said "S.M.C.," drive to school and play volleyball. Then I would come home, work, go for a swim, work some more, run on the beach, work again, fix dinner with Bruce and go to sleep.

We were the only couple to reappear together at the volleyball net, week after week. The others were constantly shifting partners, and as one player said, five days with the same woman was "the same as five years." I thought Bruce and I were an island of sanity on this beach, but as the summer progressed, I began to understand why he was not scarred. He had very little compassion for people in trouble. "There's nothing in life that's worth being unhappy about," he used to say. "You choose to feel pain. You can choose, just as easily, not to feel it."

"What if someone dies?" I said.

"I wouldn't mind dying. And I wouldn't be sad if you died."

He did not want to hear about frustration. He did not want to know about writer's block. He did not think I should feel jealous if he dated other women, and he did not believe a relationship should be work.

"I think we do too much talking," he said.

"That's funny. I think we don't do enough."

In the fall, I went to New York and in my absence, Bruce took est and fell in love with one of the women at the volleyball net. When I returned, he told me it

9

was time for us to break up because there was "no more cheese in the relationship."

I moved to a different part of the beach. A month later, I ran into Bruce with still another woman, whom he introduced as "the love of my life."

So much for that dream.

My mother sells real estate in Los Angeles. So do my aunt and three of my mother's closest friends. This business has always been appealing to women because there are no prerequisites, except passing a test; you can start at any point in life; you can set your own hours; and you have the potential to earn far more than was possible for women, until recently, in other fields.

My sister and I grew up with an aversion to the words "real estate." It meant my mother was never around on Sunday because she was "sitting on a house." It meant violent swings in her mood and our fortunes. Often, she would dash out of the house on a moment's notice to show property, canceling a date to take us to the movies. We never knew if she would return in a terrible mood or exultant, "I made my deal!"

At seventeen, I left Los Angeles and did not return until I was thirty. During the interim years, I grew to have contempt for people who spent money on houses and furniture, expensive cars and first-class airline tickets. I thought it was more interesting and adventurous to travel second class, if not to hitchhike. I visited and wrote about communes where "free land" was the ideology. It sounded right: no one should be able to own the land, any more than people could own the sky or the sea. One of my friends refused to buy a country house offered to him at a very low price, because, he said, "Owning property is theft, and in any case, it would put us in the camp of the ruling class." Another friend gave away her fifty-thousand-dollar inheritance. She believed that God would provide.

My sister, after college, became a gym teacher and lived communally in the San Fernando Valley. She ate only vegetables, practiced yoga, made God's-eyes out of yarn and sticks and rode long distances to march in peace demonstrations. She found, very quickly, that she didn't like teaching—being in a position of authority over children. So she quit her job, sold all her belongings and bought a one-way ticket to the South Seas.

In 1978, my sister began selling real estate in Hawaii. Her guru was a Chinese broker who gave her a life plan: use the commissions you make on sales to acquire one piece of property a year for ten years; then sell half the properties, pay off the mortgages on the rest, retire and live off the income. In her study at home, in what used to be a sewing and pottery room, was a sign:

Y.C.S.A.S.O.Y.A.

"What does that mean?" I said.
"You can't sell anything sitting on your ass."
We spent half of our vacation time driving around Oahu, looking at homes. The irony was so overpowering that we did not speak about it.

My own interest in real estate had begun the year I moved to Venice. In the previous twelve months, I had moved nine times. I was recently divorced, writing a book and free to live anywhere. I tried Bridge-hampton, Santa Fe, Berkeley, Mill Valley, the Holly-wood Hills, until the cycle of searching for perfect places, packing, moving, unpacking, installing phones and setting up bank accounts became so cumulatively unbearable that I didn't care where I landed, so long as I didn't have to move again.

The way to ensure such rootedness, I thought, was to buy a house of my own. For a year, I walked up and down the lanes of Venice. I, who had always dis-paraged the acquisition of property, was spending days with a broker named Milt, who was twenty-six, had a coarse mustache and little higher education but a winner's instinct for beach real estate.

Everything we looked at was old, dark, cramped, in terrible condition and ridiculously expensive. The same houses, if not so close to the beach, would have been considered uninhabitable. I was about to give up when I went to see a two-story Victorian house, and the minute I stepped in the living room, my heart be-gan to race. Sunlight was pouring in through a wall of many-paned windows. The house had a Franklin stove, hardwood floors that needed refinishing, a large kitchen that needed remodeling, two primitive bath-rooms and three eccentric bedrooms. I looked at Milt and said, "I want it."

"Keep your pants on," he said.

We made an offer, which was rejected. We made another offer—also rejected. "We got no deal," Milt said. "I won't let you pay a dollar more. It's not worth it." For the next two days I was miserable. Every time I drove past the house I felt a stab of longing and regret. It was a year since I had broken up with Bruce, and I was involved with a ballet dancer named Tommy, who had little money himself but whose father owned casinos and land in Las Vegas. When Tommy saw what was happening, he sat me down and said: "Pay the owner what he wants. Next year, it'll be worth even more."

I instructed Milt to make a third offer, which was accepted. "I bought a house!" I told friends, but everyone except Tommy thought I was crazy.

My lawyer said, "I'd never pay so much for that piece of junk."

My mother said, "You lost your senses. You got so excited, you couldn't see." She began to call me every few hours with new objections. "How will you fit your bed in the bedroom? Why should you have to pay for the termite repairs? The seller should pay."

By the time the escrow papers arrived, my enthusiasm had reversed itself and I was in a panic. I was sinking my life savings into an old, broken down house half eaten by bugs, and I would have to rent out the upstairs to meet the payments. What if the real estate market fell through? What if the house needed massive repairs? How would it hold up in an earthquake? What if I couldn't find a tenant and couldn't pay the mortgage? Hadn't my parents seen their friends dispossessed in the Great Depression?

At night I lay in bed and shook. Tommy said I was having "buyer's remorse." So there was a name for it. I found that comforting. I knew the panic was unrealistic but I was helpless to stop it. More was at stake than the purchase of a house. It was a statement about myself.

"He used to be a radical leader. Now he's an actor in soap operas."

"She tried to burn down the Bank of America at Isla Vista. Now she's a vice president at Universal."

It is a cliché, a joke, something we are past feeling anguished about, but the fact is that a considerable number of people have passed through a door and come out wearing different clothes, and this transformation has taken place almost without comment. People who, in the flowering of the Sixties, gave their children names like Blackberry and Veda-Rama have changed them to Suzy and John. The parents are "getting our money trip together." If they are successful, they are buying homes, Calvin Klein suits and Porsches and sending their kids to private schools to avoid busing.

Not all have come through the door, of course. There are still groups of New Age people in places like Berkeley, Oregon, Hawaii and Vermont. They are still dedicated to social change, still wearing beards and flowing shawls, still holding symposiums where they talk about holistic health care, living closer to the earth and creating communities where people can love each other and share and cooperate. But their numbers are dwindling and few young recruits come along.

Those who have crossed the line cannot help but feel some irony and bafflement about "the people we've become." They retain an awareness, however faintly it is pulsing, that the acquisition of material wealth does not necessarily bring satisfaction, but that awareness is fading rapidly into unconsciousness.

On a Sunday in May, 1979, I am walking on the boardwalk in Venice with a friend, Andy, who is, in fact, a former radical student now an actor in soap operas. Andy lives next door with his girlfriend, Sue, who works as an accountant while Andy tries to find parts in television. In 1969, Andy had stood in the front lines, arms locked together with others who were occupying University Hall at Harvard. Today, he could pose for a life insurance ad, but ten years ago, he wore a mustache, a torn leather jacket and a headband over thick black hair that fell to his shoulder blades.

On that night in 1969, when police broke down the doors of University Hall with a battering ram, Andy was clubbed and carried off in a paddy wagon. The next day, head wrapped in bandages, he joined the strike that shut down the school. In June, his parents took time off from their jobs in Cocoa, Florida, to drive up North to see their son graduate from Harvard. But ten minutes into the ceremony, Andy walked out with about three hundred others, to protest the racist imperialist policies of Harvard University.

In the years that followed, Andy founded an alternative high school in the Roxbury ghetto, lived in a therapeutic community for chronic schizophrenics, worked on an organic farm, ran an assembly district for George McGovern and joined a commune of twelve who were sailing around the world.

Somewhere down the line he took an acting workshop, and decided to settle in Los Angeles. By stages, his appearance and then his values began to change. When I met him, in 1976, he was getting ready to break down and buy a suit—a custom-made suit from a tailor on Rodeo Drive, not from Good Will. He had decided he wanted to star in movies that would "alter the culture." He had also decided he wanted to be richly rewarded by the culture.

"Sometimes I lie in bed and think about how I've changed," Andy says. "I wouldn't want to live in, or even walk through a ghetto today. And I've become a racist about Arabs. Their oil money flooding in here is driving up the prices of everything—houses, gas.

Did we think we wouldn't have to worry about such things?"

I feel myself sinking. "I suppose our commitment wasn't that sincere."

Andy disagrees. "Mine was. I gave up years of my life working to make society better. Those were years I could have been earning money and advancing in a career."

We notice a commotion on the mall in front of the Venice Pavilion. The usual crowds are skating and wheeling, but in the center, twenty people are standing in a circle, holding signs. "Stop Nuclear Power." The leader of the group is on skates and has bloody knees. He starts a chant, "Hell no, we won't glow," but the voices barely carry over the roller disco music.

A lone TV cameraman is photographing the group. Some of the spectators are laughing and calling insults. "Smoke a joint, guys, and mellow out." I feel embarrassed, the demonstrators look so silly and ineffectual, and yet I know that this is how things begin.

Andy says, "What is the point, who are they reaching here?"

We turn and walk away in troubled silence.

I am invited to speak at colleges about the "Sixties in America" and the "Changing Roles of Women." I am not invited to places like Harvard and Yale. I go to Florida State University and Spokane Falls Community College. The staff in charge of scheduling speakers at these colleges are usually "Sixties people" who want to keep the flame alive. The main reason I accept the engagements is that they give me a chance to spend time with students. I have often thought that the spirit of an era is most clearly expressed by those in college at the time.

This particular generation, who were students in the Seventies, never managed to acquire an identity. No one figure, like the Beatles, Elvis Presley or Sinatra, emerged to galvanize and articulate their sensibility. No one was king, and no one was hanged in effigy. The students seemed too bland, even, to merit a name. At best, they were thought of as "the careerists," an ambitious, uninspired flock who trotted as quickly as they could down paths they hoped would lead to good jobs and success.

A speaker's visit to a college has a set choreography. I am met at the airport by two or three nervous undergraduates, who want to make a contact with the outside world. On the ride in, I cannot bear the twitchy silence, so I ask about their school. "What do students here talk about and think about?"

The question throws them—they are not used to anyone caring. One young woman in Florida says, after a moment of blankness, "Just themselves."

During the lecture, I try to paint a picture of what it was like to be young in the Sixties. If the speech works, the students sit rapt. They were born in 1960, or later, and the decade sounds as fantastical and remote to them as the Roaring Twenties did to me. After the speech, we go to a local restaurant, and the same students who were tongue-tied before are now impatient to give their opinions. Some feel frustrated at having been born too late. "We waited for our turn, and it never came," an eighteen-year-old in Boston said. She was angry at my generation for failing her. "How can you blame us for not running with the ball?" she said. "It's you who disappeared, left nothing behind and went into real estate."

A larger proportion of the students I met, however, responded with some variation of: "Yuk. Who'd want to do that?" A premed student at Wisconsin said, "I could never take off my clothes in public and pop pills, like you did at Woodstock." His friends agreed. "All that running in the street sounds ridiculous."

They said they were raised in a time of chaos and want order restored, They want assignments, reading lists, grades. What impressed me was that going to college these days is not a lot of fun. For one thing, it's hard financially. Everything is expensive—tuition, rent. Many have to work full time and, to conserve money, live at home.

From the moment they enroll as freshmen, they are pressured to make a career choice. They are told they must sacrifice their personal interests for "marketability." They must learn to think about what will "look good on the résumé." To change majors in midstream is disastrous—"You won't graduate in four years."

For women, there no longer seems to be the option of biding one's time until marriage. A student in California told me, "What I'd really like to do when I graduate is get married and have kids, but my sorority sisters would give me so much heat! They say you have to work or you have no identity." She gave a shrug. "So I'm applying to law school."

Of all the visits to colleges, the one I remember as most poignant and unsettling took place at a private co-ed school in Oregon. After the lecture, I went to a pizza restaurant with three women students and two women professors. The students sat on one side of the booth, the working women on the other. The three of us on one side were in our thirties, unattached and without children. One professor taught English, the other psychology. We were aware, and not entirely comfortable with the knowledge, that the students were looking at us, hoping to assay their own future.

The three students were attractive, graceful, obviously talented and hard-working. But they were worried they would not be able to find jobs. Pam, who had long red hair which she kept pushing behind her ears, said, "I'm afraid of not being able to make enough money to survive. I'm afraid of starving."

I tried to reassure her. "Nobody I know has ever come close to starving—not even free-lance writers."

"I realize that," Pam said. "But somehow it scares me. I've had to live on popcorn and pancakes because I've run out of grocery money."

The students talked about how much they wanted to be successful: to be paid well, rise to an important position in a corporation and have influence, prestige, power.

"Does love figure in this picture?" I asked.

Pam rested her chin in her hand. "I can't imagine that I would ever meet a man I would want to spend my life with. I think you would grow in different directions."

The three on my side of the table exchanged looks of surprise. Among us, we had been through five marriages and five divorces, and we still believed it would be possible to find a mate who would endure.

"What about children?" I asked the young women.

Rebecca, a brunette who wore oversized horn-rimmed glasses, said, "I'm afraid that if I have a child, my ambition will disappear. Somehow, magically, I'll be transformed into a woman like my mother—a housewife, trying at forty to figure out what she's doing with her life."

Lucy, the third student, said, "I'm not willing to give up years of my career for the sake of children. Men won't do it."

19

Once again, the three on my side were surprised. Deanne, the psychology professor, said, "I used to feel that way, but as I've gotten older, I realize the price I've paid for my independence. I feel deprived that I don't have a family. I see a whole generation of women I know getting stuck without children, and it's sad."

Pam twirled a strand of hair around her finger. "We may not feel that way." As the hours passed, I learned that all three students live alone—something the three of us would never have considered when we were in college. I asked about the young men they know. Pam: "The guys at this school have a lot of charm, but they're jocks. The women are more intellectual."

"Those types are not exactly made for each other," I said.

The young women laughed. "Yeah. The three of us are celibate."

"Don't you get lonely?" Deanne said.

Pam shook her head. "We have too much work."

The window of my study in Venice looks out on a building of single apartments. The average tenant stays six months, and I can tell where he or she is in the cycle by the state of the front yard. If there is a new resident in the building, the yard is full of young plants. They are carefully watered and begin to flower and then overnight everything turns brown. Weeds spring up, until the ground is so dry that nothing will grow on it and people throw beer cans and trash on the lot. The old tenants leave without saying good-by, and new ones arrive and begin to clean up. I watch them installing stereos, hanging wind chimes and putting out lawn furniture. Home at last: the good life by the beach.

One of the tenants this year was a man of thirty, Don, who taught phys. ed. in junior high school. After weeks of nodding to each other across the lane, we struck up an acquaintance. Sometimes we would sit on the beach together, or have a quick dinner on the Venice pier. Don was exceedingly attractive in a California way: blond hair, blue eyes, a pleasingly symmetrical if not terribly interesting face, and a body kept in wondrous shape. Every so often, preteen girls who had followed him home from school would tiptoe up to his door, ring the bell and, squealing with laughter, run away.

I liked to hear Don talk about teaching. He said the seventh-graders need to be disciplined, "or else it's *Lord of the Flies*. The kids are confused and can't keep things organized. They're always losing stuff. After a seventh-grade period, we have to go through the locker room and collect their junk in boxes." The eighth-graders, he said, are gaining confidence and want to test their limits. "They need to be smashed down." The ninth-graders "know what they can get away with, and you can actually teach them stuff."

A few months went by that I didn't see Don, until he appeared one Sunday night with a bottle of tequila. "I'm glad you were home," he said.

"Why?"

"I've been alone all week. I went skiing by myself. Every night I just sat and read, or daydreamed. I drove back today, and I thought I'd stop at Death Valley and take pictures of wild flowers, but there weren't any. So I came on in." He was staring at his lap. "I didn't want to be alone."

"I know what you mean."

"Do you?" He looked surprised.

I nodded.

"I'm in pain. Do you believe me?"

I realized, from the question, that people do not tend to take very seriously the pain of a blond gym teacher. "Yes," I said. "You want a close relationship with someone and you can't have it."

He let out a sigh.

I said, "It's been six months or so since I was close with anyone."

Don said, "It's been three or four years for me. And I have this fantasy—of having a home, a wife and kids. It's very strong. But it's not happening."

I said it seems puzzling: he's so attractive, warm and good humored. He meets and dates so many women.

He shrugged. "I could say the same about you."

Being unattached these days can be such a maddening business. You will have what feels to be the most intimate encounter: there is dazzling promise, blunt truth spoken, laughter and wonderful communication and you will never see the person again. Sometimes it lasts a few weeks, then one or the other calls in sick. I have observed the pattern in myself: infatuation turns suddenly and without warning to aversion. A friend said it comes over her in waves. "I hate the way he walks, the way he chews. I can't wait to be alone, but in a few days I'll get lonely again." It is nothing short of a disease, and those who have it tend to gravitate toward others with the same affliction.

On a weekend in July, I sat out by the lifeguard tower with Don, the gym teacher, and two of his friends. All three had been married and divorced, and every week, they would get together and recount their little disaster stories.

David, who is a doctor, described spending the

night with a woman who turned out to have silicone breasts. "When she lay down on her back, the breasts didn't move. They felt like silly putty. It stopped me cold, man. It was like making love to a goddamned lamp or something."

The others howled with laughter.

Don reported that a teacher he'd been dating had just told him she wouldn't be seeing him as often. She was starting a new job and giving first priority to her career. Don said, "I grew up thinking my wife would cook while I was out running the school district. It's sad to think I probably won't have kids now."

"What makes you so sure?" I said.

"Who's going to raise them?"

I said there must be women who would want to stay home with children, at least part of the time. But Don disagreed. "Women who are interested in raising kids are dogshit."

I looked at the other men. Was this serious? Allan, a lawyer with an Afro, did not seem to be listening.

"Hey Al," Don said. "Where are ya?"

Allan said he had been thinking about a woman he'd met at a dinner party. "At first I didn't think much of her, but as the evening progressed, she became more beautiful. She had a real nice smile, which turns me on. There was a gentleness about her. I liked her voice, and I liked what she was doing. I've been thinking about her all day."

"You gonna call her?" Don said.

Allan thought a moment. To my surprise, he said, "No."

"Why wouldn't you call her?" I said.

He tipped his head from side to side. "Just because I like someone doesn't mean I want to get into a scene."

23

I had a fleeting urge to have at him. What is wrong with these men? But David and Don seemed to empathize with their friend. David, the doctor, said, "You can't satisfy the women out there. No point trying. Anything you do will be criticized."

Once, while I was doing research for a film, I spent a day with David on his rounds at the hospital. He has a sensitive face, blue eyes and dark hair that looks black against the white doctor's coat. David treats very sick people—many are terminally ill—with kindness and concern. He is always overscheduled and yet remains cheerful. Every case requires him to make decisions that will prolong or curtail life. He works grueling shifts with no relief, and often goes home and falls asleep in his clothes with the lights on.

In his free time, he is adept at one-night stands. When we sat by the lifeguard tower, he described his operating procedure at singles bars. "The first thing is the preening—you've got to do everything you can to make yourself look great. Because it's real competitive. Make sure you smell good. Blow your hair dry. Your clothes should be casual but stylish."

"How long does it take you to get ready?" I said.

"About an hour. That includes shaving. I have to put in my contact lenses. Take a shower. Powder my balls."

"Come on."

"I have to—Johnson's baby powder—otherwise I get a rash from my bikini underwear."

When he leaves the house, he takes a leather shaving kit in which he has packed:

> razor
> contact lens solution
> K-Y jelly

aspirin
rubber ("in case the bubblehead
   forgot to take her pill")
address book

"You always go to her place, if you can. Then you control when you leave. You don't get stuck with her all weekend." He said the first moves in the bar are most important. "You have to feel the woman out, learn what her fantasies are. The best approach is to ask a lot of personal questions, without giving her a chance to know that much about you. Later her talk about her problems and nod understandingly. Because really, people love to talk about themselves."

Don said, "What if she starts to get upset about her problems?"

David: "At this point, it's a good idea to commiserate; either share, or manufacture some sort of similar experience."

"You're good at this, aren't you?" I said.

David: "I'm pretty good at being very understanding."

"Do you ever make it clear you just want to fuck?"

"Not really, no."

"Why?"

"It's never worked for me. My basic assumption is that women don't want one-night stands. They want an emotional experience. So I make her feel like she's the most fascinating and unique person I've ever met."

"What if she is a fascinating person," I said. "What do you do then?"

"Either fall in love. Or run."

Don and Allan started hooting and slapping their legs. "Run like hell!"

REAL PROPERTY

Now you rich people listen to me,
Weep and wail over the miseries
That are coming, coming up on you . . .
Your life here on earth has been filled
With luxury and pleasure,
You have made yourself fat
For the day of slaughter.

"Warning Warning," by Max Romeo

The only music I follow with any excitement these days is reggae from Jamaica. I cannot abide the monotony of disco, and I'm tired of listening to albums from the Sixties. Reggae music is alive; it has melody, wit, a hypnotic jungle beat and lyrics that burn with righteous fire.

Most reggae singers are Rastafarians—members of a mystic religion; they smoke ganja, worship Haile Selassie and believe that they are the lost Children of Israel who will one day return to Zion. On that day, the rich will eat each other alive and the blessed will survive. The Rastafarians sing about Jerusalem lost, and the temptations of dwelling in Babylon. The imagery seems relevant to me, and became even more relevant after I visited the actual Jerusalem in 1976.

In recent years, I have traveled to Israel so often that people have begun to think me odd. I keep returning for many reasons, one of which is that I find in Israel a sense of belonging to a family—the ancient family of Jews. To achieve this feeling in America, I would probably have to join a synagogue and come to some decision about observing the Orthodox laws. But in Israel, all one has to do is be present. Hebrew is spoken. Everywhere one is reminded of the biblical past. The week has a rhythm emanating from the Torah given to Moses at Sinai. On Friday afternoon, a quiet descends on the cities. Buses stop running, shops close. No newspaper comes out. Nobody works. Everyone, even the most irreligious person, has to be aware that the Sabbath has arrived and that this day will be different.

Life in Israel is in diametric contrast to life in Southern California. Israelis who are my age have fought and survived two wars. They still serve in the reserves. They know how to handle a gun, fix a jeep, find water in the desert and apply first aid to someone with a chest wound. Most of them were married in their early twenties, had at least two children and stayed married. To remain single after a certain age would make them an oddity.

In 1978, I spent a summer at Mishkenot Shaananim, a magnificent residence for artists and writers run by the city of Jerusalem. For two months, I did not hear a single remark about diet or jogging. I found great conversation—Israelis love to talk and laugh—about ideas, politics, history, "the conflict," music, art, books. But there was an absence of personal revelation.

I spent one Sabbath with a couple who lived in a farmhouse outside Jerusalem. The husband was German and the wife a sabra. Every Saturday, their closest friends would come by with their children to swim and eat a potluck meal. The day I was there, four couples sat around the table in the garden, eating roast chicken. I asked our hosts, the German and the Israeli, how they had met. The husband told a story, and I noticed that all other conversation at the table stopped. When the husband had finished, one of his friends said, "We never knew about that." For years, they had been going on trips and celebrating holidays and taking care of each other's children, and they had never asked one another how their marriages began.

Israel is beset with internal problems and in no way a paradise, but life there has an intensity and meaning, derived from having a common enemy and a sense of purpose in history. The most radical critics of the government will have no qualms about serving as officers in the reserves. There is no contradiction in being a left-wing pacifist and a soldier, because if people fight, it is to protect their homes and friends.

Israelis are reminded, almost daily, that human life is transient and relationships are not replaceable. Having a family becomes a matter of critical importance. I never ceased to be moved by the sight of muscular Israeli men playing with their children. One I knew, Gidon, was a commando in the navy and drove heavy machinery on his kibbutz. He had spent a year in New York, and told me he was puzzled by the attitude of people there. "All the men and women are interested only in their own careers," he said. "They don't want children." Gidon, who is twenty-eight, has two daughters and a newborn son. "Who says children take away your freedom? I have my family, and my work, and tell me, what is a career"—he held up his baby son—"compared to this?"

> Have a good tomorrow,
> Buy real estate today.
>
> —a billboard in Marina del Rey

Six months after I moved into my house in Venice— the house for which everyone thought I had paid too much—realtors began to knock on the door and ask if I wanted to sell. The longer I stayed, the more they

28

offered. After a year, the price of the house had doubled and after two years, I had earned more money just by living there than I had in my entire writing career.

It was phenomenal. The money was insurance for the future and I wanted more. I began looking in the Marina Peninsula at condominiums on the sand. My house was a short walk from the beach, but as Bruce Jay Friedman wrote about such homes: "It's either on the beach or it isn't . . . The fella who is 'a short jog away' is in the same boat as someone who has to be brought in by Concorde."

What I saw on the Marina Peninsula was shocking. The condominiums had been built with no concern for aesthetics or quality. They were like shoe boxes, long and narrow, with thin walls and sprayed acoustic ceilings aptly called "cottage cheese." The selling feature, of course, was that the front windows opened onto the surf. If you faced the ocean and forgot about the apartment, it was fine; but the apartments themselves were abysmal.

The price of one of these two-bedroom boxes was four hundred thousand dollars and up—the price you would pay for a nine-room house with a pool and tennis court in another part of the city. The realtors insisted, however, that the prices, outrageous as they were, would only go up. "Beach property is better than gold. They can mine more gold, but they're never going to make any more oceanfront."

I saw nothing that I would not have been embarrassed to own, and in any case I came to the conclusion that I could not afford to move. That is the Catch-22 about real estate: your house has gone up, but if you sell it, where are you going to live? If you buy another house, it will cost far more than what you received for your old house, the interest rate will be higher and you'll be stuck with a whopping overhead. So people tend to stay where they are and remodel. But they cannot stand being left out of the game, so they refinance their homes and use the cash to purchase income units, or join limited partnerships or get together with three friends and buy a house for speculation.

What has resulted is a feeding frenzy. Policemen, plumbers, film directors—everyone is making more in real estate than in the profession he was trained for. When a new "for sale" sign is posted on Pacific Avenue, cars screech to a halt. I am no less guilty than the others: I am tempted to quit work, cancel dates and run out if a broker calls to tell me about a "great deal." What is fueling this madness is anxiety about the future, and the wish for tangible security. Marriages may not last, political movements come and go, even money loses its value but the land gains. A woman I know, who recently quit her job as a public defender to become a realtor, put it this way: "I'm looking for something in real estate: freedom." The only problem with this kind of freedom, of course, is that you can never have enough.

> "I think there's going to have to be a reorientation of what people value in their lives."
>
> —Jimmy Carter,
> Camp David Summit, 1979

"I just made a major purchase," Andy told me on the phone. "Roller skates."

"You didn't."

"Ninety-five dollars." He laughed sheepishly.

"Now I can float along with the rest of the flakes."

Once Andy had succumbed, it was only weeks before I followed. I had seen beginning skaters hobbling along the bike path and falling into trash cans, but I figured they had never skated before. When I was eight, I had lived with a skate key around my neck, and had been particularly skilled at taking the steep driveways on our block. But a long time had elapsed since I was eight.

I rented a pair, laced them on, stood up and rolled away. Just like that. I could not do tricks but I could move right along. I thought I had discovered a new and delightful way to keep in shape, and promptly bought myself some Road Skates.

The next Saturday, Andy and I left our homes in the morning and rolled a mile down the bike path. Despite the claims we had heard that skating is good for the legs, I did not find it strenuous. Andy agreed, "I'm not even sweating." The sensation was more of dawdling: mindless, effortless. It was pleasant, with the surf shooting in the air and gulls flapping overhead. We decided to skate back to Venice and have lunch at the Meatless Mess Hall.

The crowds on Ocean Front Walk were thicker than I had ever seen. People were skating down slalom tracks made of beer cans. A man crashed into a tree. A girl on a bike hit a boy on a skateboard. Bums and shopping-cart people were rummaging through the trash cans. A woman in a powder blue Mercedes had ignored the "Motor Vehicles Prohibited" signs and pulled onto the boardwalk. The license plate on her car said, "Moist 1." A policeman was giving her a ticket. He wore his beach uniform: shorts, a holster with a .38 and a T-shirt that said "L.A.P.D."

I saw two women I knew from the movie business,

Sandy, a producer, and Lois, the token female vice president at a studio. Both are paid more than sixty thousand dollars a year. Sandy was wearing shorts, platform shoes and a blouse so low-cut that her breasts were spilling out. She said to me, "How's your life. Are you in love?"

"No, are you?"

"Are you kidding? I can't even get laid."

Lois said, "Forget it, you can't get laid in this town. I go to parties and take home phone numbers of women. I may have a guy for you, though, Sandy. He's an old friend."

"Yeah?"

"He's not that smart."

Sandy: "Can he move it in and out?"

Lois made a so-so gesture.

"Fuck it," Sandy said. "If this goes on much longer, I'll die of vaginal atrophy. Give me his number."

We said good-by, laughing, and I looked around for Andy. He was talking with a tall redhead, whom he introduced as Carl—"We used to be roommates at Harvard."

Carl was saying, "I'm playing the game of the Seventies: corporate executive."

Andy laughed. Carl explained that he had formed a production company and just finished shooting a movie for television.

"Great," Andy said, sounding not all that happy.

Carl: "I'm going to Cannes next week."

"That is fantastic," Andy said, but the word "Cannes" had struck him like a body blow.

Carl said, "Look, I spent ten years starving. Now I want to get even."

Andy: "I know the feeling."

Carl said, "Hey, let's have lunch. Keep in touch."

"Sure," Andy said. "And, uh . . . congratulations on your success."

As we began to skate away, I could tell Andy was upset. He was racing, making quick turns and plowing through people who were idly talking. I let him move ahead. Just before the Meatless Mess Hall, I saw a bump in the asphalt. I thought I could take it the way you take a wave in water skiing. I rolled up the rise but at the top, my skates continued flying upward instead of down the other side. Before I could think, my feet were in the air and my back hit the concrete, four feet down, smack! I blacked out for a second, and when I came to, I could feel the impact in my chest, head, teeth.

"Are you all right?" someone was asking.

"I don't know." I had no wind. I was afraid to move, afraid I had crippled myself. Was this dumb, I thought. What a price you're going to pay. Andy had to half-carry me home and drive me to the emergency room, but the x-rays showed nothing broken. I had bruised and badly swollen tissue, but with ice packs, followed by heat, I was told, I would recover.

For the next two weeks, I minced around painfully, unable to stand upright. I began to notice people on the boardwalk wearing casts on their arms and legs. One retired surfer on our block took a terrible spill and dislocated his shoulder. Still he went skating, wearing a brace. "Why?" I said. "Anytime you fall, you hit concrete." He shrugged. "What else is there to do?"

Every day, there was at least one call for an ambulance and somebody was carried off on a stretcher. Then in June, an eighty-six-year-old woman, Ann Gerber, was killed on the boardwalk when she was run over by a twenty-five-year-old bicyclist, who explained later, "She got in my way."

An emergency meeting was called of the Los Angeles City Council. On the boardwalk, it was war on wheels: shouting and pushing erupted between skaters and bicyclists and joggers and senior citizens over who had the right of way. The skaters had the numbers, and were gaining each day. People were skating to the bank, to the laundromat, to restaurants, to walk their dogs.

The City Council voted to ban skating on parts of the boardwalk, but people disobeyed.

"No skating on the boardwalk!"

"Up yours, ya jerk!"

A ninety-two-year-old woman struck a skater with her cane when he cut in front of her. "I'm living here twenty-five years," she shouted. "You should be ashamed."

I was driving home from the doctor's. I stopped at the light on Venice Boulevard and Pacific Avenue. A girl was waiting for the bus—an Oriental girl wearing a leopard skin bikini and thin high heels. She was carrying two electric guitars. Where could she be going on the bus? The light changed. As I started to move, a man who had a beard on one side of his face and was clean-shaven on the other, stepped off the curb. I hit the brakes. I nearly ran him over. You're going to have to be more alert, I thought. There are crazy people, and wouldn't it be terrible to hit someone. I saw a picture in my mind of the man lying under my car. If it had happened, if he was actually under the car, I thought, what should I do? Drive forward, or backward, or leave it there and try to jack it up? My thoughts drifted on, and soon it was time to pull into my carport.

The space is narrow, so I made a wide arc, glided through the turn and was coming to a stop when, clunkety clunk, I felt the car roll over something that sounded like a metal trash can. What was it? Why hadn't I seen it?

I stepped out of the car and got down on my knees. A man was lying under the car. A wino, flat on his back, dressed in a green plaid shirt and a woolen cap and brown shoes. I screamed. Should I drive forward, or backward . . . His legs were behind the rear wheels, extending out across the driveway. I had to have driven over his legs. I looked for blood.

"Are you all right?" My voice was high, like a shriek. "Did I hurt you?"

"No," he said fuzzily. He seemed to have been in a drunken sleep.

"You must be hurt."

"No I'm not."

"But my car . . ."

"Nahhh," he said in the slurred, combative manners of drunks. "If I was hurt, I'd know it."

He was struggling to raise himself. "I wanted to sit down here . . . think about shit."

Suddenly he jumped to his feet. I jumped back and screamed.

Andy, who had heard the commotion from next door, came running over.

The wino said, "What do you know goddamnit! I been in Venice longer 'n you. This is my home."

Andy said, sounding friendly, "You like it here, huh?"

"Yeah. I got shit on my mind, I wanna sit down, nobody's gonna stop me."

I said, "I'm just glad you weren't hurt. It scared the . . . life out of me."

The drunk swayed in my direction. "Awww, I'm sorry, miss, I didn't mean to bother you."

An urge to laugh came over me. This made the drunk laugh too.

"What's your name?" he said.

Pause. "Sharon," I lied.

"Okay, Sherry. Take it easy." He pulled his cap down and started to walk away, without apparent limp or pain.

"How could this be?" I said to Andy.

"I don't know."

"I must have driven over him."

"You did. I saw it from my window."

The drunk reached the corner, turned and disappeared. As I stood there, I realized that I was thirty-five and I was still waiting, expecting I would soon wake up from all of this.

1979

2

Last Days in Sinai

"The Jewish approach to life considers the man who has stopped going—who has a feeling of completion, of peace, of a great light from above bringing him to rest— to be someone who has lost his way."

Adin Steinsaltz
The Thirteen-petalled Rose

The sky erupted with lightning on the morning of March 26, 1979, the morning a peace treaty was signed between Israel and Egypt. Although it was spring in Jerusalem, hail poured in my window and pelted the floor. All day, there was tumult in the heavens: rain, then sunlight, then the crack of thunder and the whistling of winds that tore the purple blossoms off the Judas trees.

It was weather announcing the climax of a drama: the first agreement of peace between Arabs and Jews in the four-thousand-year history of the two nations. I had flown to Israel, eager to be present at this turning point, but there was to be no dancing in the streets. What most Israelis felt was loss and uncertainty. One man, an early settler who had fought in the War of Independence, said, "I should be happy, and I'm not and I don't know why."

Some complained that the peace process had dragged on so long that the signing was an anticlimax. Many were worried that the terms of the treaty could be "fatal" to Israel; that peace with Egypt would not last, and even if it did, "we still have Syria, Iran, Iraq, the P.L.O., terrorists . . ."

Only one Israeli I knew was happy, the novelist A. B. Yehoshua. "This *is* a historic moment," he said, "but people don't realize it yet. The treaty means normalization, and Jews have thrived on being abnormal, on being in conflict with everybody else."

What made peace so difficult was its price: relinquishing the Sinai Peninsula, a critical piece of real estate three times the size of Israel. The Sinai had given Israel a sense of having a cushion between itself and its largest enemy; also, the Sinai exerted a strange, inexplicable psychic hold on all those—and I was one of them—who had spent time in it.

A week after the treaty was signed, I set out on a comprehensive tour of the Sinai, my fourth trip to the region in less than three years. From the first, I had found it the most spectacular wilderness I had ever seen. It is an unusual desert of stark red mountains falling away to beaches, coral reefs and sea. But it was more than scenery that drew me to the region. The Sinai is the site of legends as old as the imagination of mankind. Every time I had been there, the Sinai had given me a link to those legends and through them, the Jewish past. It was in this desert that Moses and the Children of Israel wandered for forty years, until they could regain the Promised Land. It was here that the Ten Commandments were given to Moses; it was here that the Jews became a nation, and saw and heard the Divine. The desert is, in many ways, a metaphor for the Jewish heritage: vast, harsh, inspiring, trying, ultimately unknowable and sacred. As pleased as I was about peace, I felt some pain, knowing this might be the last time I would see the Sinai in Israeli hands.

My traveling companion for the first leg of the journey, Hirsh Goodman, had stronger feelings. Hirsh is thirty-two, the military correspondent for *The Jeru-salem Post*. He came to Israel from South Africa when he was seventeen. Within a year, he had to fight as a paratrooper in the Six-Day War; then he was married, had children, fought again in 1973, and is still an officer in the reserves.

Hirsh is a short man, but fit and strong, with dark hair and the most expressive brown eyes. He is an hour late to pick me up—I have been waiting on a corner—but before I can scold him, he jumps out of the car and shouts, "Where have you been? Let's go!"

We meet Hirsh's photographer and a military escort, then drive west from Tel Aviv and across the northern edge of Sinai. The northern half of the peninsula—which, apart from the Mediterranean coast, is a nightmarish waste—has been the site of more wars than any other territory on earth. Because it is a strategic bridge between Asia and Africa, it has been attacked and occupied by invading armies since the early Bronze Age.

As we approach El Arish, Hirsh points out trenches in the hills. "This was a major battlefield in the Six-Day War," he says. Most of the men in his brigade were eighteen. "None of us dreamed we'd live to be thirty. Even if Israel won the war, we were sure we'd have to fight another. In America, you were saying that people over thirty were useless. But to us, living to be thirty was fabulous—it was reaching the golden land."

The road passes orange groves and fields of date palms reaching to the sea. "You see a beautiful beach?" Hirsh says. I nod. "I get the smell of death in my nose." He describes the first time his troop went into battle. "It was a hundred and ten degrees, the wind was howling and everything was burning: flesh, tanks. Even the sand was burning. It was the first time we saw our friends dying. It was horrifying, but we didn't have time to think. We were running on pure adrenalin.''

When the firing was over, twelve hours later, they headed for the beach, hoping to jump in the water and rid themselves of the blood and stench. They raced up a sandy hill, but at the top, the troop of eighteen-year-olds stopped cold. The sea they had hoped to bathe in was full of corpses.

The asphalt road is now so hot that a tire ruptures. We stop in El Arish to have it repaired. El Arish is an Arab town, with donkeys and barefoot children in the dusty streets. Egyptian flags are flying over most of the houses, in preparation for the return of the town to Egypt. "Blessings on this new time!" the merchants greet each other. Sand is blowing in our eyes. Hirsh says, "I never fought for El Arish to be part of Israel. I just hope this isn't the last time I'll be able to drive down this road." The treaty calls for "open borders," but no one knows how freely Israelis will be able to travel in Sinai.

We leave the Mediterranean coast and drive south, into the heart of the northern plateau. The roads are restricted to the military here, and every few miles we must clear an army checkpoint. No one has ever lived in this part of Sinai except nomadic Bedouin, and armies.

A *hamsin* is blowing, raising the temperature unexpectedly to a hundred and five. The *hamsin* is a hot, poisonous wind that plagues the Middle East. It is theorized that a *hamsin* caused the darkness that lasted three days in Egypt just before the Exodus. During a *hamsin*, the air turns brown and viscous.

The wind is so loud that we cannot hear each other speak. The road is half buried under sand, and Hirsh warns that unless it is cleaned soon, the road will disappear.

It is hell we are driving through: monstrous sand dunes, littered with rotting carcasses of tanks, planes, helicopters, bombs, mines, grenades and the skeleton of an ammunition train. The Israeli army with its camps and airfields and underground bunkers and radar screens is like a pulsing, deadly, gray-green presence.

We emerge, twenty-four hours later, at the tip of Sinai, Sharm El-Sheikh. We blink and inhale. We have come from the graveyard into an earthly paradise. Brilliant red mountains give way to rolling sands, date palms, and a sultry turquoise sea so still you can hear the slap of a large fish as it jumps out of the water. Raffi Magnes, the photographer, says, "You can never capture what we see now in a photograph. Not with a wide angle lens, not with anything. Because what you feel is the vastness."

Hirsh says, "I'm sick. I can't give this up." In the past twelve years, he has come with his wife, children and friends at every opportunity to scuba dive and camp on the Sinai coast. "This place is a paradise for divers—the clearest water, the most abundant marine life in the world. It's become an important part of our lives. I don't want to own it, I just want to visit it freely, the way we do now. But if we have to wait months for visas, if the roads are not maintained, if we can't get clean water, if the gas stations won't operate, if the Egyptians limit our freedom of movement . . ."

His voice trails off.

"I'm sad, Raffi."

Raffi says, "What do you think of our treaty now?"

There is silence in the car. Hirsh says, "I'm behind it one hundred per cent."

"You are?"

He nods. "If it comes to a choice between my pleasure at diving and having to fight another war, I'll give up Sinai."

If the Sinai coast has had the strongest pull on Hirsh Goodman, it is Santa Katerina, in the remote mountains of southern Sinai, that has most affected me. After leaving Hirsh at Sharm El-Sheikh, I fly there.

The area is called "Santa" after Santa Katerina Monastery, a fortress-like retreat for Greek Orthodox monks built in the sixth century. Santa is believed to be the setting of key events in the Exodus story. On my first visit to the monastery, I am shown a raspberry bush—believed to be the actual burning bush through which God spoke to Moses. Above the monastery are red granite mountains, one of which is thought to be Mount Sinai, where Moses received the tablets. Below Mount Sinai is the er-Raha Valley, where six hundred thousand Israelites are thought to have camped while they waited for Moses to come down.

Before 1967, there was nothing at Santa but the monastery and the wilderness. When the Israelis came, they opened the area to the world. They built an airstrip, roads, an army base and a field school for the Society for the Protection of Nature in Israel. More than twenty young people have been living at the field school and guiding people through the mountains. The head of the school is Abraham Shaked, whom I met on my first trip to Sinai.

Shaked is a bearlike figure, thirty-one, with a fuzzy brown beard and glasses. He is thoughtful, generous, but difficult to know, not quick to reveal himself. He is called exclusively, even by his mother, Shaked, with the accent on the last syllable. When I arrive at Santa, he is preparing the field school for a reunion at Passover.

"This will be our last seder," he tells me. He has invited all the people who have worked at Santa to come with their parents, families and closest friends. Dorm rooms and tents are being set up, and extra Bedouin cooks have been hired.

Shaked seems stoical about the return of Santa to Egypt. "I knew we couldn't stay forever. I've always said I'm willing to give back all the territories, if it means peace." But he admits, "I can't really get it through my head that we're leaving. I'm like a cancer victim, hoping until the last minute that a cure is going to be found."

He invites me to join him and several friends on a jeep trip through undeveloped regions to the west. For the Israelis, it may be the last opportunity to visit this area. For me, it may also be the last chance to see something, learn something, find something residing in the Sinai mountains, although what that is I cannot say.

There are to be six of us: myself; Shaked; his girlfriend, Dorit; another couple— Ari and Yona, who met at Santa and were recently married; and Dado, a sixty-year-old Yemenite Jew, a member of a kibbutz, who is writing a study of the Bedouin.

We will be gone six days. We are taking only these provisions: a crate of tomatoes and onions, a sack of flour, a sack of rice and six jerry cans of water. "No worries," Shaked says with a smile. "Everything is planned." I learn, later, that we will be relying partly on the hospitality of Bedouin. In addition to the food, there are cans of gasoline, extra tires, tools, a medical kit and a shortwave radio for emergency. The gear is piled in the rear of the jeep and strapped down with ropes. Around 4 P.M., we are ready to set off.

Three ride in front, three in back; we rotate places but it is assumed that only the men will drive. Once we have left the er-Raha Valley, there are no roads. The jeep rolls right across sand, or over dry riverbeds called wadis. Those in front have a fine view, but in back, it's like being shut up in a covered wagon. The jeep has open sides, but an overhanging canvas top makes it impossible to see much, except what's at eye level.

"Try to sit like this," Dorit says. "I don't want to miss this beautiful wadi." She leans way out over the side, as if hiking out on a sailboat. I follow, but it becomes tiring and I sit back inside.

Dorit is ten years younger than I, but there is an easy understanding between us. She has an agreeable, natural beauty: a heart-shaped face, tawny skin and blue eyes set wide apart. Her parents are Hungarian. They met in Auschwitz and, after the war, went to Israel, where they married. "They never speak about the camp," Dorit says.

When she was twenty-two, Dorit lived in Australia, much of the time in an ashram of the child guru Maharaj-Ji. I have never lived in an ashram, but I have known that sense of euphoria when one feels lit from within, believing one has found a liberating truth. "Was blind but now I see." And I have known, as has Dorit, that point when the brightness falls, until it is spoken of only in the past tense. When Dorit reached such a point, she could not stay in the ashram. "Everything had been so wholehearted. I couldn't go on, feeling anything less."

Our resting place for the night is Bir Ikna, by the orchard of a Bedouin called Suleiman. The orchard, with its wells and fruit trees, rises up as a comfort station in the emptiness. Suleiman carries our supplies to his wife so she can cook rice for our supper.

The Israelis admire the Bedouin for their ability to survive in the desert, and for the tranquil, unhurried rhythm of their lives, but at first, I have difficulty understanding this admiration. The teeth of the Bedouin are rotting and caked with brown scum. The children's hair is wretched and filthy, and they don't swat away flies, so the insects cluster in the corners of their eyes. The women seem haunted, jumpy. "They are shy," Dado says. "They are afraid of outsiders, so they hide themselves."

The Israelis travel through the desert wearing as few clothes as possible—shorts, sandals and tank tops—but the Bedouin weigh themselves down with layers. The men wear long cotton gowns, called *gelabya*, and over them—even in the most extreme heat— wool jackets, cut like a man's suit jacket. No one knows the reason for the layers; one theory is that it prevents them from losing body water.

The Bedouin women wear robes of black, which absorbs the light. Their hair is braided and dressed with camel urine, then molded into a horn that stands up over the forehead. The face is covered, except for the eyes, with a *burga*, a black cloth adorned with bangles.

I watch as Dado plays with a group of Bedouin children. He is a happy sight, in his olive green cap and olive shirt buttoned across his large belly. Like the Pied Piper, he carries a bag filled with pencils, pads, Band-Aids, tape recorder, nuts and sweets. He has been roaming the Sinai, talking with Bedouin, for six years, and is now so trusted that he is even permitted to interview the women

Dado explains that when they are young, Bedouin girls take care of the goats. They leave the tent at first light, wandering at will after distant grasses, singing to the goats and throwing little stones, not returning until dark. This pastoral life is halted when the girl begins to menstruate. Her face, once left free, must be covered, and as soon as possible, she is married, usually to a relative. Her duty is to produce many children. She is no longer allowed to leave the tent except to fetch water, and is forbidden to speak with men outside her family.

The wife of Suleiman remains in her tent while the rest of us gather in the orchard. We lie in the sand, watching the mountains before us glow with paradisal light. At this time of evening, the desert is a wonderland. The air is perfumed with mint. A white camel stands, reaching up with its neck to feed on an acacia tree. Bells tinkle. Far up the wadi, Bedouin girls in long black veils seem to float like ghosts over the sand.

Our supper is brought to us: stacks of hot pita, a platter of rice and a bowl spilling over with fruit from the garden—pears, almonds, grapes, plums, apples, figs and dates. We eat with our fingers, and accept the ritual glasses of sugary tea. A wave of contentment flutters about our circle.

Dorit sighs. "It's like a dream. This is how I picture our ancestors living, when they were nomads. It's like walking back in time."

Five years ago, if someone had told me I would be tracing the path of my Semitic ancestors across the Middle East, I would have laughed. I had little interest in being Jewish, and no interest in Israel. I would have said, then, what many of my friends who are American Jews say now: it has no relevance to me.

Although I grew up in a Jewish neighborhood, I longed to disinherit myself—as was the pattern in the Sixties—from tradition, family, the past. Being Jewish was little more than an ethnic i.d. tag. It meant chicken soup and bagels, but it also meant nose jobs and vulgar bar mitzvahs and obsessive comparison shopping. As for the Jewish religion, the brand dispensed at our reform temple was diluted and bland. In seven years of "Sunday school," I don't remember anyone speaking about God. We were taught about anti-Semitism and the Holocaust and the need to be vigilant because it could happen again. But I don't remember any discussion of prayer or the inner experience of truth.

When I visited Orthodox synagogues, the very air seemed sour and chill. The Orthodox lived by archaic rules they had carried from the shtetl. On the high holy days, I was required to accompany my family to Reform services, which were inevitably boring. When I left home at seventeen, I wanted never to enter a temple again.

And yet I was a seeker, walking with a staff. There was a spirit in me that was restless, eager to travel any road if it might lead to truth or transformation. And there was another spirit that followed the first, quick to announce, "See! It didn't work, it didn't last." I would pan a little in different streams—psychedelic drugs, Hindu meditation, est, Tai-chi Chuan— but although I found much of value, I never stayed very long.

In 1976, I made an unplanned trip to Israel and came home wearing a Star of David. In Jerusalem, I had seen a variety and majesty to Judaism that I had never known existed. I met people who approached the tradition with searching intelligence, and were honest about the limits of their belief. What I saw was that Judaism offered rich metaphors which could be used to find one's inner light.

I also had the shock of physical recognition—seeing the gene pool from which I had come. The people on the streets were all Jews, but their faces and manners reflected the cultures where they had grown up. The British Jews were pasty and formal. The Russian Jews had bodies like whales. The French Jews were chic and birdlike. The Moroccan Jews resembled Arabs and had families of thirteen children, sleeping on the floor. The American Jews had a look all their own—lax and pampered. Yet beneath the patina, I could see the same facial features, the unmistakable Semitic archetypes.

Wherever they had wandered, the Jews had refused to bend, quit, mix in. Even those who did not believe in God had resisted, under pain of death, relinquishing this link. Why? Other civilizations fell into extinction, but the Jews not only clung to their culture in exile, they kept building, rooms upon rooms.

When I returned home, I enrolled in Hebrew classes. My friends were amused. "Don't worry," they told each other. "She got through Ram Dass. She'll get through this one too." I laughed with them, but set about planning to return to Israel for a longer stay. I would be a guest at Mishkenot Sha'ananim, a residence for writers and artists run by the city of Jerusalem. There I could study, absorb, read. But the plans had to be arranged a year in advance, and by the time they came due, I had moved on.

During that year, I had become immersed in Babylon: money, publishing, real estate. I could scarcely remember why I had wanted to live in Israel. So, I thought, was my interest in Judaism to be no different from the other trips? Was I doomed, by my very American-ness, to a pathetically short attention span?

I returned to Jerusalem, for no other reason than that I had made the plans. It was the season of peace, and I felt lost and alone. I made a stab at studying Hebrew intensively. For what? I fled from rabbis who wanted me to enter a yeshiva for penitents. I could not follow rules! I decided, operating not by reason but instinct, to return to the Sinai desert. I had been there before on camping trips, and it had never failed me. Surely, somewhere in the desert, I would be able to pick up the thread.

"Boker tov." Good morning, Shaked says, as he walks about our sleeping forms. It is 4:30 A.M. Suleiman has already made a fire, and by the time we are dressed, he has cooked a stack of pita.

We drive up into the Zaituna mountains and leave the jeep to hike. The first sun washes everything gold: sand, mountains, sky. I have always loved the desert, more than any other natural environment. I feel as if I could walk farther, climb higher, breathe more deeply. The starkness makes it possible to see details: a bright blue lizard; a single palm tree, fronds splayed in the breeze like a spider's legs. Sir Richard Burton wrote of a journey through the Sinai in the nineteenth century:

> In such a country, every slight modification of form or color rivets observation; the senses . . . prone to sleep over a confused mass of natural objects, act vigorously when excited by the capability of embracing each detail.

51

The wadis that run through the Sinai like veins are filled with plant life. As we hike, we pass thickets of camomile, sage, thyme, rosemary, mint and oregano. The air is so rich with fragrance that breathing is a delight: in and out, every step fills the head with spice and perfume.

After an hour, though, my feet become sore. I have not brought proper hiking boots, only sneakers, and I can feel the rocks beneath my soles. By 6 A.M., the sun is scorching. The Israelis have a sound they make: "*Ooo-wah*." Shaked trots back and forth, making sure that everyone is drinking enough. "You better drink three gallons of water a day," he says, "otherwise you could die of dehydration."

By 9 A.M., it is a hundred and twenty degrees. Every time I spot a sliver of shade, I move into it, pressing myself against the rock so that as much of my body as possible will be covered. I crouch there, panting, sweating. We have, by now, gone through all our canteens and we still have an hour's hike to the jeep. Shaked keeps checking the trees. "The palms are a sign there's water. Their roots don't go very deep." Sure enough, in a few yards he finds a well at the foot of a tree. There are wasps and garbage floating on the surface. No matter, we lower a rusty tin can and take turns drinking, then dousing our heads.

By eleven, we are back at the jeep, pouring water from the jerry cans down our throats, as if pouring water down a car radiator. Dado fixes me with a knowing smile. "You see, the desert is not romantic now. It is serious." I nod, dully. He points out camels, sitting with their noses pointed toward the sun so that their flanks—the broadest expanse of skin—will not be directly exposed. A baby camel sits in the shade of its mother. Black goats huddle under an acacia tree.

Dado says, "At this time of day, everything hides from the sun."

Ari: "Except crazy Jews."

We are lying on the floor of a Bedouin "guesthouse." The phrase is a euphemism. The guesthouse is a stone shed, smelling of sour goat's milk. On the floor are donkey turds and patches of black fur. "It is not four stars," Ari jokes. But we are grateful for the shade.

Ari, who is compiling a book on the Sinai, takes photographs and notes. He and Yona are never far apart. They whisper and kiss, leaning against each other in their matching kibbutz hats. Soon after this trip they are going to Berkeley so Ari can study for a Ph.D. in ecology.

While we wait out the heat, we talk about what will happen to the Sinai in the next few years. Shaked hopes to persuade the Egyptians to permit the guides at the field school to continue their work: conducting research, preparing maps and educating people about conservation.

Dado says, "Excuse me, you are naïve! The Egyptians will never agree."

Shaked says, "We can try."

Dado: "You don't know the Arabs as I do. It was a tragic mistake to sign the treaty. The Arabs are unstable, their governments can change overnight. If Sadat goes and someone like Khomeini of Iran comes to power, we could be wiped out in hours."

Dado belongs to the founding generation, for whom the memory of the Holocaust, when there was "no alternative," is still alive. The dream of this generation was to build not only a new country but a new type of Jew: tough, heroic people who would live with one hand on the sword, one hand on the plow.

I met a woman of this generation in Jerusalem. She had come to Palestine in 1938, when she was twenty. She camped in a mosquito-infested swamp, clearing rocks from the fields. She learned to ride a bike with no hands, and would pedal down the road, holding a book with one hand and smoking with the other. "The breeze was blowing through my hair and I was reciting poetry, hoping someone would see me," she remembers with a laugh. The work was hard, there was little to eat, but tangible progress could be seen each day. The field of rocks and malarial swamps turned into clear brown earth. Soon there were tractors, combines and the most advanced irrigation systems, while a few miles away, Arab farmers still worked their plots with hoes. I asked this woman if she ever had dark moments, wondering what would have happened if she had stayed in England. Had she done the right thing? What was it all for?

"No," she said. "In a word. I was a Jew, building the State of Israel."

The founders tried to implant this clarity of purpose in their children. Shaked describes how in school, "We were brainwashed to love Israel. We were taught that you can't trust anyone, no other country will help you, you have to do everything yourself, and you can do it better because you are *smarter*."

I ask if he's aware of the stereotype about Israelis: they're arrogant.

Ari says, "Of course. We were programmed to be proud."

From the first grades of school, the Israelis are taken on bus tours to learn about their land. Wherever you go in the country, you see groups of long-legged children, singing songs, equipped with canteens and colored hats and always escorted by soldiers. The children learn to cook out and sleep out. They are taught that the bravest and best among them will be chosen to be pilots and tank commanders. The Israelis have a privilege that other Jews through history did not have: the opportunity to take up arms to defend themselves. By fifteen, boys are eager to volunteer for fighting units. Dorit says her younger brother was heartbroken when he learned he could not be a pilot because he wears glasses.

After the wars of '67 and '73, however, many came home disabused of their illusions. Many did not come home. Dorit says, "When we graduated high school, we used to joke: 'See you in the graveyard.' But I can't tell you what a shock it was when our friends didn't return."

It was after the '67 War that Shaked came to the Sinai to take refuge. He had seen the rot in the floorboards of Sparta. Israel was a war machine gone mad, like the sorcerer's apprentice, shooting and marching, no longer certain why. He answered an ad for guides to work for the Society for the Protection of Nature. "I had never been to the Sinai, but it was love at first sight."

The Sinai was virgin wilderness then—no roads, no means of communication. "Every trip was an adventure. You never knew when you would arrive home." Shaked and other guides struggled to keep the Israeli government from bulldozing mountains and building gas stations, but it was a lonely fight. "Taming the wilderness was always the main goal of Zionism," Shaked says. "In school, we used to sing a song that went, 'We'll cover this land with a dress of cement.'"

Shaked has written a proposal, which he hopes to transmit to Egypt, that southern Sinai be made a nature reserve, "an international peace park."

Ari is pessimistic. "I don't think the idea of conservation exists in any Arab state."

"No matter," Shaked says. "This is not an Arab-Israeli problem. The wilderness belongs to everyone."

By the third day of our journey, my body is sore from riding in the jeep: endlessly bumping, banging, rolling, slamming. We drive and hike, drive and sleep, and I'm beginning to think that nothing more significant will happen on this trip.

Today we are heading for Umm Bugma. It is a ghost town, sitting on a black plateau overlooking the Gulf of Suez. The old road has been washed away by flash floods, but the Israelis are confident we can make it up the mountain in the jeep.

We start on the washed-out road and the jeep stalls. The fan belt has broken. There is no spare part and nowhere to obtain one. Shaked and Ari rummage through the tool kit and end up cutting a piece of rubber to improvise a new belt.

The road becomes worse as we climb, with gaps over twenty feet long. The drop-off is now so frightening that I can't bear to sit on the down-side of the jeep.

We come around a bend and see a boulder blocking the road. Ah, that's it, we're going to have to turn around now. But Ari has other plans. He wants to drive the jeep up the side of the mountain around the boulder. If the wheels should slip, he'll fall straight down the cliff. I suggest, "We don't really have to see Umm Bugma . . ." but Ari cuts me off. "Nothing is impossible."

Everyone starts gathering stones to lay a road—two parallel tracks for the jeep's wheels, with a gulf in between. It takes half an hour, the temperature a hundred and sixteen and the high sun producing a hellish glare. When the road is built, Shaked stations himself ahead to give directions. Ari, alone in the jeep, maneuvers onto the makeshift tracks. The jeep pitches back and forth, the radio antenna waving like some mad tail.

Rocks begin to slide away from under the wheels. I cover my mouth. What is the point of this? Another few yards and the left front wheel slips out altogether. "Give it gas!" Dado yells. The jeep jumps the gap, lurching through air until all four wheels land hard on the old road. We scream and cheer.

Exalted, the group climbs back in the jeep, and all the way to the top we never slow down. When obstacles appear, Shaked jumps out, runs ahead to heave aside a rock and jumps back in. The rest of us laugh and applaud.

Ari says, "Did you ever do this in America?"

"No."

"Now you see why Israelis are proud?"

At sunset, we sit on the edge of a cliff, happily eating watermelon we received from a Bedouin. A sign says, in Arabic and English, "Welcome to Umm Bugma." The sign is pocked with bullet holes. We toss the melon seeds into the canyon below, a canyon which, I'm told, the Children of Israel may have passed through on their way out of Egypt.

There are two theories about the course of the Israelites through the Sinai. The northern theory has them crossing the top of the peninsula to Kadesh Barnea. The southern theory—more commonly accepted—has them crossing the Great Bitter Lake, moving down the coast of Suez and across Wadi Firan to Santa Katerina.

Because they left nothing behind but footprints, there is no way to determine what route they took. The mountain now called Sinai was identified in the fourth century by the first Christian hermits who came to pray in caves in the desert. They made their identifications largely by intuition, but the labels were not challenged until 150 years ago. Since then, archaeologists have proposed a dozen theories about the site of the true Mount Sinai.

To me, the argument is irrelevant, for I see the mountain as a meditation point, a physical trigger that sets one re-imagining a magnificent legend. What strikes me about the Exodus story is that it is a parable of such extremes: miracles and disasters; leaps and falls. Above all, it is a story about faith.

According to biblical legend, the Jews, soon after the miraculous crossing of the Red Sea, wanted to return to Egypt. I can picture them: city dwellers, struggling through merciless heat with no food or water. God had to keep intervening to sustain them, first by creating a well that never ran dry, then by causing manna to fall.

Each time a new threat occurred, the people lost their faith completely. They forgot all the miracles and threatened to rebel against Moses. Then a new miracle released them and they regained their faith and gave thanks.

God waited three months after the departure from Egypt before revealing himself on Mount Sinai. During this time, he made the Children of Israel physically pure: the blind regained their sight; the deaf could speak; all those with diseases were healed. He made them morally pure as well, so the Torah—the sum total of Jewish wisdom—could be given to a healthy and prepared people.

No generation before or after has witnessed what this generation did. The entire tribe, not just one prophet but six hundred thousand together, heard the visible and saw the audible. It is said that the soul of every Jew who has lived or is yet to be born was present at Sinai.

On the morning of the revelation, the sky erupted with lightning. The mountains smoked and trumpets blared through the camp. When the Jews approached Mount Sinai, God lifted the mountain and held it over their heads, threatening to dump it on top of them if they did not accept the Torah. Angels descended and gave each person a crown and robe of purple. All of nature stood still: no bird sang; no animal lowed.

God spoke: *"Anokhi."* It is I.

The Israelites turned and ran for twelve miles. Weeping and quaking, they pleaded with Moses to be their intermediary with God, to receive the rest of the Torah. They could not take the direct flames, but they had become transfigured. They had never known a greater joy.

Now, here is where the extremes come into play. Forty days later, when Moses had not come down from heaven, where he was learning the Torah from God, the people imagined that Moses was dead. In their panic, they discounted the entire revelation on Mount Sinai. They decided their experience of the One Almighty God had been an illusion. They wanted a physical object to worship, like the idols carried by the Egyptians, and so, they built a calf of gold.

This lapse back to the worship of idols had more disastrous consequences for the Jews than anything else in their history. Every anguish that followed was a result of worshipping the golden calf. Moses pleaded with God to forgive the people, which he ultimately did, agreeing to deliver them to the Promised Land. But the Israelites lost their crowns of glory.

That the greatest sin came after the greatest exaltation—that is what I cannot cease thinking about. This pattern of extremes is seen in the secular history of the Jews as well: the Holocaust, followed by the birth of the State of Israel, after 1900 years of exile. The Israelis often joke that they have a manic-depressive country. "Why are we either so high or low?" After Sadat's visit to Jerusalem in 1977, there was delirium and dancing in the streets, but as the peace talks dragged on, the people crashed. "We conceded too much," they mourned. "We've jeopardized our security."

This same high-low cycle is a strong and perplexing current in me. I often feel as if I am a fish of the deep, who swims, from time to time, into a shaft of sunlight, continues swimming and finds himself in the dark. No matter how bright the light, the dark returns, and when it is dark, I believe it will always be dark.

I suppose it is for this that I find such sustenance in the Exodus story—seeing the paradigm enacted in mythic proportions. I am amused when I read that the Israelites, after asking Moses to be their intermediary, regretted their decision. They wanted to see the Divine presence once more.

Why? Moses asked.

Because, they said, what we heard directly from God is rooted in our hearts and we remember. What we learned from you, we forget.

Dorit and I are sitting on a cliff above Wadi Sahoo. It is night, and in the darkness below, the young men of the Chamayda Bedouin tribe are dancing in rows. The first line chants and claps, seven beats. The second line answers and claps, seven beats. The white-gowned figures ripple and sway, the song is raw and mesmerizing and we want it to go on forever.

A trio of masked women pass before us on their way to fetch water. Dorit says, "Their life is so simple. Sometimes I go and stay with them in the mountains. Then you can see how peaceful they really are."

"Do you think you could be happy as a Bedouin woman, completely subservient?"

She laughs. "No, we can't go back to that."

The women pass by again with their water bags. They notice us and stop, a Greek chorus in shrouds.

"Are you alone, Sara?" Dorit asks.

I think to tell her about the various relationships I keep myself in, but instead say, "Yes, basically. I'm alone."

Dorit: "That sounds good to me. I'll tell you, there's not much difference between Israeli men and Bedouin men."

At twenty-five Dorit is unusual, wanting to be alone in a society where the pressure is to marry young, have children and stay married. The towns of Israel look like baby hatcheries. On every street, there are masses of pregnant women, fathers pushing strollers and toddlers screaming, "*Ima!*" Mommy! In the founding generation, women fought to drive tractors, but in the second generation, most Israeli women have chosen to keep house and raise children. Women serve in the army but in clerical posts, never combat. Half the women in Israel do not complete grade school. Dorit says, "They're happy just to have a husband who's alive. If you have children here, that's all you have to do. You're a success."

I have heard many explanations for this, one being that in a country where people live with political uncertainty, terrorism and imminent war, there is a craving for stability and "normalcy" in private life.

While I was in Jerusalem, I had met a literary critic visiting from Harvard. Taking hold of my arm, he had said, "You've got to *do* something about the condition of Israeli women. They rarely speak, their job is to serve and clean up. It's appalling." But I had said to this professor: "I'm not sure I represent a better way."

Our final day is spent almost entirely in the jeep. In the hottest hours, between eleven and four, the light is shrieking like an air raid siren. Everything you see—mountains, trees, plants—has lost its color. There is nothing of interest, nothing of beauty. My head is full of rubbish: old wounds, fears are dug up like bones to be chewed on. This trip has been a washout. I shouldn't have come, I'm sorry I did and I'm sure they're sorry they asked me. Nothing has happened. Nothing but riding riding riding. Same pink rocks, same palm trees, same gardens with black rubber hoses snaking through the sand.

My nose is bleeding again from the dryness. When I wipe it, the blood is mixed with sand. The jeep raises clouds of sand and we are coated with gritty pink dust. We pass the canteen, but it's hard to drink while the jeep keeps bumping. Dorit says, "Can we stop and rest?"

Shaked: "Not yet, little girls."

I want to shout, "Don't you know how miserable it is back here! We can't even see, we might as well be driving through New Jersey." But shouting would be too much effort.

Shaked must sense my distress, for he tells me to sit up in front. I'm more comfortable there, but I start to see sheep, oversized sheep where I know there are only rocks. I close my eyes for relief, and nod off. "Pecking," the Israelis call it, describing the way the head will jerk and the mouth plop open.

"Okay, you can get out now." We have stopped, at last. "You better drink water," Shaked says, "and say hello to the sheik." What sheik? A lean brown figure, a limp handshake. I accept a pitcher of water, stumble over to a tree and faint.

At four, they wake me for food. Eating hot rice with our fingers revives us. There is a marvelous breeze, and not far away, I'm told, there is a place to shower—a camel watering trough.

We shoo the camels away and stand in their grungy trough, pulling up water in a goatskin bag and heaving it on each other. *"Ooo-wah!"* With the shower, all stickiness, sweat, odors and bad humors fall away. We are innocent and clean, like the desert regaining its color in the fading light. I want to walk through it, drink it all in. I'm not ready to end this journey now. I've passed through a barrier and want to go on. I've become accustomed to the riding, the sleeping on sand, the cooking on Bedouin fires, the drawing of water from wells.

During the final drive, I don' want to miss a detail, and concentrate to fix them in my mind. I lean out the side of the jeep for a better view. Suddenly Dorit disappears. "Girls, try to sit like this!"

She is perched on the side rail, her body completely outside the jeep, holding on with her hands to the top. In seconds, Yona and I are up with her. We have an unobstructed view of the sky turned fuchsia and the mountains taking fire in the setting sun. The wind blows in our faces and we are rushing through space, free.

"We don't need the boys anymore!" Dorit shouts.

The jeep begins to slow, and stops.

"*Yeladot!* Girls! You have to get down. It's too dangerous."

We stay in our places. Dado says wryly, "We cannot control them anymore."

I suggest a compromise. "Let us sit on top until the sun sets, and then we'll come down."

"No."

We tighten our hold on the top of the jeep.

"Okay, we'll stay right here then," the men say, and lie down in the sand. Dorit slips into the driver's seat and tries to start the motor. The men jump up and block the car. Shaked grabs the keys away from the ignition. That's it. The women have no choice but to concede.

Dorit says, "I told you Israeli men are like Bedouin men."

Ari says, "At least we're not impotent."

"You'll never get away with this in Berkeley," I tell him, but I have to laugh.

The air turns cool as we make the ascent to Santa Katerina. It is a shock, when we come into the er-Raha Valley, to hear the generator and see the electric lights burning in the field school. The valley is full of tourists. At the army base, a speaker is playing the Beatles' "Rocky Raccoon."

It is another shock to see a mirror. My hair looks gray, powdered with sand. My skin is dark and cracked, like the skin of the Bedouin. I stand in the shower for an hour, wash my hair twice, brush my teeth twice. When the six of us meet again in the courtyard, bathed and wearing fresh clothes, we are startled. We look like different people.

Before I return to Jerusalem, I want to climb Mount Sinai—perhaps for the last time—and sleep there alone. I wait all day for the heat to subside before starting, but end up waiting too long. Hiking fast, breathing hard, I make good time until just before dark, when I miss a turn and find that I'm not at all where I want to be. I had planned to sleep in the valley of Elijah—a little valley under the summit of Mount Sinai—but I've come upon a different valley, one I've never seen.

No time to go back and find the other trail. It will be dark in moments. I roll out my sleeping bag and lie down to catch my breath. I focus my attention on the sky. It's more quieting than looking at the black forms on the ground. I hear buzzing—mosquitoes? My lip swells up from a bite. I crawl inside the bag and cover my face with a Bedouin scarf.

These are not just any mosquitoes, they are venomous Middle Eastern mosquitoes, whose bites, during my first week in Israel, blew up into boils that festered and bled.

I hunker down and zip myself in completely. This is insane: I have come up the mountain of the revelation and am lying in a sack, recoiling from petty stings. Whatever possessed me? I keep my body curled tight, afraid to move around or make noise or in any way call attention to my presence. I don't know what else I'm likely to attract.

I think about a conversation I had in Jerusalem with a distinguished rabbi, Adin Steinsaltz, about the nature of the pilgrim's search. I had gone to see Steinsaltz because I had found his writing provocative and filled with respect for individuality. Steinsaltz, in his early forties, gives the appearance of a being of the air. His walk is a light-footed sashay, his hair is red and his eyes are blue and crinkle when he smiles. He was a physicist before he began rabbinic studies.

"I had a secular background myself," he said, "so I'm familiar with the process of transition. I'm not in love with the current 'return to Judaism,' the leap into orthodoxy, because it means you have to destroy yourself."

He said the word "faith" in Hebrew has two roots: truth and practice. "Faith is something you have to practice, you don't acquire it in a jump. It's like learning to swim. There is a time when you must leave the edge of the pool, but you don't swim perfectly at once. You have to practice. It is the same with belief. I don't think you can ever have absolute certainty, where you cease to doubt, suffer, wonder."

Listening to him, I had felt a relief; my own wavering was not, as I had feared, a deficiency that would keep me forever barred at the gates. Steinsaltz said that Judaism, unlike Eastern religions, pays little attention to tranquillity and peace of mind. "That could undermine your capacity to go on." He described the way of the faithful as an endless straining after a distant light. "At every rung of the ascent, you perceive mainly the remoteness, and because of the remoteness, there is always doubt. The higher you go, the greater the doubt. It is only when you pause on a summit and look back that you can see how far you've come."

I lift my head out of the bag. The clouds are showing pale pink edges. It is 5 A.M.—enough light now to gain my bearings. I scramble up the rocks and see, from the top, another valley, and directly behind it, Mount Sinai. I think about dashing over to it, but the spot where I am standing, the spot to which I have blindly scrambled, is a perfect spot to watch the sun rise.

Cheering bursts out from the direction of Mount Sinai. Visitors from all over the world have climbed three hours in darkness to witness this moment. Streaming down from the summit is a parade of nations: Swiss mountain climbers; Japanese youth groups; Greek priests in tall blue satin hats; Israeli soldiers; American nuns.

I start the descent by way of Santa Katerina Monastery, and halfway down reach a lookout point. To my right are black mountains, creased and curled like the surface of the brain. To my left are sharp red peaks. Behind me, the Mountain of Moses, and ahead, the er-Raha Valley, that vast, twinkling diamond of pink sand, outlined in blue mist. The symmetry of form and color is so overpowering as to be painful. I feel a fragility, a trembling, as if I were a tiny presence cupped in someone's hands.

I turn around slowly, and in the turning, I have a glimpse of the line of my own life. I see myself as a child, a girl, an independent woman, a mother, and on, the line continuing ahead through my children and their children, and behind, reaching all the way back to the Israelites who gathered in this valley.

It is rare that a Jew can trace his ancestry back more than three generations. Records were destroyed in the Holocaust, and names were changed again and again. A friend used to joke that this was why Jews are so nervous. "They don't have family trees."

We can never know the course our families took from ancient Palestine to Asia, back and forth in Europe and across to the New World. But we know that all threads, no matter how tangled, originated here.

The er-Raha Valley looks today almost exactly as it did to the Tribes of Israel. Their eyes saw the same mountains; drawing breath, they took in the fragrance of these same herbs. I can link myself to a chain—the long line of the race, with its ups and downs—in which is threaded the line of my life, with its ups and downs. And I wonder, Was it not for this connection that I came back to Sinai? Was I not in search of such hints, symbols, echoes of generations?

I hear a flute song, from high in the mountains. It is a plaintive, oriental tune. I look up and see a black goat, picking its way around the tip of a red peak. Other goats follow, until there are twenty. Then a Bedouin girl appears, in a long red dress and black veil. She is hopping barefoot from rock to rock, playing her flute. I am incredulous. The cliff is so sheer I would not attempt to climb it without ropes. She sits on a rock, dangles her legs and begins to sing, to no one but the air. She stands, twirls and laughs—like the sound of silverware cascading down stairs. I am in tears.

"Come down here," I call. She freezes, and seeks me out with her eyes. "Please? I'll give you anything if you'll just come closer." I know she cannot understand my words. She looks off toward the goats. She seems to list in my direction. There is a catch in my throat.

"*Quies?*" she calls, meaning "It is good?" The word is sounded like "quiet" with an "s."

"*Quies,*" I say.

The Bedouin girl laughs. She twirls again, and the sunlight plays on the bangles of her veil. Returning the flute to her lips, she begins a new song, and skips

away to find her goats. In seconds, there is nothing at
all to be seen on the red mountain.

The following day is *Pesach:* the Passover seder
celebrating the passage of the Israelites—and all of
us—from slavery to freedom. A full moon rises over
Mount Horeb. The mountains encircling the valley are
black, the sky is royal blue. A hundred people are
streaming to the field school: guides, archaeologists,
soldiers, relatives, friends, everyone wearing fresh
white.

The seder begins with Israeli folk songs. The lights
are turned off, and slides of the Sinai mountains are
shown while a man tells the story of the Exodus. At
first I am caught up in the singing, swaying and magic
of the images. But the second of four ceremonial cups
of wine brings on acute sadness: the sense of never
being able to return. I may, in fact, come back but it
will not be the same. Is it ever?

Shaked stands, and the room falls silent. "This
seder tonight is different from all other seders," he
says, "because on this night, peace is at the door.
Peace—a word we've dreamed about for so long, and
never imagined we would see. But in our hearts, there
is the fear that peace will mean the end of our work
and our life here."

All the people who have come to Sinai in the past
twelve years, he says, have one thing in common.
"Here, and not in forty years, but almost overnight,
they became free people. Because freedom is not a
flag or a country. Freedom is discovering an unknown
land, and moving through its vastness humbly."

The peace he hopes for, he says, "is a peace where
we'll be able to be here still, to keep climbing this

country's mountains and exploring its wadis and searching out its secrets that never end."

He proposes a fifth cup of wine. The bottles are passed.

"A glass of love," Shaked says, "and hope, and *shalom* . . ."

We raise our paper cups. "*Shalom*."

"To Sinai."

1979

3

Words

BUSTED IN VENICE

It was a warm spring night in 1976, and I was at my desk, trying to write a scene in which a woman has a breakdown. The work was not going well. I wanted to convey that state of raw, animal fear in which one jumps at the sound of a kettle boiling, dogs barking, but I could not seem to breathe feeling into the words.

I sat there, scratching phrases, crossing them out, twirling my hair, when I heard a sudden crash in the patio at the rear of my house. I looked at the clock: 12:45 A.M. I was alone, and the houses next to me were dark.

Thud, thud—it sounded like people were beating the walls of the house with sticks. Then I heard footsteps. My heart began to pound. I ran to the back door screaming, "Who is it!"

"Police."

I opened the door; before me were two men in plain clothes, carrying guns and high-powered flashlights. They had walked through my carport, pushed open a gate and entered a patio enclosed by a seven-foot fence. They asked if I had reported a burglary. I hadn't. They said a call had come from number eighty-five . . .

"This is fifty-eight. Eighty-five is down the way and across the street." I wanted them to leave quickly. I glanced to the left. The policemen swung their flashlights to the left. There, in a pool of chalky light, stood three marijuana plants, five feet tall.

"You're on private property," I said. "Don't you need a warrant?"

"No, not now. We're conducting an investigation of a felony."

I looked at the policemen. One had a sad hound's face, the other seemed like an overweight lifeguard, blond, heavy-chested, officious.

"Are these plants yours?" the sad hound asked.

"I, uh, no . . . a friend left them . . ."

"You alone here?"

"Yes. Please, can't you just forget about this? There's a burglary down the street."

The policemen caught each other's eyes.

The sad hound shook his head. "I don't think so. We couldn't turn our backs on something like this."

"I want to make a phone call," I said.

"You can make it from the station."

I asked if I could bring my work along.

"No."

Several of my neighbors had heard the noise and come to their windows. As they watched, the policemen handcuffed my arms behind my back. "Try to keep your hands still," the officious blond said. "If you move 'em, the cuffs will get tighter." We drove in a squad car to the Venice police station, then to the Van Nuys Women's House of Detention. I felt angry, foolish; I had been warned about growing the plants but I had felt invulnerable, behind my fences.

I worried about how much money this was going to cost to untangle. I was behind schedule on a book, and my income had fallen so low I was eligible for food stamps. In 1976, possession of less than an ounce of marijuana had been decriminalized in California. Anyone caught with a small amount was given a citation, like a traffic ticket, but cultivation was still a felony. It was absurd: you could have marijuana but you could not grow it, buy it or sell it.

At the Van Nuys jail, I was made to undress for a skin search. "Bend over and spread yourself. Now squat on your heels." I tried to think of it as calisthenics. In my clothes again, I was asked to sign a card having something to do with fingerprints.

"What am I signing exactly?" I said.

"You don't have to sign if you don't want to," the matron said.

"Okay, then I won't."

"That's great." She smirked and stamped "REFUSED" all over the card. "The judge will love that."

"Wait, you didn't explain . . . !"

She made a hush sign and took me away to be photographed. "How tall are you?" she asked. "I always wanted to be tall. Look at this chile," she said to a guard. "She could be a model."

I was put in a cell with a pay phone on the wall and told I had five minutes. I called a friend who was an entertainment lawyer. He arranged for bail—five thousand dollars—then called another friend to pick me up.

Six hours later I was home, but those six hours had destroyed all confidence I maintained that the ground beneath me was stationary. Unable to sleep, unable to work, sick with worry, I found myself in the very state I had been struggling earlier to put on paper: jumping at the sound of dogs barking.

I called several criminal lawyers, but the lowest fee I was quoted was eight hundred dollars. I did not have eight hundred dollars. Finally, a friend referred me to Paul Fitzgerald, an eccentric attorney who said he was in practice not for the money but for "the art form." Paul had defended people accused of crimes so heinous they seemed indefensible. He had been chief defense counsel for the Charles Manson family and, until 1973, had defended more multiple murderers than any other attorney in the state. The friend who referred me to Paul said, "You couldn't be in better hands."

Paul agreed to take my case for a nominal sum, and said the simplest solution was to move for "diversion"—a procedure by which first offenders are placed in a rehabilitation program instead of being tried. To qualify, I was sent for an interview with a probation officer, who filed the following report:

Appearing before the court on a first arrest for cultivation of marijuana is a 33-year-old free lance writer who is currently completing a novel on which she has almost exhausted funds advanced her. She denies any drug use, except for occasional marijuana which she smoked when she was in college. Defendant stated that the plants were grown simply out of curiosity. She has a large collection of plants, including vegetables and cactus, and stated a friend had given her some marijuana seeds. She feels that her growing the plants was "a big mistake." She states that she is "enormously upset" about her arrest and placement in jail, as well as the worry she has caused her parents. She continued relating that one of the worst parts was anxiety since her ar-

*rest, which led to being unable to sleep properly
and in sum she stated she felt her violation of the
law was "not worth it."*

A week later, I reported for "intake" at the Venice
Drug Coalition, a shabby storefront on Electric
Avenue, separated by streetcar tracks from the more
chic parts of Venice. The Electric Avenue neighborhood is made up largely of Chicanos and blacks. At
the V.D.C., as it is called, I was given an eight-page
questionnaire.

"What's the longest you've been clean on the
streets?"

"How many fights have you been in this year?"

"If you *had* to make a choice, which would you
choose: uppers or downers?" I considered this; obviously, either was the wrong answer. I went with the
truth—downers.

I was told I must attend group therapy twice a week
for six weeks. At the first session, I was the only
person who was white and not there to kick a serious
addiction. The group leader, Robert Jackson, had the
missionary zeal of a reformed junkie. He was tall, gre-
garious, opinionated, and possessed an earthy way of
making an adage his own: "We always think the grass
is greener when we drivin' by on the freeway. But if
you stop and go walk on it, there's yellow grass!"

There were seven in our group. The first to be questioned by Jackson was May, a heavy woman with
puffy lips and gray hair tied with a ribbon. She wore
a flowered sack dress and white slippers, and spoke
in a groggy voice. May was addicted to uppers; she
said she had been taking Dexedrine for twenty years,
and had cut down recently from twenty capsules a day

to eight. She had been hospitalized and given shock treatments, unsuccessfully. Despite the Dexedrine she slept all day.

"What are some things you like to do?" Jackson asked.

"Nothin'. I'm too tired to enjoy anythin'. I have a tired mind."

I thought of Peter Handke's line about his mother in "A Sorrow Beyond Dreams:" "Tired/Exhausted/Sick/Dying/Dead."

The man next to May had stolen a color TV set from his grandmother so he could "get down," then fallen asleep with a cigarette and burned down half his house, killing his cousin. He looked sullen, hopeless. Another man had just been "popped" for dealing heroin to minors; he had been on heroin himself since thirteen. He was on methadone presently, but having trouble "holding my mud."

Jackson came around the circle to me. "What's happenin' with you, baby?"

I shrugged.

"You just gonna sit here and observe us?"

"No, I mean . . . I grew some plants . . ."

"We know that's bullshit, we don' have to talk about that. But you gotta contribute somethin' or we gonna sit here all day. Ain't there nothin' in yo' life that's causin' you grief?"

What could I tell this group? I'm having writer's block? I wake up with fear and tremors when I realize I have to face the typewriter again?

When Jackson learned I was a writer, he sat upright in his folding chair. "That's it! Next week, you gonna bring us a piece of the book you're writin' and read it to the group."

I had never read my work to anyone, and was particularly sensitive about reading unfinished work. "Look at it this way," a friend said. "It's a test. If you can hold their interest, you've got it made."

It was a test I failed. I read a six-page excerpt, during which everyone nodded off and I kept hearing Jackson say, "Wake that brother up." Jackson, however, was pleased, and confided that he wrote poetry which he wanted me to read.

As the weeks passed, I almost grew to look forward to my trips to the V.D.C. I became involved in the stories of the people there and they in mine. After the group, the daily bouts I faced with words seemed, for a brief but blessed time, less formidable.

I still had to find a way to "contribute," so I began, in the remaining sessions, to talk about my relationships with men. This held their interest. Not only did they stay awake, they vied to give me advice. I told them I had recently fallen in love with a man who was married, someone I had known for many years. It was a situation in which I had promised myself I would never become involved. It was a violation of principles, and yet, once it had begun, I had difficulty stopping it. "I can't help thinking," I told the group, "being with this person makes me happy. How could something that makes me feel so good . . . be bad?"

A thin man with ravaged skin nodded understandingly. "That's what I used to say . . . about heroin."

1979

JOAN DIDION

Her office is a chamber in which to dream waking dreams. It is a small, spartan room where the curtains are always drawn. There are props and cue cards. While she worked on *A Book of Common Prayer*, a map of Central America hung on the wall. Set out on a table were postcards from Colombia, a newspaper photo of a janitor mopping up blood in a Caribbean hotel, books on tropical foliage and tropical medicine and a Viasa airlines schedule with "Maracaibo-Paris" circled in blue. "Maracaibo-Paris—I thought those were probably the perimeters of the book," Joan Didion said.

I have been making the drive for six years and it never seems shorter: forty miles up the Pacific Coast Highway to Trancas, where Joan lives with her husband, John Gregory Dunne, and their daughter Quintana. Once past Malibu the landscape changes. Wild mustard and cactus grow on the hills, and the oceanfront is no longer a protected bay, it is a seacoast.

I associate Joan Didion with the house in Trancas. The living room has a floor of large, square terra-cotta tiles, white brick walls, a redwood ceiling and a wall of glass doors looking out on the Pacific.

Joan enjoys "forms," and an evening in her home has a curve as carefully plotted as the narrative of one of her books. Orchids and oil lamps are placed about the room. Drinks are served by the fire. Joan wears a long dress, white thong sandals and a flower in her hair. Her sandals slapping on the tile, she walks to the kitchen where she completes preparations for dinner, consulting a menu written on a white pad:

> Artichokes Vinaigrette
> Roast Loin of Pork w/ Orange Sauce
> Corn Souffle
> Crème Caramel

On a Saturday in February, I drove to Trancas to conduct an interview with Joan, with some apprehension. She is not what one would call a virtuoso conversationalist. We taped four hours, of which she said later, "Two hours were pauses." As I set up the machine, John Dunne wandered into the living room wearing a blue bathrobe. "I got the Saturday jits," he said. "I got anxiety crawling over me."

He asked Joan, "Do you have any Coke? Then I'll disappear, so I don't answer all your questions for you."

She brought him a Coca-Cola. When John had returned to his study, we settled on the couch. Joan was wearing a light blue sweatshirt and faded jeans. Her reddish-blond hair was parted in the center. She smoked Pall Malls, or twisted a blue rubber band around her fingers, and at times her sentences trailed into a soft, rapid laughter.

JOAN. How are we going to go about this, in terms of talking naturally?

SARA. There are a lot of things I know that I'm going to ask anyway.

J. So we'll do it like a regular interview.

S. Yes, I even have a list of questions. I figured that was the only way, otherwise . . .

J. (Laughing) Otherwise we'd end up cooking.

S. I thought we'd talk first about the origins of *A Book of Common Prayer*.

J. In the spring of 1973, John and I went to Cartagena, Colombia, and the entire trip was like a hallucination, partly because I had a fever. It seemed to me extraordinary that North America had gone one way and South America had gone another and I couldn't understand why. I kept reading that they had more resources than we had, they had more of everything and yet they had gone another way.

S. How would you define the other way?

J. Obviously they're not industrialized, that's one way. Also, in North America, social tensions that arise tend to be undercut and co-opted quite soon, but in Latin America there does not seem to be any political machinery for delaying the revolution. Everything is thrown into bold relief. There is a collapsing of time. Everything is both older than you could ever know, and it started this morning.

S. Did you read García Márquez, *One Hundred Years of Solitude*?

J. Yes, yes, it's so wonderful. I was overcome by the book when I read it, but when I went down there, I realized the book was far more social realism than it was fantasy. The element which had seemed to me fantastic was quite reportorial.

S. Did you have a technical intention for this book?

J. Yes, I wrote it down on the map of Central America. "Surface like rainbow slick, shifting, fall, thrown away, iridescent." I wanted to do a deceptive surface that appeared to be one thing and turned color as you looked through it.

S. What about the repetitions of phrases?

J. It seemed constantly necessary to remind the reader to make certain connections. Technically it's almost a chant. You could read it as an attempt to cast a spell, or come to terms with certain contemporary demons. I can't think what those demons are at the moment but there's a range: flash politics, sexual adventurism.

S. What has been your experience with politics?

J. I never had faith that the answers to human problems lay in anything that could be called political. I thought the answers, if there were answers, lay someplace in man's soul. I have had an aversion to social action because it usually meant social regulation. It meant interference, rules, doing what other people wanted me to do.

The ethic I was raised in was specifically a Western frontier ethic. That means being left alone and leaving others alone. It is regarded by members of my family as the highest form of human endeavor.

S. Do you vote?

J. Once in a while. I'm hardly ever conscious of issues. I mean they seem to me like ripples on an ocean. In the life of the body politic, the actual movement is going on underneath and I am interested in what's going on underneath. What *Life* magazine used to call "the quality of life in our time" is determined not by who is in the White House but by economic forces.

The politics I personally want are anarchic. Throw out the laws. Tear it down. Start all over. That is very romantic because it presumes that left to their own devices, people would do good things for one another. I doubt that that's true. But I would like to believe it.

S. Do you feel identified with Charlotte and Grace in this book?

J. I think you identify with all your characters. They become your family, closer to you than anybody you know. They kind of move into the house and take over the furniture. It's one of the difficult things about writing a book and leading a normal social domestic life.

S. What is the effect of seeing people and getting a lot of stimulation?

J. It's quite destructive. Either you sit there and just close off, or if you do become engaged in what is going on with other people, then you have lost the thread. You've turned off the computer, and it is not for that period of time making the connections it ought to be making.

I really started thinking of my mind mechanically. I almost heard a steady humming if it was working all right, but if it stopped for a couple of days then it would take a while to get it back.

S. In "Why I Write" [a lecture delivered at the University of California at Berkeley], there's a confidence expressed about the process of writing that I know you don't always feel.

J. I didn't express confidence so much as blind faith that if you go in and work every day, it will get better. Three days will go by and you will be in that office and you will think every day is terrible. But on the fourth day, if you do go in, if you don't go into town or out in the garden, something usually will break through.

S. How do you feel when you wake up?

J. Oh, I don't want to go in there at all. It's low dread, every morning. That dread goes away after you've been in there an hour. I keep saying "in there" as if it's some kind of chamber, a different atmosphere. It is in a way. There's almost a psychic wall. The air changes, I mean you don't want to go through that door. But once you're in there, you're there and it's hard to go out.

S. I'd always assumed that after you'd been writing for a number of years, that fear would disappear.

J. No, it doesn't. It's a fear you're not going to get it right. You're going to ruin it. You're going to fail.

The touchy part on a book—when there's not the dread in the morning, when there's the dread all day long—is before it takes. Once it takes, there's just the morning dread and the occasional three days of terrible stuff, but before it takes, there's nothing to guarantee that it's going to take.

There's a point in a novel where it shifts gears or the narrative won't carry. That point has to come before a third of the way through. It goes into overdrive. There are some novels you pick up and start reading and they're wonderful. Maybe you have to go to lunch or something and you get to page seventy and never pick them up again. You're not moved to keep turning pages. That's the narrative curve, you've got to allow, around page seventy or eighty, to give it enough thrust to send it out.

Imagine a rocket taking off. There's a point at which it drops its glitter or glamour and starts floating free.

S. How do you feel about a book while you're writing it?

J. I try to hold my opinion in suspension. I hate the book when I'm working on it. But if I gave way to that thought, I would never finish the book and then I would feel depressed and useless and have nothing to do all day.

S. Have you ever not finished a book?

J. I've put things aside at forty pages.

S. Did you get depressed?

J. Yes. There's a certain euphoric mania at first when you think you've made the right decision and are really taking charge, but it sort of lies there as something you haven't finished. And you always wonder if maybe you had pushed a little harder, it might have broken through. I mean it's a failure. So starting anything, there's a great chance for psychic loss.

S. How did you feel after finishing *A Book of Common Prayer*?

J. I was tired, so tired. I didn't want to read it. I haven't read it. I like it, though, in an abstract way. It's like a dream again.

S. I take it success and failure are important issues for you?

J. Yes, I suppose they are. I don't want to do anything that I don't do well. I don't want to ski. (She laughs)

S. What about tennis?

J. I do play tennis, not well, but I've moved into thinking of it as a way of getting color on my face and mild exercise, not as playing tennis. I haven't learned to serve yet. Every once in a while my teacher brings it up, but it takes too much coordination. He brought it up again last week and I was on the verge of tears. I was furious, because I was really hitting the ball across the net pretty well.

S. Could you talk about your writing method?

J. When I started this book, I wrote the first paragraph and continued for about three pages. Then I got scared and started skipping around and writing odd things.

S. What did you get scared of?

J. Scared I couldn't sustain it. So I started writing odd bits here and there, and then I stopped being so scared, when I had a pile of little things that appeared to be in the same tone as the beginning of the book. I just went back and started writing straight through until about page forty. By then the book was taking a slightly different direction. It was clear there was a narrator, for example. I had not intended there to be a narrator. I was going to be the female author's voice. I the author was going to tell you the reader the story. But the "I" became so strong that it became a character, so I went back and rewrote those forty pages with that narrator.

As the story developed, things kept changing, and you can push ahead for a little while knowing that those things are wrong back there but you can't push too far or you lose precision. It doesn't matter to you as much, if you know it's wrong back there, so I started over again. I started over about twelve times. I wanted to start over when I went to Sacramento to finish it, but I didn't have time.

S. You always go to Sacramento to finish your books. Is that a ritual?

J. It's very easy for me to work there. My concentration can be total because nobody calls me. I'm not required to lead a real life. I'm like a child, in my parents' house.

S. Do you have a room there?

J. Yes. It's sort of a carnation pink, and the vines and trees have grown up over the windows. It's exactly like a cave. It's a very safe place. It's a good room to work in, it's a finishing room.

I once tried working in John's office here and I was beside myself. There were too many books. I mean there was this weight of other people's opinions

87

around me. I worked in the Faculty Club in Berkeley for a month and it was very hard to work there because I didn't have the map of Central America. Not that Boca Grande is on the map, but the map took on a real life in my mind. I mean that very narrow isthmus.

One of the things that worried me about this book was that there were several kinds of weather. It took place in San Francisco, the American South and Central America. This sounds silly but I was afraid that the narrative wouldn't carry if the weather changed. You wouldn't walk away from the book remembering one thing. The thing I wanted you to walk away remembering was the Central American weather. So all the things I had around my office had to do with Central America.

S. Where did you get the title?

J. It seemed right. *A Book of Common Prayer* was very important to this book. Why, I had no idea. At one point, my editor, Henry Robbins, asked what the title meant. I made up some specious thing and told him, I don't remember what I told him, something to the effect that the whole thing was a prayer. You could say that this was Grace's prayer for Charlotte's soul.

If you have a narrator, which suddenly I was stuck with, the narrator can't just be telling you a story, something that happened, to entertain you. The narrator has got to be telling you the story for a reason. I think the title probably helped me with that.

S. Are you as skeptical about religion as you are about politics?

J. I am quite religious in a certain way. I was brought up Episcopalian, and I stopped going to church because I hated the stories. You know the story about the Prodigal Son? I have never understood that story. I have never understood why the prodigal son should be treated any better than the other son. I have missed the point of a lot of parables. I have much too literal and practical a mind, they just don't appeal to me, they irritate me.

But I like the words of the Episcopal service and I say them over and over in my mind. There's one particular phrase which is part of every service: "As it was in the beginning, is now, and ever shall be, world without end. Amen." It's a very comforting phrase to a child. And to an adult.

I have a very rigid sense of right and wrong. What I mean is I use the words all the time. Even the smallest things. A table can be right or wrong.

S. What about behavior?

J. Behavior is right or wrong. I was once having dinner with a psychiatrist who told me that I had monocular vision, and there was no need for everything to be right or wrong. Well, that way lies madness. In order to maintain a semblance of purposeful behavior on this earth, you have to believe that things are right or wrong.

S. What authors have influenced you?

J. As far as influence on a style goes, I don't think you're influenced by anybody you read after age twenty. That all happens before you start working yourself. You would never know it from reading me, but I was very influenced by Hemingway when I was thirteen, fourteen, fifteen. I learned a lot about how sentences worked. How a short sentence worked in a paragraph, how a long sentence worked. Where the commas worked. How every word had to matter. It made me excited about words. Conrad, for the same reasons. The sentences sounded wonderful. I remember being so excited once when I discovered that the key lines in *Heart of Darkness* were in parentheses.

James, whom I didn't read until I was in college, was important to me in trying to come to terms with the impossibility of getting it right. James' sentences with all those clauses had to do with keeping the options open, letting the sentence cover as much as it could. That impressed me a great deal.

S. What determines what you read now?

J. When I'm working, I don't read much. If it's a good book, it will depress me because mine isn't as good. If it's a bad book it will depress me because mine's just as bad.

I don't want anybody else's speech rhythms in my dream. I never read *Ragtime*. I opened the first page and saw it had a very strong rhythm, so I just put it away like a snake.

S. There's a certain aesthetic to the way you live. You once talked about using good silver every day.

J. Well, every day is all there is.

S. Do you admire elegance?

J. Yes, because it makes you feel better. It's a form. I'm very attached to certain forms, little compulsive rituals. I like to cook, I like to sew. They're peaceful things, and they're an expression of caring.

S. Could you talk about what you refer to as your shyness?

J. I'm not particularly sociable. I like a lot of people and I'm glad to see them, but I don't give the impression of being there. Part of it is that I'm terribly inarticulate. A sentence doesn't occur to me as a whole thing unless I'm working.

S. Isn't it a surprise to people who read you and expect the same fluency in your conversation?

J. I don't know what they expect but they certainly

don't get it. (Laughs) I don't know why, and I don't know what I can do about it and it is easier for me to just write it off and try to do better at what I do well.

S. I once asked if you liked living in Trancas and you said you found it a hostile environment.

J. The only really benign climate I've ever been in is Hawaii. All other climates strike me as hostile.

S. What makes Hawaii benign and Cartagena, Colombia, not?

J. In the Caribbean, there is rot, real rot. Hawaii is a tropic without rot.

S. Are you sure?

J. Well, there's mildew. The place just strikes me as benign. It is sweet, it smells pink to me, it smells like flowers. It is a pink environment and it makes me feel good. This is an arid environment. This is a desert. There's cactus growing across the highway. If the cactus started on that slope going down to the ocean— I think about it all the time, about the cactus coming across the Pacific Coast Highway and starting on that slope. I would really be upset. So far we do not have cactus on that slope. I don't like the desert. I don't like dryness, I like everything to be wet.

S. What was your fantasy about owning land in Nevada?

J. It was the last place where you could have enough land so that as far as you could see, you owned it. It was relatively cheap. Land in southern Nevada was selling as recently as five years ago for three dollars an acre, in nine-hundred-thousand-acre pieces. Obviously you couldn't grow anything on it, you couldn't graze on it, but as far as you could see, it was yours. Nobody else could come on it.

S. What would you do on it?

J. Just look out. (Laughs)

S. Is it important for you to live near the ocean?

J. I don't think so. I like the horizon out there, I like the flatness, which is the same flatness you get if you're looking out on nine hundred thousand acres in southern Nevada. There's a straight line across there and it's easy to keep your bearings. But I hardly ever go down to the beach.

S. Why?

J. Well, usually I'm working.

S. Is John your editor?

J. Yes, we edit each other. A lot of people wonder how we can edit each other and live together, but it works out very well. We trust each other. Sometimes we don't agree. Obviously you never want to agree when somebody tells you something doesn't work. I don't mean that kind of not agreeing. That's just when you're tired and it's midnight. I mean, sometimes, even on reflection, we don't agree, and there is a tacit understanding that neither of us will push too far. Each of us is aware that it would be easy to impose our sensibility, particularly our own style, on each other. And so there is a tacit agreement not to push beyond saying, "It doesn't work. This is how to fix it." If there is still a substantive disagreement, it's never mentioned again.

S. Are you more interested in writing fiction these days than nonfiction?

J. I'm trying to do a nonfiction book now. I have always sort of wanted to write a book about California water. I'm interested in water, the pipes that water goes through, the mechanics of getting the water from place to place. I could look at a flume all day. I love dams, the way they are almost makes me weak, it's so beautiful.

There's a thing they do on the water project that I

would like so much to see, that I've never had any reason to set up an appointment and go see. Farmers, say, in the Imperial Valley, order their water ahead. You have to put in your order the week or the night before, and then there's a ditch rider who goes down the ditch and opens the valves to each ranch, and lets a certain amount of water go through. Technically that interests me. I don't know what I could do with it. Maybe I would like to be the person who opens the valves and lets the water through. Because it interests me and all I know how to do is write, I have thought about writing a book about California water, but I have mentioned it to a few people in New York and they have not been terribly interested.

S. You could have chosen to live anywhere, New York, the South. Did you pick Los Angeles because you think it's interesting?

J. I love it here. It has a kind of energy I like and a kind of inertia I like. It's a very good place to work. The weather's all right, and the place is neutral, it has for me no social overtones whatsoever.

S. Do you like to drive?

J. No, I can't stand it. I hardly ever drive. People are always calling me up for a quote on the freeways. I could probably number on both hands the times I've driven freeways. I can only enter a freeway if it's at the beginning, I can't enter it at a normal entrance or I freeze, like a child at the top of a slide. Freeways are so tricky for me that I am obsessed by them. When I've driven one, I think I've really flown the Atlantic, gone to the moon, and I replay it in my mind: exactly what lane I was in and where the crossover was. The two pages about the freeway in *Play It as It Lays* came out of that obsession.

S. Are you intrigued with the movie community?

J. It interests me as an industry, you can watch it working. I like following the moves of the particular game. I like movie people. If I lived in Detroit, I would want to see automotive people. I would want to know what the moves were.

S. Why do you write for movies?

J. One reason, obviously, is for the money. It's specious to say you could make the same amount of money writing a book. You can't write a book every year, but you have to keep on living every year. A lot of writers support themselves by teaching and lecturing. I don't like to do that. It uses up far more energy.

S. What about the frustrations—deals falling through?

J. If your whole conception of yourself depended on whether or not you got a movie going, you might as well go up to San Francisco and get sad and jump. But ours doesn't. Our real life is someplace else. It's sort of a game. Also it's very gratifying, it's fun, at least a first draft is fun. It's not like writing, it's like doing something else.

S. Do you think it's proper or feasible to write about sex in an explicit way?

J. I don't think anything is improper in fiction, that there's any area that can't be dealt with. I don't in point of fact know very many people who deal with sex well. The only person who deals with sex in an explicit way whom I can read without being made profoundly uncomfortable is Norman Mailer. I know that's not an opinion shared by many. Mailer deals with sex in a very clean, direct way. There's no sentimentality around it. He takes it seriously.

I tend to deal with sex obliquely. There is a lot of sexual content in *Common Prayer*, there was quite a lot in *Play It as It Lays*, too, but it was underneath. I'm just more comfortable dealing with it as an undertone.

S. Some people complain that your female characters are passive drifters who lead purposeless lives. Do you see Charlotte Douglas that way?

J. No, I don't see that about any woman I've written about. I think there is a confusion between passive and successful. Passive simply means passive and active means active. Active doesn't necessarily imply success. Charlotte is very much in control there in Boca Grande when everyone else is running out. She knows just what she's doing.

S. She doesn't seem to have a center, something in herself for which she's living.

J. Obviously the book finds her at a crisis. I don't know too many people who have what you could call clearly functioning centers.

S. You have your work, that sustains you no matter what, and devotion to your family.

J. They could all fall apart tomorrow. This is not a problem peculiar to women, it is a problem for all of us to find something at the center. Charlotte finds her center in Boca Grande. She finds her life by leaving it. I think most of us build elaborate structures to fend off spending much time in our own center.

S. Do you think of yourself as sad or depressed?

J. No, I think of myself as really happy. Cheerful. I'm always amazed at what simple things can make me happy. I'm really happy every night when I walk past the windows and the evening star comes out. A star of course is not a simple thing, but it makes me happy. I look at it for a long time. I'm always happy, really.

S. How do you feel about getting older?

J. I'm a very slow writer and I could count, if I wanted to, which I don't, the number of books I will have time to write. I work more. I work harder. There is a sense of urgency now.

1977

JACQUELINE SUSANN

The Eastern Airlines 7 A.M. shuttle from New York to Washington takes off exactly one hour late. In a front aisle seat, Jacqueline Susann, a tall, slender woman, stares ahead through a mask of makeup: black penciled brows, heavy false lashes, orange lipstick and a black shoulder-length fall made of Korean hair. Her body is clothed in Pucci designs of yellow, purple and pink. The woman who has made the word "doll" a synonym for pill opens a small gold box and takes out a pink tablet. "I'm going to take a wake-up pill."

In her baritone voice, she explains that she decided to take the early shuttle instead of flying to Washington the night before because of her poodle, Josephine. "She's fifteen, and if I'm away overnight, she has to have a sleep-over." Jackie washes down the pill with Binaca, and begins flipping through *Harper's Bazaar*.

Beside her is her husband, Irving Mansfield, né Mandelbaum in Brooklyn, thin, with a small, round face that carries an anxious expression although it is usually smiling. Irving was once a press agent for Eddie Cantor, then producer of "Arthur Godfrey's Talent Scouts." He is now head of the campaign to promote Jackie's second novel, *The Love Machine*.

"Jackie, we wanna be organized," he says as the plane descends through sheets of rain. Irving carries a bag of Jackie's dresses and a hatbox full of makeup and hairpieces. In the limousine, Jackie puts on gray bubble sunglasses. "Where's the schedule, so I can see if I need another wake-up pill?" They check the guest list for a party that evening which will feature a Love Machine Cocktail—crème de cacao, vodka and Pernod—and a Love Machine Cake decorated with two clasped hands like the jacket of the book. A publicity aide says, "May I suggest that you'll get everyone sick if you serve that drink." Irving says, "How about we put a Spanish fly in it, and have the rolls made up like phallic symbols? Ha ha ha. That's funny, isn't it?"

They arrive at the Shoreham Hotel, where the American Booksellers Association is holding its annual convention, minutes before a press conference has been scheduled for out-of-town newspapers. Jackie walks in with a smile. There are twenty men and women in the suite, and none smiles back. After a period of silence, Dan Green, publicity director for Simon and Schuster, asks the first question: "How does it feel to have another book on the best-seller list?" Jackie talks animatedly, perched on her chair. No one in the room takes notes. A man in the back asks, "Do you read reviews?" Jackie says, "I'd like to have the critics like me, I'd like to have everybody like what I write. But when my book sells, I know people like the book. That's the most important thing, because writing is communication."

Jackie describes her writing routine, Irving tells a joke at which no one laughs, even though he adds, "That's funny, isn't it?" At the end, Ivan Sandrof of the Worcester, Massachusetts *Telegram* says, "What do you think is the reason for everybody reading your book, apart from the obvious?''

"What's the obvious reason?" Jackie says.

"Sex, pure and simple."

Jackie says it is not sex that sells her books. "I'm a today writer. The novel today has to compete with television and the movies. It has to come alive quickly and be easy to read. When people tell you they couldn't put the book down, that is good writing."

The sex in Susann's books is minimal by contemporary standards. Although a girl is undressed by page three, lovemaking is described only in vague terms. Instead of using naturalistic language, Jackie's characters employ prudish euphemisms. Men refer to their sexual organs as "Charlie." Women talk about getting "the curse." Jackie says, "I can't stand being clinical. You don't have to say, then he took out his thing and put it in her vagina. For adults, all you have to say is, he took her in his arms."

Michael Korda, Jackie's editor and the editor-in-chief of Simon and Schuster, feels Jackie's promotability is the key to her success. Without promotion, he says, the book would probably sell a hundred thousand copies, "but it wouldn't have the great impact it does." *Valley of the Dolls* sold 356,000 in hard cover and ten million paperback. "Jackie has succeeded where no one has before in tapping all the modern means of communication in one great campaign—movies, television, newspaper interviews, magazines, commercials, all cleverly bound together. Most novelists are not promotable. They don't go on tours because they wouldn't know what to do."

In the Eastern half of the country, critics and interviewers approach Jackie with condescension. Jackie says, "They walk in with the attitude—how dare you be a best-seller." During a Toronto television show, a young woman said, "Don't you ever wake up in the middle of the night and realize you haven't done anything that is really artistic?" Jackie said, "You're sick. Do you wake up and think you're not Huntley-Brinkley?"

Once she has crossed the Continental Divide, and especially in Los Angeles, the feeling toward Jackie changes. Susann is called America's best writer. One man told her his wife had started referring to his sexual organ as "Charlie." "You're adding words to our language."

Jackie is almost uninsultable. A snide question, a bitchy interview, brings out the best in her. She reads vicious reviews and grins. "I think it'll sell a lot of books." On the David Frost show, critic John Simon asked Jackie in his *echt* Central European accent, "Do you think you are writing art or are you writing trash to make a lot of money?" Jackie said, "Is your name Goebbels—you act like a storm trooper." She called him "Simple Simon," a joker, a publicity hound—"How many people have even heard of you?"—all the while Simon kept shouting, "That's not important. Will you just answer the question. What do you think you are writing?" Jackie tried another tangent, saying Simon was "rather nice looking" even though his hair was thin. Simon said, "Cut out all this soft soap. I can smile through my false teeth like you." Jackie bared her teeth and hit them with her finger. "Look, they're caps, not false." Simon kept pressing. Jackie finally said, "Little man, I am telling a sto-ry. Now does that make you happy, huh?"

The one publicity tool Jackie has given up is the autograph party. "When you appear at a bookstore, you are at the mercy of any sex maniac who gets in line. They can say, 'Wanna fuck, baby?' " Irving says, "They've said the worst things. I've had to acquire the sixth sense on a T-man. In a Detroit bookstore, three guys were standing in a corner. They were daring a friend to go up to Jackie and say, 'Your book stinks.' I spotted it a mile off."

Jackie accepts interviews from all publications, all media, no matter how small or limited their reach, unless she or Irving suspects the writer is out to do a hatchet job. She turned down *The Village Voice*, columnist Dick Schaap and *Saturday Review*. "I tried to turn you down," Jackie told me. For months, she will give six or more interviews a day, repeating the same stories with unfailing enthusiasm.

At the American Booksellers Association in Washington, Jackie has set aside an hour and a half for William Silverman of the Detroit *News*, who is writing a cover story for the Sunday magazine. He asks Jackie to pose for photographs. "I want something that's sexy and glamorous, but I don't want it to be vulgar." Jackie says, "That's marvelous." Irving shakes his head. "The problem is, this is not a glamorous background. There's no satin, there's no damask."

Silverman, a grandfather in his sixties who has the shape of a large panda bear, drops to the rug and lies on his stomach, kicking one foot up and resting his chin on his hand. "Could you be like this, like you were writing?" Jackie obliges, adding, "You know, I write like this every day." Irving dozes for a while, awakens with a smile and sings, "If you can talk to the animals."

Silverman asks Jackie how her success has affected her marriage. "When people work with each other, not in competition but together," she says, "it's like a dance team." She jumps up and strikes an arabesque with her white-stockinged legs. "You could say Irving and I are Nureyev and Fonteyn." She waves her arms. "We are the Burtons. We are anything that is two people working together."

When she turns aside, Silverman says to me, "Do you believe that?"

Dan Green interrupts the interview to tell Jackie people are crowded around the Simon and Schuster booth in the exhibit hall, where she is scheduled to autograph copies of her book. Because of a feeble air-conditioning system, the hall is steaming hot, with thin red carpets and silver tinsel hanging from the ceiling. A double line radiates out from the alcove where Jackie is seated. Irving says, "Never in the history of the world has there been a writer with this charisma." The people in line—bookstore owners, salesmen, jobbers, editors, publishing executives—wait for more than two hours, clutching yellow pieces of paper on which they have printed their names so Jackie can write personal messages. "For Isabel Smith. All my best."

One of the first in line is Lloyd Severe, a supervisor at Martindale's bookstore in Beverly Hills. "Frankly, this is not exactly my type of book, but my wife wants it." Asked what accounts for Susann's popularity, he says, "There's only one word for it. People like thrills."

Irving, in his yellow, green and pink Pucci tie and Gucci shoes, says they have given away six hundred books. When they arrive at the suite, the figure has grown to eight hundred. That evening it is one thousand. A bottle of champagne is brought to the room. Michael Korda, a wiry British blond who wears a bright blue suit, a red handkerchief, a black belt with gold metal studs and blue motorcycle glasses, walks in and kisses Jackie on both cheeks. "Do you think we'll make number one?" she says softly. "Of course we will," Korda says. Jackie drinks the champagne in a water glass with ice cubes. Irving makes the toast: "To the first author who's gonna be back-to-back number one on the best-seller list."

In the Chatelaine Room of the Mayflower Hotel, fifty bookstore owners, managers, and buyers from department stores have bypassed the Love Machine Cocktail for whiskey or gin. Since publication of her first book, a biography of her poodle called *Every Night, Josephine!*, Jackie has cultivated friendships with booksellers. She calls some of them her best friends.

A shout goes up when Jackie appears at the party in a turquoise voile dress. A strawberry blond book buyer from Oregon grabs her arm and pumps it. "I want to shake the hand of the lady that's been makin' me so much money the past two years." The book buyer, an angular, freckled woman, wearing a black chiffon dress with ruffles, says she doesn't think *Love Machine* will sell as well as *Valley of the Dolls* because "it's an over-again, the same jenner. [Genre?] It's Jackie's husband that puts her across with all that Madison Avenue hoopla, and I love it! The pa-toy they speak! [Patois?] It's just marvelous. I don't care what's in the book as long as it sells."

Irving and Jackie move to a different table for each course—crab cocktail, vichyssoise, beef en brochette, wine and cake. When the Love Machine Cake is wheeled out with seven candles, Jackie carries it around the room. "For a finale, I fall into it." She and Irving leave just before 10 P.M. to catch the last shuttle back to New York. As they settle in the limousine, Irving swivels around. "Jackie, will you stop already with these goddamn books! Ha ha. That's funny, isn't it?"

The Mansfields live in a three-room apartment in the Navarro Hotel overlooking Central Park South. The décor is theatrical, with black lamp bases in the shape of human torsos, red shades, ivory linoleum floors and a large bar. The walls are lined with photographs of Jackie with celebrities, Irving with celebrities and celebrities who have appeared on television shows Irving has produced. On a late Friday afternoon, just before leaving for California, Jackie is having caviar and imported Russian vodka, straight, with her press agent for *The Love Machine*, Abby Hirsch, a fashion-conscious young woman who radiates self-assurance and efficiency. Abby's salary is paid by Simon and Schuster, which guaranteed to spend seventy-five thousand dollars promoting the book, and has spent considerably more.

The Love Machine dominates Simon and Schuster this year. In the reception hall, red and white buttons with the book's title are pinned to the rubber tree plants. Michael Korda has written on the walls of his office in blue ink: "Three bottles of Dom Perignon, '59 or '61, *The Love Machine*—150,000 advance. Sixteen ounces of caviar when we reach number one." Korda says the advertising budget for *Love Machine* is larger than for any other book they have published. In addition to Abby, they use a press agent in California, Jay Allen, and a full-time press agent in New York, paid for by Irving.

Both Abby and Michael Korda, like Jackie, wear around their necks a gold chain with the ankh, an

Egyptian symbol of life, which Jackie made the motif of *The Love Machine*. On television, Jackie likes to describe how Cleopatra carried the ankh—a cross with a loop on top—as a symbol of eternal sex. Two New York designers have started production of ankh necklaces, pins, wrist and ankle bracelets, and there is talk of a Love Machine perfume. The Mansfields have avoided these projects. "It's a little too much," Irving says. "Jackie's a writer, an artist. Inside this little breast beats a heart that is not as commercial as people think."

The Mansfields' life-style has not changed since they struck gold in publishing, because they have always lived well. They commute between Central Park South and the Beverly Hills Hotel, where they have had the same suite—at seventy-eight dollars a day—since 1959. Jackie does not cook. In Los Angeles they eat at Chasen's, in New York at Sardi's, Danny's Hide-a-way, "21," and, if they are feeling informal, P. J. Clarke's. They are city animals and have no desire for a yacht or a country estate. On Sundays in New York, they like to walk to the out-of-town newspaper stand in Times Square, have breakfast at Nathan's—two dozen cherrystones for Jackie, two hot dogs for Irving—and go to a movie like *The Green Slime*.

Like the characters Jackie has created in her books, she and Irving seem to be rootless, tieless. Jackie writes in *The Love Machine*: "Nothing is as dull as a woman without a past. And once you know all the details there is no past. Just a long, dreary confessional." Jackie and Irving have sealed off their own past with vague and contradictory references. Jackie often says she was born in 1963, the year her first book was published. When a reporter asked her age, Jackie said, "You could say I'm a young woman in her thirties." The reporter looked up. Jackie smiled. "*Newsweek* printed my age—it's forty-two." Jackie looks younger than forty-two; her figure is slim and her hairpieces are set in youthful, shoulder-length flips.

I accepted the age of forty-two until I met an actress who said she remembered Jackie from the theater in the late 1930s. When I called other theatrical figures, I found they were reluctant to talk of Jackie's past. One woman said, "Jackie will be furious if this gets out. She doesn't want the country to know she's been around all that while. She doesn't want to shock the country. If I looked as well as she does, I'd be proud. I'd want everyone to know how old I was."

Programs on file in the Lincoln Center Performing Arts Library show that Jackie appeared in Max Gordon's production of Clare Boothe's *The Women* in 1937, in *She Gave Him All She Had,* and *When We Are Married* in 1939; in *My Fair Ladies* and *Banjo Eyes* with Eddie Cantor in 1941, and in *Jackpot* in 1944. She was not playing child roles. As the reluctant actress put it, "You can't put two and two together and get forty-two."

A subject Jackie and Irving never bring up is their son. When questioned, they say the boy is sixteen and in school in Arizona. In Jackie's novels there are no children (except for an occasional infant), no families living and growing up together. She creates a fantasy world of stardom, wealth and power. The hero of *The Love Machine*, Robin Stone, works his way from delivering news on a local television station to controlling the national network. In the process, he is loved by, without loving, a model, an actress and the blue-blooded wife of the chairman of the network. Although the story is set in the 1960s, there is no mention of Vietnam, the generation gap, racial tensions, urban riots, inflation. The book, like *Valley of the Dolls*, is an escape hatch from the news.

Susann's characters experience no guilt about sex or anything that might be considered "sin." When a girl loses her virginity, or a baby through abortion, she gives it no more thought than if she had lost a tooth. Because all the characters have miserable, bathetic fates, the reader can feel his own values have been upheld.

A young man with green eyes and an easy smile is sitting on the couch in Jackie's suite at the Beverly Hills Hotel. "I saw a lot of myself in Robin Stone," he says. Irving says, "So did Peter Lawford." The young man says, "I've learned to hide my feelings and not show emotions ever since I was little." He turns on a tape recorder. "This is Dick Spangler. My guest on 'The Forum' is Jacqueline Susann. Miss Susann, you've been criticized as not being the best writer, although you are the best-selling writer." Jackie says, "Way back they didn't think Shakespeare was a good writer. He was the soap-opera king of his day. They called Zola a bad writer, a journalistic writer. Everything changes in writing. I think James Joyce is a bore. *Ulysses* is a bore. In fiction today there is no time to do great exposition on a landscape. Writers like Harold Robbins, Leon Uris and Irving Wallace have given the novel new life, new excitement. They're storytellers. That's the place for the novel today."

Breakfast is brought in on a tray. Jackie drinks iced tea and cuts off pieces of a kosher salami she was given by a television sponsor. She removes the butter from the tray and puts it in her refrigerator. Irving says, "Would you believe it? A woman as rich as Jackie stealing butter?"

Jackie and Irving have been in Beverly Hills for two weeks, visiting bookstores, radio and television stations. Jackie has been on television more hours in the past two years than most actors. For a spot on "Hollywood Squares," she is driven to the NBC studios in Burbank with five costume changes, since a week's worth of programs are to be taped in one night. In the back of the studio, the stars—Wally Cox, Shirley Jones, Jack Cassidy, Vincent Price—pop in and out of their dressing rooms as if they were playing a slapstick comedy.

"Hey, Vince."

"I just bought a house on the beach."

"Look at my new dog."

On the set, the warm-up man, burly, red-faced, with dandruff on his shoulders, bellows at the audience, "Hello, my name is Ken Williams. I'm from Baltimore. Where are you all from?"

"Eddyville, Iowa." "Mayville, Tennessee." "Mount Eric, North Carolina." This is Jacqueline Susann country.

Peter Marshall, the emcee, introduces Jackie. "You ladies know all about this guest. She wrote *Valley of the Dolls,* which sold a couple books, and *The Love Machine,* which just knocked *Portnoy's Complaint* off number one on the best-seller list. Which shows, if you write family, beautiful, sweet things, you're gonna make a buck." The audience is signaled to laugh.

The game is played like ticktacktoe. Each star sits in a separate box of a large orange steel contraption. Two contestants try to earn boxes by picking a star, listening to the star answer a question posed by the emcee, and then deciding whether the star is right. If the contestant is right, he gets the box. The first to win three in a row gets two hundred dollars, and possibly luggage, a car, a vacation, or a mink coat.

The contestants, chosen from the audience, are all young, cleancut, not overly bright. A large portion of the questions are based on articles in *Ladies' Home Journal* and *Woman's Day*. Jackie is asked what Benjamin Franklin used as his pen name for *Poor Richard's Almanack*: Richard Benjamin, Richard Small, or Richard Saunders. Jackie says, "I'm going to guess— Richard Saunders." The contestant says Jackie is wrong. Jackie squeals when told Richard Saunders is right. "You should have trusted me," she says to the contestant. "One writer with another." On the last show, when Jackie is introduced in her blinking orange box, she mouths the words, "Hello, Mother." Mrs. Susann watches the program every morning in Philadelphia.

They finish just after 11 P.M., and the producers, directors, and several of the stars drive to the home of Mary Markham, an independent producer, on Beverly Drive. It is a lavish house of excessive symmetry. There is a fake fire blazing in the den, where Jack Cassidy is playing pool. Mary's dog, a white cockapoo, is running through the house bumping into furniture. Three men begin playing a dice game called "Canoga" over the long, sunken bar. Jackie is the first of the women to join, throwing dollar bills into the pile. She wins the first two games, and claims the cash pot with a smile. Irving sits on the couch saying, "No, no!" as the cockapoo laps at his face. Cassidy confides in Jackie that he wants to write a book. Jackie says, "You should. I think any good actor is a good writer, because he is able to mimic life."

*　　*　　*

Jacqueline Susann is compulsive about writing, as compulsive as the legendary British popular novelist who was said to keep a rigid schedule of writing five hours a day. If during that time he finished a novel, he would type "end," insert a new page and type the title of the next book. Jackie has already written a first draft of a new novel to be called *Once Is Not Enough*. She writes the first draft in the period between the time she finishes a novel and the day it is published and she embarks on the promotion tour. "Then I don't return to an empty typewriter."

Even after the film rights of *The Love Machine* were sold for a million and a half dollars, even after the book had hit number one, Jackie continued to plug it as if she were an unknown author. "Maybe it's my bag, but I feel I have to keep going around and doing it." She was autographing books for Higbee's in Cleveland when she learned *Love Machine* had made number one. Her response was, "We've gotta keep it up there." Irving says that with Jackie staying number one is a matter of pride. "Simon and Schuster wanted us to hold off publication for a month because *Portnoy's Complaint* was so hot. But Jackie said no. She wanted the title shot. She's a natural going competitor."

Irving has taped on the wall of their bathroom in the Beverly Hills Hotel a cardboard facsimile of the *New York Times* Best Seller List of June 22, the first week *Love Machine* was number one. "It's great to watch when you're on the head," Jackie says. "It makes you relax. It's good for the soul."

Irving looks up from his copy of *Variety*. "That's funny, isn't it?"

1969

4

A Happy Family

THE NELSONS

The show opens with a picture of the white colonial house in Hollywood where the Nelsons actually live. "The Adventures of Ozzie and Harriet, starring the entire Nelson family. Here's Ozzie . . ." One by one, they come out the door smiling and form a row by the front hedge: father, mother, David and Ricky. "America's favorite family, the Nelsons." For twenty-two years on radio and television, the Nelsons seemed the most perfect expression of the ideals invested in the American middle-class family. They were not just acting, it was felt, but portraying their natural selves. People wanted to believe in the Nelsons and to live vicariously with them. Women wrote in for Harriet's recipes and clothes patterns, and asked for designs of the kitchen, where the family was seen nearly every show having the most convivial dinner hour. The imprinting of the Nelsons on our national consciousness is unique, because three or four generations have identified with them. A large group were fans of Ozzie as a bandleader in the Thirties, when Harriet Hilliard was his featured singer. For many, the radio shows in the Forties are irrevocably associated with growing up. For me, it was television in the mid-Fifties. Others

adored Ricky as a rock-and-roll singer, and stayed
with the program into the Sixties. The Ozzie and Har-
riet shows were almost always built around problems
which, in the end, proved not to be a problem at all.
A traffic ticket turned out to be a Christmas card from
the police. A flat tire was revealed as a trick to arrange
a surprise party. How reassuring, then, it was to hear
Ozzie say, with his Howdy Doody smile: "You see,
there was nothing at all to worry about."

Ozzie and Harriet are alone in the house in Hollywood, eating dinner in front of a color television set
tuned to the evening news with the sound off. As they
talk, their eyes flick to the screen, to images of Nixon
and a mob of youths waving signs. Harriet reads one
of them aloud: "Killer . . . cops." Ozzie nearly drops
his fork. Harriet says, "It's like a nightmare. Is this
the United States? I don't know where we're going,
it's so frustrating." Ozzie runs a hand through his
blond hair. He speaks in a strong voice that carries
through the house. The words come out in a breathless
rush, except those he wishes to emphasize, which are
carefully enunciated. "There seem to be more *de-*
pressed people now than any time I can remember.
Don'cha think? I wish Agnew would stop the alliter-
ations and all, but I do agree with a lot of what he
says. I think it's terribly hypocritical of radicals to
demonstrate for free speech for people they agree
with, and to *shout down* others. Through permissive-
ness, we've allowed too many people to *shout down*
other people."

Since they stopped filming their show in 1966, Ozzie
and Harriet have had long hours to think. Ozzie, who
produced, directed, starred in and helped write the

114

program, stays up until five in the morning, reading magazines, doing the daily crossword puzzle, watching the late talk shows and reading several books at once. He and Harriet are Republicans. "Fortunately we agree on most things," he says. They spend half their time at Laguna Beach, where Ozzie swims a mile a day and plays volleyball with the teen-agers. "They grew up with our show and feel a rapport with us." Harriet has learned to cook, after decades of pretending on television, and does yoga exercises to a talking record. She is willow slim and wears elegant pants suits, with her red hair brushed in a French twist. While on TV, her style was more frumpy. "You fall into the trap of the character, you know. I always had to be the little brown wren on the show, cooking, dusting, wearing aprons, not speaking out. I found myself dressing the same offscreen." She tucks her chin down and chuckles. "It's taken me a few years to become myself."

Harriet is a Daughter of the American Revolution, and she and Ozzie can trace their families back to the eighteenth century. "I'm not a joiner," she says, "but I thought it would be nice to be in the D.A.R. for my grandchildren's sake. Now it turns out things like this—ancestors, and your background—don't matter. People don't have much respect for them." Ozzie says, "I think what's happened to our family in the last four or five years is the same with all other families, no?" Harriet agrees. "There's been a whole change in the way of of living. People are peeling off early, not wanting to be part of a large family unit. The whole institution seems to be in trouble. We're just as confused as everybody else. And we all used to be so sure about what we wanted, what was good."

She makes a little frown. "We're three separate families now. It's kind of sad."

Ricky Nelson has just turned thirty-one. In a giant poster done in sepia tones, which folds out of his album, *Rick Sings Nelson,* he is wearing bell-bottom jeans, cowboy boots and a captain America jacket. He has been making a musical comeback, writing his own songs and going on tour with a country-rock band. At first, people came to hear him for laughs or nostalgia, but since his hit recording of Dylan's *She Belongs to Me,* he has been acquiring a new following.

Rick has twin three-year-old boys and a seven-year-old daughter who say "Hi Pop" to him now. His blond wife, Kris, is a painter of primitives which are owned by, among others, Jackie Onassis and Luci Johnson Nugent. They live with children, three dogs, three cats, a maid, nurse, four cars and a Volkswagen bus in the Hollywood hills, five minutes away from Rick's parents.

"It's really weird to be over thirty," Rick says, with a soundless laugh. "I feel like I'm eighteen." He looks eighteen. His face is Indian red, from lying by his swimming pool, and his blue eyes have a trusting, unmasked innocence. Unless he is around people he knows well, he is quiet. In an interview, his response to many questions is silence, an intake of breath, and then "Yu"—hanging somewhere between "yup" and "yuh." He has always been a repository of slang ("I don't mess around, boy," was his trademark in the Fifties), and these days he uses "into," "scene," and "do a number."

From the time he first said "Hi Pop" on the radio at the age of eight, Ricky was a hit. He was givn all the funny lines on the show, and everything—sports music, laughs, girls—came easy. At sixteen he became a pop singing idol, faking his way at concerts knowing only three guitar chords. For five years, every record he put out was a million seller. Then came the Beatles and psychedelic music, and Rick briefly went on the nightclub circuit, singing *Mame* and snapping his fingers at the Latin Quarter and other places "where they have jokes on the napkins." He never stopped recording, and eventually found a new direction. He was not devastated by the fall from popularity because, he says, "The years of consistent, wide acceptance gave me a positive attitude about myself. I don't have to have a hit record to feel good."

Rick says there is no generation gap between him and his parents. "Just an age gap. We're as close as any family could be. Family worked in our situation. It had to—we were forced to get along because we saw so much of each other. I always loved my family and felt they were there to back me up. I still do."

David Ozzie Nelson, thirty-four, is waiting for me at the Nelson family office, called "the bungalow," in Toluca Lake. It is a four-room cottage on a blinking thoroughfare lined with drive-ins and franchised restaurants. David, while working on a film in West Virginia, grew a beard and mustache, which add interest to his Pleasant Valley face. Although he has a bad cold, he chain smokes.

"A lot of families are trying to make a transition, in morals and values, from the Fifties to the Seventies," he says. "In our family, there was no generation gap, and I think it's too bad. Because I was a little old man at thirteen. I was polite, tried never to offend anyone, and I felt this great responsibility, because I wasn't just me—I was a quarter of a thing. Whatever

I did, I felt the burden of three other people and all the crew who worked on the show. I wasn't a truck driver's son who could go out and bust people if he got mad.''

When the family show was canceled, David set up a production company, and is trying to establish himself as a producer and director. About a year ago, he told his parents he didn't want to see them as much, while he was trying to get on his feet. "I can't listen to my father forever—he can't direct my life and my career indefinitely. The cord should have been broken years ago, but at thirty years old I was still on that show saying, 'Hi Mom, Hi Pop,' every week.''

David says the Nelson family and the TV program were "totally separate. One was real and one wasn't. For your sanity, you had to keep that clear. Rick and I had to distinguish between our father and the director telling us what to do. If we got the lines crossed that's where the arguments started, and I would end up putting my fist through a wall behind the set, because I was that angry.'' The Nelsons grew into the habit, David says, of maintaining their television image for the public, even when off camera. "We would keep up the front of this totally problemless, happy go-lucky group. There might have been a tremendous battle in our home, but if someone from outside came in, it would be as if the director yelled, 'Roll 'em.' We'd fall right into our stage roles. You'd get to wondering which was the true thing. It's an awfully big load to carry, to be everyone's fantasy family.''

David decided a few years ago that it was time to drop the pretense. He and his wife June would be at the beach, or doing a play in summer stock, when strangers would approach them and say, "We tried to have a family like yours, and we failed." One woman said through tears that her husband had left home, and the children were in trouble with drugs. June would tell them, "Listen, the show was a fairy tale. They were all stories. Nobody has a family like that. They don't. It's ridiculuous."

David says, "I find it hard to believe that, with all the social changes of the last few years, the collapse of the Nelson family will shock anyone." He says he thinks Rick, though, has an "undying loyalty" to the family. "Let's say the Nelson family as the great American pastime is sinking. Ricky is likely to dive in and try, until his last breath, to prop the whole thing up. I'm likely to stand on the rocks watching, with my arms folded, and say, 'I told you so.' "

Imagine, as I have been trying since I met the Nelsons, what it would be like to grow up before thirty million people, playing yourself, but speaking lines someone else has written for you. To keep your sanity, as David suggested, you would need to establish a separate identity. But many of the steps you would take to grow and differentiate yourself from the family would be reflected right back on the program. When David became a trapeze catcher in a circus, it was used in the show. Rick's singing was incorporated. When they married, their wives came on playing themselves. Everyone outside the studio believed and treated the Nelsons as if they were the characters on television.

It is difficult to remember any single episode in "The Adventures of Ozzie and Harriet," because for twenty-two years they did absolutely nothing except live together. No one ever knew what kind of work Ozzie did. There were no references to the world, no hint of changes in the country from Truman to Eisenhower to Kennedy to Johnson. What one remembers of the show is a tone, an attitude, a lulling sense of security about the family. A friend of mine used to do an imitation of the show that was delivered with smiles and automatic turning of the head:

"Hi Mom,"
"Hi Ricky,"
"Hi Mom,"
"Hi David,"
"Hi Pop,"
"Hi Sons, Hi Harriet,"
"Hi Thorny,"
"Hi Oz, Harriet, Dave, Rick . . ."

Everyone in the family had the same skin tones, and spoke with the same inflections. All the stories had happy endings; there was never meanness or real anger. There was also nothing that would pass for sexual passion. The boys never kissed their dates, and all Ozzie and Harriet did was walk arm in arm, although Ozzie points out with pride, "We were the first couple on television to sleep in a double bed." The values which permeated the show were unequivocal: mother is the backbone of warmth and support, but her place is in the kitchen; be wary of neighbors; keep up with the Joneses; solve your problems by family teamwork and above all, love, honor and obey your parents.

The wild success of the show in the Fifties was attributed to the fact that it was "natural," "spontaneous," "the real thing." One newspaper critic wrote, "It's the dream of what the American family should be." *Time* magazine said, "On and off the air, the Nelsons are Mr. and Mrs. Average Family."

All the articles published about the Nelsons asserted that they were indeed, in private life, the model family: they resolved all conflicts by talking; they did everything together—swimming, cribbage, charades, football, and breakfast each morning at seven-thirty; and neither boy caused his parents "a moment's serious concern."

As I read through the clips about the Nelsons, the thought that they were in life as they were on the screen was more frightening than the fantasy that Ozzie drank on the side, or that the boys tried endlessly to run away from home. The truth, as always, fell somewhere between.

The major difference between the television family and the Nelsons who lived in Hollywood was that in the first house no one worked; in the second, life revolved around work. The boys went to public school and afterward reported to the studio. They had dinner at home, then Ozzie went back to work on scripts and editing. They shot all day Saturday and had Sunday to catch up on homework.

Rick, as a teen-ager, was uncommunicative. "He used to make people nervous, because he hardly talked," Harriet says. David was more of an extrovert, "Mr. Personality." Ozzie was not the stammering patsy he played on television, but, in David's words, "a human dynamo. I never saw him not take the stairs two at a time. He had so much energy and drive, it made you tired." David says whenever he or Rick would say, "Hi Pop," they could never get eye contact with Ozzie. "He'd be staring at your hair. It was always too long, too greased up, not combed right, something." The Nelsons were not close with any of their neighbors. On the show, Thorny, played by Don DeFore, was always popping over the back fence to needle Ozzie. There actually was a Thornberry family in the house next to the Nelsons, and

Ozzie took the name of the character from them. "But I was not a pal of that Thorny," he says. "I did have some friends like that at the L.A. Tennis Club."

The show was a more accurate picture of New Jersey in the Twenties than Los Angeles in the Fifties. Ozzie conceived and wrote it with memories of his own boyhood in Ridgefield Park: the malt shop, the corner drugstore, back-fence gossiping and community dances which the family would attend together, taking turns at the punch bowl. There are no malt shops in California; David and Ricky used to hang out at drive-ins, and wouldn't dream of attending a dance along with their parents.

In the twilight years, from 1960 on, the show diverged more radically from the Nelsons' personal life. Ricky and Kris were portrayed as married students, struggling through college, when Rick had barely managed to graduate high school. David was shown going to law school, while on his own he was traveling with a circus act. The public, of course, continued to believe the show was reality. When I saw my grandfather recently, he said he had always like the program because "they were both good boys. They got good educations, and the older one became a lawyer." I told him David was not really a lawyer, and he said, nodding gravely, "That's a disappointment to me."

Now the cycle is beginning again, as a new generation grows up with the Nelsons on daytime reruns. The history of the Nelson family is a classic American story, and to go back through it is to feel the roots and branches of our social mythology.

Oswald George Nelson was born in Jersey City in 1907. His family moved to Ridgefield Park, and Ozzie grew up in a Gothic shingled house with a wide fron porch over which, several times a year, a large American flag would be draped. His father, who was of Swedish descent, worked in a bank, and liked to produce amateur theatricals. Ozzie, the middle of three sons, sang in minstrel shows for the Elks and Masons, took an interest in all sports, crafts, music and reading.

When asked what books shaped his thinking as a youth, Ozzie lists: *Tommy Tiptop,* the Horatio Alger books ("I read just about all of them"), the Rover Boy books and *David Copperfield.* By the end of his adolescence, Ozzie was equipped to fulfill the American dream. At Rutgers University, he was: quarterback on the football team, varsity letterman in swimming and lacrosse, college welterweight boxing champion, head of the student council, captain of the debating team, president of his fraternity, art editor of the humor magazine and leader of a band in which he sang and played saxophone. He also did well enough in his studies to be accepted at Rutgers Law School. But during his last year of college, his father died, and to pay his tuition at law school Ozzie performed with his orchestra at proms and deb parties. By the time he earned his degree, the band had become so popular that Ozzie decided to continue with it. Their regular appearances at the Glen Island Casino in New Rochelle were broadcast over what was then hailed as a "coast-to-coast radio network."

In 1932, Ozzie thought a girl singer might be a great gimmick for the band. He saw Harriet Hilliard in a short film, *Musical Justice,* arranged to meet her and persuaded her to join the team. Three years later they were married.

Harriet's real name was Peggy Lou Snyder. She was a stage baby, born in Des Moines, carried in front of the footlights at six weeks by her parents, Roy Snyder and Hazel McNutt, who used the theatrical name Hilliard. She traveled the Midwest with them, learned to sing, dance, perform vaudeville and drama.

Ozzie Nelson's band toured the country in a bus, playing one-night stands, sleeping until noon and driving on to the next town. They were always paid in cash, and Harriet lugged it around in a leather satchel called the "nanny goat" until they could deposit it in a bank. On the road, Harriet leafed through ladies' magazines, cutting out pictures of homes. "I never had a real home and always wanted one," she says.

Ozzie, who did not smoke or drink, was attractive in a wholesome way. His face had a puppet-like quality, with a perpetual smile, the mouth opening and closing as if operated by strings. He and Harriet made a specialty of boy-girl duets, where they would exchange lines of patter. They also appeared on radio shows in New York, and Harriet began to appear in feature films.

In 1940, after their two sons were born, the Nelsons moved to Hollywood. When looking for a house, they passed up the Tudor estates and Doric palaces that dotted Beverly Hills for a white Cape Cod house on a dead-end street, just above Hollywood Boulevard. Harriet furnished it with Early American antiques, needlepoint cushions, ticking clocks, rocking chairs and lampshades with ribbons. Ozzie and Harriet made films together—*Take It Big, Honeymoon Lodge* and *Sweethearts of the Campus*—and were regulars on the Red Skelton radio show. In 1944, when Skelton joined the Army, Ozzie wrote a script for a program based on his own family, auditioned it and, in two days, the International Silver Company signed up as the sponsor.

"The Adventures" began with professional actors

playing the parts of David and Ricky. Ozzie was presented as a well-meaning, befuddled oaf because, Harriet says, "he had to be that way for the show to be comedic." In 1949, the boys were playing tennis with Bing Crosby's son, Lindsay, who told them he was going to be on the *Ozzie and Harriet* Christmas show. The boys had a conference in their room. "Let's go tell them we want to be on too," Ricky said. The Nelsons agreed to let them try out at a rehearsal. "They got such tremendous laughs," Harriet recalls, "that we dismissed the actors and the boys took over. When an actor gets his first laugh, he's hooked. It's as if he's tasted blood."

Ricky, who started out by just saying, "Hi Mom, Hi Pop," was too small to reach the regular microphones, so he sat at a special low table. Sometimes he would forget where he was, and begin humming, or take off his shoes. The studio audience roared. Ozzie hurried over and said, "Son, those are not the kind of laughs we want."

At home, the boys never heard their parents have an argument, but the brothers were constantly brawling and rolling over each other. They would get into shouting matches of "Oh Yeah?" "Yeah!" "Oh Yeah?" "Yeah!" Ozzie would walk in and separate them. Rick says he was "great bait" for his father, and could get him into screaming arguments over inconsequential things. David never participated, and would tell Ricky later, "Why don't you just keep your mouth shut?"

Ozzie and Harriet were determined not to favor either of the boys, but the public went crazy over Ricky. Ozzie says, "People would come up to us and say, your David is a good boy, but this little Ricky. He's the cutest thing we've ever seen. And they would brush David aside. Harriet and I tried to make up for it by giving David attention, and I think we may have overcompensated." David says he never felt his brother was favored. "He got all the laughs, made all the money and had all the success in singing, but there was one thing he never had—he was never older than I was. That was sort of a saving grace."

The Nelsons did not, as the myth goes, have breakfast together. "We were all on different schedules," Harriet says. But dinner was an important ritual. They ate in the formal dining room and were served. The boys were required to wear coats. Ozzie would conduct spelling bees and play "geography." Despite his drills, neither Ricky nor David did well in school. David was thinking about football and Rick was preoccupied with music. He would lie on his back by the record player for hours, listening to symphonies, jazz and top-forty hits. He had a set of drums when he was eight, and went on to the clarinet, guitar and piano.

Both boys had endless cycles of lessons: horseback riding, swimming, tennis, karate, ice skating and, for Ricky, tap dancing. The one mainstream American practice the Nelsons did not follow was going to church. Harriet describes herself as "deeply religious," but says she does not believe in formal religion.

Harriet did not believe, either, in sex education for children. She assumed it would come naturally. David says, "The first news I got about the birds and bees was from Will Thornberry next door, when I was seven. His explanation was a disaster! I resolved not to ever let it happen to me. All I knew about girls was that they were bad football players." In junior high, he and his friends would spy on girls' gym classes when they were showing films about menstruation. One day he came home and found a book placed on his bed. "It was called, *The Egg and I,* or something." He took the book into Ricky and said, "Do you know what you have to do when you get married?" Ricky recalls, "I knew about it, I don't know whether I was for it, but I wasn't shocked."

In 1952, Ozzie decided to move the family program to television, and made a film, *Here Come the Nelsons,* as a pilot. David cried when he saw the first rushes. "All the things Ricky had been teasing me about were true. I was fat, husky. I never held myself in as high regard after that." Hotpoint was the sponsor for two years and then alternated with Listerine (those wonderful folks who gave you the jingle: "He said that she said that he had halitosis").

For two years, the Nelsons had shows on both radio and television, but they were fascinated with the new medium. They moved into the living room for dinner so they could watch TV as they ate. Their ratings were good from the start, and the family made five hundred thousand dollars a year. The boys had absolutely no sense of the fortunes they were amassing. Ozzie channeled their salaries directly into trust funds, which would give each, when he was twenty-one, a quarter of a million dollars. In the meantime, Ozzie doled out pocket money—five dollars for David, fifty cents for Ricky.

Ozzie and Harriet did not socialize with others in the industry. They wanted a "normal, average home life," and planned all activities around the boys. They gave them elaborate birthday parties, took trips together and Harriet was hostess at a yearly New Year's Eve party for both boys and their friends.

In 1954, when David graduated high school, the

Nelsons made their first venture outside the United States. Ozzie booked passage on a Swedish boat, the *Kungsholm*, from New York to Goteborg, Sweden. In the middle of the Atlantic, he gathered the family on deck and gave them a little talk. "I told them the 'ugly American' image so many Europeans have is not a true picture of Americans," he recalls. "I said, let's be one family who will make people think, the Americans aren't so bad. Let's be considerate, thoughtful and adaptable."

When Ozzie looked over the railing at Goteborg, though, he suddenly realized he was in a city where he could not speak the language. In America, wherever the Nelsons had gone, Ozzie says, "There was always a Mr. Ass Kisser to meet us at the airport, take care of our arrangements and see us settled." He and Harriet watched the dock workers calling to each other in an incomprehensible singsong, turned and exchanged looks of imminent panic. "Where's Mr. Ass Kisser?" A chauffeur from the hotel appeared, speaking perfect English, and Ozzie engaged him for their stay in Sweden. From that point, he wired ahead to every city for an "American-speaking chauffeur" to meet them at the airport.

In Sweden, the distant branches of the Nelson family gave a luncheon for their American relatives, but they couldn't communicate. In Paris, the Nelsons discovered wine and champagne—"We got smashed every night," Ricky says. In London, Ricky, who had just turned fourteen, had his first sexual encounter. "I thought I was super grown-up, and kept saying to David, 'Let's go out and get some broads.'" The night before they left Europe, Ricky, David and an American friend drove around East London picking up prostitutes. When it was Rick's turn, he kept passing the girls by. "I was scared to death. Finally, the two guys got fed up, parked the car, went out and got a woman and brought her back. She opened the door and grabbed my hand. There was no getting out of it." Ricky did a bravado act, though, slinging his arm around the woman and waving, "See ya later." David says, "I thought he'd never come back alive." Ricky says the woman was "really nice to me. I didn't want to leave! The guys had told her I was a young French water skier, and she kept wishing me luck. When we got back to the hotel, though, I couldn't look my mom in the face. I remember thinking, 'She knows.' "

After the trip, Ozzie and Harriet never journeyed outside the country again. "I have no desire to," Harriet says. "I've traveled my whole life. When we have to go on the road now for work, we stay at Holiday Inns. We love the impersonalness of them."

Ricky, during his teen years in Hollywood, underwent a personality change. He shot up to six feet—the tallest in the family—and withdrew, shedding his "little Jerry Lewis" skin. David says, "He went into a shell for a while, then glommed onto the Elvis Presley image and fashioned himself as a skinny sex fiend." David, at the same age, had chosen Pat Boone for his model. "I thought kids were looked upon with most favor if they opened doors, were polite and said 'Yes, sir.' I figured I could do that easily. It was nothing to me to bow down to people who, I knew, didn't deserve the courtesy." David's friends in high school were equally straight. They went steady with "nice girls," played football and belonged to a club called the Elksters.

In Los Angeles, until fairly recently, every high school had ongoing social clubs, which conducted rush, pledging and initiations that were far more cruel than in most college fraternities. Every year, there would be a scandal when one of the clubs would paint pledges green and drop them nude on Hollywood Boulevard. At school, each club had a special bench in the yard, where they would meet at lunch. They wore medallions and jackets with the club's name on the back, held dances and rented cabins in resorts for Easter week.

The Elksters all knew Ricky because they used to swim in the Nelsons' pool and stay with them in Laguna. When Ricky started Hollywood High, he naturally began hanging out with them. In midsemester, they had their big voting meeting, and the next day told Ricky he had been blackballed. His friends were accepted, but Ricky was felt to be a little too "fast." He still winces at the memory, and didn't tell his parents about it for years. "It was really degrading to me, because they were all, like, friends of mine. I vowed to myself I'd get back at those guys, and I did."

Another club, the Rooks, asked Ricky to sit on their bench. They were more of a car club; members wore sideburns, black leather jackets and motorcycle boots. "They looked good to me," Rick says. "I was always a greaser at heart." He let his hair grow, coated it with Brilliantine and combed it in eight parts, with a crest swirling over the forehead. He used a needle and India ink to tattoo "R. N." on his hand. "I was really out of control then, with the Rooks," Rick says. "We would cruise Hollywood Boulevard and choose off people we thought we could beat up. We were arrested for stealing construction lanterns. We thought we were really bad. Most of the guys did end up in jail—they went on to bigger things, like armed robbery."

Rick's new image created problems for the show. In that period, "juvenile delinquency" was the great national horror, and Ozzie, like many other Americans, wondered if rock-and-roll music had anything to do with it. Rick had to keep his hair degreased for the program. "That's when my character became different from the TV role," Rick says. "But it wasn't that different. I mean, I was a *nice* greaser."

Rick's singing career came about by accident. There was a girl named Arline, blond, tan, "developed," who was highly prized by the Rooks. She was seventeen, a year older than Rick, at a time when a year's difference meant a great deal. He took her out a few times, but, he says, "She didn't particularly like me. I really dug her, probably because everybody else liked her." One night he was driving her home through Laurel Canyon, taking the curves fast so she might fall against him, when an Elvis Presley song came on the radio. "She did this whole big number, and I thought to myself, and then said out loud, 'I'm making a record myself.' She just laughed and it made me mad. I decided I was going to make a record any way I could, just to show her."

When he got home, he went in to his father and made the arrangements. He cut a record of "Fats" Domino's "I'm Walkin'" with studio musicians on the TV set, and Ozzie sent it out to record companies. Verve released it, and at the same time a special "Ozzie and Harriet" show was written to showcase Ricky singing. The program was called *Ricky the Drummer*, and at the end Ozzie introduced the number as "a rhythm-and-blues song." Within a few weeks, to the shock of the Nelson family, the record sold a million copies, and Ricky was, before the end of his first year in high school, a national idol. Arline (remember Arline?) told the Rooks that she wanted to talk to Ricky. Finally she called him up and drove by the house. Ricky says, "It was a great moment. I had a chance to really cool it and say, 'Gee, I'll try to call you sometime, when I can swing it. We'll see.' "

Ricky did his first concert at the Ohio State Fair in the summer of 1956. When the plane landed, he looked out and saw three thousand people behind a chain-link fence, and said, "I wonder who's coming in, a politician or something." When he walked out, the fence crashed down and the crowd ran toward him. "It was really frightening. I'd always felt like I was in a fishbowl, because of the television program, but there had never been anything like this frenzy for me. When I realized what was going down, though, I loved it. It was great."

Ricky toured the state fairs, usually performing in a white suit and white buck shoes. His guitar had flowers painted on it and his name. "You can't really hear an open guitar, unless it's miked, so I would just go out and grab some strings," he says. There was little drug use in the rock world then, but there were groupies, mostly older women who waited around the hotels. Rick says, "It was nice to know you could just, like, take your pick. But you couldn't touch the real young ones who screamed and drooled on you."

When he came home from that first tour, Rick says, "I felt really alone. It had been such a power trip, with people saying, 'Mr. Nelson' right and left. Then suddenly I was back living with my folks, getting the same old numbers like, 'Pick up your clothes.' It was a depressing time, because I couldn't tell anyone about the experience without sounding dumb. I couldn't explain to people about crowds biting me, and tearing off my shirts. I had teeth marks all up and down my arms."

In Hollywood, carloads of girls started to drive by the house every night and honk. Harriet had nightmares about people breaking in, and had an electric fence installed. Rick left Hollywood High for a private school, because, he says, at Hollywood, "just walking down the hall was like making an appearance." When he got to be eighteen, Rick moved in with David, who had dropped out of U.S.C. and was living in a studio apartment in the hills.

David's nickname was "Mother," because he liked everything neat. Ricky moved in with a beagle and an elaborate wardrobe and created chaos. "He would take off his clothes and they'd stay in one lump," David says. "I'd ask him to go out and get something for dinner, and he'd come back with bonbons and a case of Cokes. He lived on cherry cough drops for years."

Rick still has eccentric eating habits. He fasts for three or more days, then eats plates of hamburgers and ice cream. He doesn't like salad ("it's like eating a leaf") and has always hated water ("it's like drinking a toilet"). When he lived with David, and later with Charlie Britt, an actor who played football with the L.A. Rams, Rick started to sleep in the bathtub. When the water turned cold, he would reach up with his foot and turn on the hot faucet. Charlie says the first time he found Rick in the tub, "He looked like a prune, man, from six hours hanging out in the water."

When Charlie moved in with Rick in 1960, Rick's sexual tastes ran "heavy on carhops." Charlie took him aside after a few months and said, "Look, the quality of girls coming up to the house has got to improve, because I can't take it." So a scheme was devised. Actresses were picked from the Players' Directory, and a network secretary called them in for interviews. Rick and Charlie would just happen to be in the office when the girls showed up. This went on for a while, and then Charlie noticed that Rick had his eye on Kristin Harmon, the sixteen-year-old daughter of football star Tom Harmon. The Harmons were friends of Ozzie and Harriet, and Kris, since she was eleven, had dreamed of marrying Rick. Charlie prodded Rick into asking her out, and after their first date, he says, "Neither ever looked at another person." They were engaged for a year, and Rick had to take Catholic instruction. He was twenty-three when they married, she was seventeen. "I'd had my fill of dates," Rick says. "I wanted a wife and a house and children, the whole number. I didn't have one doubt about Kris. We really got along well."

During the years Rick was defining himself through music, David had leaned toward testing himself physically. He played football, raced midget cars and body-surfed in forty-foot waves at Laguna. "If somebody said there's a cliff to dive off, I'd always try to see if I had the guts to do it," he says. He made a number of films, and in 1960 played the role of a trapeze catcher in *The Big Circus*. The first time he tried climbing to the platform, he nearly blacked out from vertigo. By the end of the film, he was so involved with the trapeze act that he continued to work out at a trapeze rig in Thousand Oaks.

"Trapeze is the greatest high anybody could experience," he says. "It can be as beautiful as a ballet, with the feeling of freedom you can only get when you're suspended sixty feet up in the air." David joined a trapeze group called the "Flying Viennas" and for four years, when he was not shooting the TV series, performed with them in Europe and the States. "I had dreams of reviving the golden age of the circus. I also felt I was getting down to the roots of show business—entertaining a group of people directly, with immediate feedback. As an actor, you may have an inner feeling about whether you're doing well, but you really have to wait for reviews and other responses. In the circus, you know on the spot—the trick works, or it doesn't."

During his time with the circus, David saw a red-haired actress named June Blair in a film, and asked his father to hire her for a show. David took her out, on and off, for several years and decided she was the woman he wanted to marry. The wedding was held in the chapel of Forest Lawn Cemetery, with a large reception at the Nelsons' home. June was an orphan, and had worked her way into films by starting as a secretary at Technicolor.

When I met June, at David's colonial-style house in North Hollywood, she talked nervously in a sugary voice, her eyes off focus. After a while, though, she seemed to relax. Having never been part of a family, she said, "I felt overwhelmed coming into such a huge and famous family, and then being on public display as the new bride and daughter-in-law."

Ozzie suggested she join the show as a regular—the first addition in twelve years. June says the idea seemed wrong, but she didn't want to say no to her new relatives. "It proved devastating. Everything was too fast. I didn't even know David that well—I had to get used to him, used to marriage, used to the family, while being directed by a man I was told to call 'Dad' and working with my new 'Mom.'"

June appeared for two seasons, then dropped off to

take care of their young son, Danny. She and David went to a psychiatrist, despite the fact that Ozzie had always had a bias against doctors, psychiatrists and medication. "Until recently, he wouldn't even take aspirin," David says. "He feels the whole country has been overmedicated."

Kris came on the show in 1963, the season June left, and stayed for three years. She says she had no problems whatever. "I thought of it as just a part. Everyone was terribly nice to me, and Ozzie and Harriet were the easiest in-laws in the world. Totally nondemanding." June returned for the last season, because, she says, "I missed acting terribly, and we thought it would help the family situation."

During the final years, David directed a dozen of the shows and began to develop ideas which conflicted with his father's. David says Ozzie directed by ear. "If he heard a line that didn't sound right, he would deliver it himself and ask the actor to imitate it, rather than talking about the mood and atmosphere and what should be going on. It's an old-fashioned technique, and amateurs respond well to it. But after I made films where I saw actors had something to contribute, that they weren't just cattle, we ran into problems."

David says his father accused him of not knowing his lines and not caring about the show. "I was a conscientious actor, and I knew my lines. But Dad was putting up some kind of block, and every scene became a hurdle. He'd play some kind of game where I would have to blow the lines. I never convinced him that I did know the lines."

Few others realized what was going on. Kent McCord, who played a fraternity member for five years and stood in for Rick, says, "I don't think anyone was aware of the tensions between David and his father. I guess it was a question of proven success versus new ideas. You just don't tamper with something that successful, when the formula has worked that long." Rick urged his brother to just say his lines, take his pay and split. "Our roles were completely reversed from the early years," David says. "Now Rick was telling me, 'Why don't you just keep your mouth shut?'"

Darkness falls early in Hollywood in November. Walking up to the Nelsons' white, Cape Cod home, it is all so familiar. Harriet opens the door for me, in a blue pants suit with a gold heart around her neck. We sit in the den, with its black-and-white checkered floor, and after a few minutes, Ozzie's voice, half-frantic, booms down the stairs: "I'll be right with you, all right? You go ahead if you want." Harriet calls back, "It's okay, dear, we're having a swell time. We'll be glad to see you when you join us."

We sit down to dinner around a coffee table in the living room, facing the television set. Erma serves us plates that might have come right off the "Ozzie and Harriet" show: breaded chicken breasts with brown gravy, mashed potatoes and peas. For dessert, there are miniature lemon pies.

I ask to hear records of the early radio broadcasts and see films of some of the shows. The Nelsons have copies of every program they have made, indexed and filed in the pool house. Ozzie picks a record at random and stands facing the machine. Halfway through the sketch, he turns to Harriet: "I have no recollection of this at all." Harriet says, "Neither do I." They run a film, and Ozzie says, "I've forgotten every bit of this one too." Both the radio and television shows seem hopelessly dated, but many of the comic bits still work. Ricky has a knack for bringing off a punch line, and the others share a great sense of timing. I find myself laughing at the corniest situations, and Ozzie repeats, heartily, "Thank you, thank you very much."

Ozzie seems to love talking, and runs on, dropping quotes from books, magazines and films, swinging on tangents that shoot him so far he has to stop and re-orient himself. Ozzie says he believes the American capitalist system is the best form of government in the world. "We could move toward a purer democracy, I think, but if the revolutionaries go any further, we'll have a police state." The Nelsons have always wanted to stay in the American mainstream, to have an average family and be like everyone else. "We like to think of ourselves as middle-of-the-road," Ozzie says. "Doesn't everybody?"

On a hot, clear Hollywood day, Rick Nelson boards a plane and, five hours later, steps off into the icy winds of Boston, where he and his band will perform for a week at a nightclub called Paul's Mall. The first night, there are about three hundred in the audience— somewhat older than the usual crowd.

Ron Ross, twenty-six, is standing alone at the bar. "I guess most of us are here because Ricky grew up in our living rooms," he says. "It was nice to watch that happy family, even though we didn't quite have such a family."

Rick slips out in the darkness wearing a chamois leather Western shirt, python boots and a guitar strap with long suede tassels. The spotlight comes on, and— click!—he is Ricky Nelson of the "Ozzie and Harriet" show. Cute, irrepressible, he makes teen-age wise-cracks and Donald Duck noises. "Here's a song I hope you'll remember. Ooops, I hope I'll remember it."

After the set, Rick is accessible to anyone who wants to walk into the dressing room. A balding man asks for an autograph and grunts, "You doin' this for kicks or what?" Rick says, "No, it's just what I do." A brunette in a velvet dress asks Rick if he wants to "rap and relax, later." There is a twenty-year-old salesgirl named JoAnne Linstrom from Bedford, Massachusetts, who has been a fan of Rick's since she was ten. Allen Kemp, the lead guitarist, tells Rick, "This girl's out there with some pictures she took of you in Atlantic City." Rick says, "I don't wanna see 'em. Well, okay, sure, let's see 'em." JoAnne has long dark curls, and is wearing a brown mini-dress with a big white collar. She speaks with such a thick Boston accent that, Rick says, "I can only understand every fourth word, but I just keep nodding yeah."

When he goes on for the second set, JoAnne tells me, "I've been in love with that guy since I was little. I wanted to marry him. His music just hit me, and I never missed the show once. Then he faded out, disappeared, but I never got interested in any other star. I want to see him make it all over again."

JoAnne has a dream about Rick and the Nelson family that has haunted her sleep for a decade. "I'm sitting out in front of his mother's house. It's a big white house with a fence around it, and trees. Suddenly, his brother and father open the door and invite me in to have cookies and milk. Rick comes downstairs and has a glass of milk with me, and then starts playing his songs. He looks at me with those big blue eyes, and Ozzie and Harriet and David come over and pat me on the head and smile, and I'm right in the middle—me—almost like a part of the family myself . . . and then it's over."

Which is where the dream ends.

1971

THE MAN
WITH TEN WIVES

In the month of June I crossed the Virgin Mountains to the great red desert of southern Utah where I found a man called Joseph who had ten wives. Word of Alexander Joseph had spread throughout the land. It was said his wives were beautiful, talented and strong. It was said that he could sleep with three in the afternoon and have "a perfectly warm sexual experience with a fourth at night." It was said that he had been kicked out of four states, that three hundred men had taken blood oaths to kill him, and that the FBI and IRS were stalking him but he was armed to make his stand, squatting on federal land.

His wives, it was said, lived in peace and without jealousy. They spoke differently than most women of their time. They knew their place, and because I did not know mine, I drove across the desert to seek out the Josephs and find the flaw in their story.

Numbers

What is shocking about this country is that there is no shade anywhere. No trees, nothing but salmon-colored sand that stretches to the next mountain range. From this expanse rise pinnacles of rock, red mounds and crooked fingers pointing at the sky. Pilgrims in the hills see angels and whirlwinds, and if you turn on your radio you will hear the word of God.

Glen Canyon City, where the Josephs live, consists of several dozen trailers, at Stop 'n Shop and an old cafe, the Red Desert Inn, which the Josephs own. When I pull off the highway, a teen-age girl is sitting on the porch of the cafe. Gnats swarm in the air. She draws a map in the sand and marks an X. "That's where Alex is sleeping," she says. "He sleeps until noon or one."

I follow her directions down a gravelly road until I reach a green house, the only proper house in town. It is a small wooden box with a tar-paper roof and four cottonwoods stuck in the front yard. Alex and three of his wives live here, I learn, and the other wives live across the road in two trailers.

I knock on the door of the green house. Joan Joseph, who calls herself Jonie, lets me in and then sits down, sleepy-eyed, in a Naugahyde rocker. The furniture is tacky, all nylon and Formica, except for two Navajo rugs. As Jonie blinks and rocks, the house begins to fill with young women in bathrobes, giggling children, babies, cats and dogs.

Judy Joseph, who has an expression of sweetness and buttery-yellow hair that falls to her waist, makes coffee.

Jonie asks what size shoes I wear.

"Ten."

"I knew it," she says. "So do I."

I ask Jonie what she is getting from this marriage.

"We're here because we love Alex and we cleave

unto him. He's a patriarch," she says. "He's our head and we do his bidding. He's the authority, but we have the freedom to accept it. It makes for a very powerful system."

The door bursts open. Carmen Joseph, who is studying for the bar and handling the family's tangled legal affairs, sticks her head inside. "Did the sheriff come by?"

"No," Jonie says.

"Where's our husband?"

"Asleep."

Carmen disappears out the door.

Suddenly all chatter in the room stops. Alex walks out of the bedroom wearing a blue satin headband, braids and jeans with a gun in the back pocket. "How're you!" he says in a voice so piercing it could carry clear to Kanab. Jonie gets up from the rocker and Alex takes her place. "If somebody doesn't make coffee," he says, "somebody's gonna be in trouble."

He turns to me. "I know you, don't I."

Jonie says, "Sara has big feet. And she's a Jew."

"That so?" He smiles. "Get her some pickles, kosher pickles."

He begins opening mail. An infant boy is placed in his lap. Judy brings the coffee and Jonie combs and rebraids his hair. Alex yawns. Two girls, Paulette and Melinda, come bustling in with their arms locked around each other's waists. Alex says, "Next time, I want you to come in separate doors."

"Why should we do that?" Paulette asks. She is the newest wife, sixteen, raised in Kentucky. She has large, spongy breasts under a tight white sweater and she looks hungry.

"So you won't come in giggling and carrying on," Alex says.

"You'd prefer that we come in frowning?" Paulette asks, leaning down to kiss his cheek.

"Yeah, if I got a preference."

I try to start the interview. "What led you to . . ."

"It's a long story," he says. "Relax, there's no way for you to pry it out of me."

Then he says, "There are eighteen million eligible spinsters in this country."

"Where did you get that statistic?"

"I made it up." He laughs and catches my eye with an implicit wink. "Lots of men don't want to get married, they don't want the responsibility. But if you matched up the population one for one, you'd come up with twelve extra women for each man. So I try to take up the slack."

He lights a cigarette. The girls nestle at his feet and Alex continues. "Monogamy in America is a miserable failure. I'm demonstrating a superior life-style— the polygamy of ancient Israel. With monogamy, you've got two people sitting there and they're different. The man's trying to bring the woman into his intellectual and social world and she's trying to yank him into her structure. The more intelligent they are and the more vitality they have, the more ferocious the battle, the more oppressive it is."

He says the worst part about monogamy is "that fifty-fifty crap. The husband should have a hundred percent responsibility to be a husband and the wife a hundred percent responsibility to be a wife. But how the hell are you gonna have fifty-fifty? If we had fifty-fifty here, it'd be ten-ten-ten and we'd spend all our time voting."

Alex says that he makes all decisions for the family

because he has the best perspective. "My wives understand that if they ever got up, as one voice, to oppose me, I'd run over them and keep goin'."

Jonie says, "I wouldn't respect him if he didn't, if he were a mouse."

"Let me show you what kind of dogmatic tyrant I am," Alex says. "I was in Ogden with two wives and wanted them to come home with me. They wanted to stay in Ogden, so I said, 'I've told you what I need you to do. Now you have the freedom to do what you want.'"

"What did they do?" I ask.

"What do you think? They came back."

Carmen walks in again with a briefcase. "We have an appointment," she says cheerfully. "Would you shave, please, Alex?" He walks to the bathroom and emerges with shaving cream smeared on his face. "People have spent thousands of dollars to come gawk at us," he says. "Know why? I'm like an ape in a zoo." He pulls the razor down his cheek. "They're afraid I might escape."

Alex is flying a twin-engine plane to Salt Lake. He has been charged with stealing a helicopter in Arizona and Carmen has drawn up a petition urging the Governor of Utah to stop extradition. I sit next to Carmen. She is twenty-three, with an easy, girlish laugh and a certain shy reserve in her blue eyes. Her hair is long and wavy and her jawline is remarkable—firm and outjutting like a prow. She wears aviator glasses, gray pants, a cotton blouse and a small turquoise bracelet on her wrist.

Carmen lived with two other Joseph wives, Jonie and Judy, at the University of Montana. They shared a house at 2411 South Higgins and were something of a legend—a house of famous virgins. Beautiful and intelligent, they were disdainful of sororities, committed to each other and to having good fun. "I wanted to reserve sex for marriage and the other girls felt the same way," Carmen says. "We were unique because the University of Montana was a super-loose place, but we always had the neatest guys interested in us."

Because she is sunny and flat-footedly good-hearted, people like helping Carmen. Her word is gold. She runs by "correct principle." As Carmen puts it: "Since I was a little girl, I believed there was a right and wrong and made it my business to seek right."

When she met Alex, Carmen saw polygamy as a hypothesis to be tested for its moral correctness. Alex told her that Jesus Christ was a polygamist. Forget Billy Graham, he said. Forget Christ being celibate. Christ was a sexy creature.

Alex told her to look up the original Greek version of the New Testament. The women who followed Jesus were referred to as "wives." It was the Romans, Alex says, who mistranslated "wives" to "women," because they wanted to outlaw polygamy.

When Carmen satisfied herself that Alex's premise was right, she proceeded:

Given that Christ was a polygamist;

Christ demonstrated a superior life-style;

To know Christ, we should live as he did;

Therefore, we should live polygamously.

The principle was correct. Carmen simply couldn't bring herself to apply it. Then her roommate, Jonie, dropped out of school and married Alex. Shortly afterward Judy did. Carmen flew to Utah to see the principle in action and became Alex Joseph's ninth wife.

146

They were married "for time and eternity" on Brigham Plain. Carmen describes her wedding night as a "pleasant interaction." It is clear by now that if there are benefits in the Joseph system, one of them is not an abundance of sex. The girls sleep together in double beds and Alex rotates, when he is not traveling or too tired. Sex is not tolerated before or outside the marriage. In an average month, each girl may sleep with Alex once, on which night her bedmate will sleep on the couch.

"All of us girls want to be mothers," Carmen says. "That's the first priority in our house." They take their temperatures and count the days, "and if you tell Alex, next Tuesday would be good for me, you can rest assured next Tuesday he'll work it out to be with you." I ask if this satisfies her. She grins and nods. "I don't feel any frustration in the least. When sex happens, there's such a specialness about it. A night with Alex is a celebration and it means three hours of uninterrupted talk. The next morning, Jonie and Judy will ask, 'What'd he say?' "

The plane tips violently as Alex loops sideways to take a closer look at a bear. I have never been sick on a plane but it is happening now. This is too much to deal with. A thirty-nine-year-old phony Indian preserved in aspic from the Sixties and all these nubile, prim girls mouthing "correct principle." Carmen is talking about jealousy. "I have eighty opportunities a day to be jealous. Maybe Alex doesn't look at me and holds hands with Judy. I can choose to be jealous and unhappy, or I can choose not to be jealous. I know this in my head." She points to her temple. "I have no reason to be jealous. It's my own insecurity. I can't be a better Judy than Judy, but she can't be a better Carmen than me."

The plane lands and I am still fighting nausea. Alex stares at me. "Are you married, Sara?"

"Divorced."

Silence.

"You live alone now?"

"Yes."

He nods. "Not too good, is it?"

Nightfall at El Brazo's Red Desert Inn. El Brazo—"The Arm"—is Alex's nickname. When he took over the restaurant a year ago, he covered the walls with pictures of people he admires: wrestling champions, George Wallace, Brigham Young and Orson Bean.

He calls me in the kitchen. "What do you want to eat? Will you have whatever I have?" I nod, visualizing a king's feast. A half-hour later Jonie brings us hamburgers and bags of potato chips.

Alex wants to talk about the differences between men and women. "There's no way in the world that men and women think alike."

"Could you be more specific?" I say. "What about decision-making, do you have a sense of how that's different with women?"

"Enough sense so I don't let 'em make any decisions."

Jonie slips beside him in the booth. "He doesn't mean that." She turns to Alex. "You let two wives make that decision to come home from Ogden."

"No I didn't, I forced the decision on them."

Jonie falls silent.

Alex leans across the table. "Let me put it to you this way. Let's say you had a horse you could reason with. And you told the horse: You get to choose who you'll belong to. This one man won't require much of you. He'll give you first-class stable accommodations and you'll have a nice pleasant life.

"Now this other man will work you from the time you're a colt. He'll feed you good hay, he'll care for you well, but he'll push you to run faster than you dreamed you could run. He'll force you to be the best horse you can be. He wants you to win the Kentucky Derby. Now which owner do you want?

"And the sad news," he adds, with mirthful irony in his eyes, "is that like all horses, no matter who owns you, you're gonna die anyway. So that's what we get in life—we get to choose our master, to choose how we're gonna be used up."

I ask Alex who owns him.

"God. I give myself to him but I reserve the right to withdraw. That's what I exercise with my wives— voluntary ownership. I reserve them the right to withdraw at any time."

Alex is playing with his gun, a .41 magnum with a silver and turquoise handle on which is carved "For Christ's sake." He points it at Melinda's nose.

"Is that thing loaded? It makes me nervous," I say. He unsnaps the clip and shows me the bullets. "Try not to be nervous, dear."

Jonie says, "It would be an honor to be shot with that gun."

The Book of Joan

I am coming to a better understanding of obe-dience to one's husband. Knowing myself in wife-liness as the helpmate and chattel property is

*neat! It feels pretty and it feels right! Being where
you belong is a liberating thing.*

from the Journal of Joan Joseph

She is, to me, the most complex and interesting of
the wives. Her carriage is elegant; she has a rounded
torso and small waist, a rosy complexion and wide
brown eyes that are mischievous, suspicious and curiously naïve. She has the kind of mind that cleaves to
powerful ideas, the kind that will commit itself to die
for a belief. As we talk, she stops periodically to seize
my notebook. "I want to see how badly you're misquoting me," she says. I suspect she is irritated. She
nods. "Alex is going deeper with you than he does
with most reporters and you're bein' an ingrate.
You're not believing him."

I ask if Alex's ideas were easy for her to believe.
"The idea of a relationship being eternal was a strain
on my brain," she admits. But then, what could eternity mean to her, sitting in a pink ruffled room at college with a shelf of great books and a diary filled with
dates? It was only after she went to live in the desert
with the dust devils and gnats and crusted walls of
rock that eternity began to seem palpable.

When Jonie quit college to marry Alex, he was a
Boy Scout leader with short hair, leading the upright
life of a Mormon fundamentalist. He was unschooled
and raw but he had the most original mind of any man
she had met. He understood her as she had never felt
understood. He told her she had been deprived of
love. What he did not know yet was that she was one
of triplets adopted at the age of three. He told her it
was a shame she had to wear makeup, she was so
pretty just as she was. Jonie wrote in her journal,

"Alex is breaking me open and I feel exposed, like so much wreckage."

She found Alex a welcome contrast to the examples of "quiet manhood" in her family—her father and brother. "The boyfriends I picked before Alex weren't mouses," she says. "They were always intelligent but I was always a little bit more so." She thought that would be true with any man she could meet, except Alex.

So she held her breath and leaped. She became a polygamous wife, knowing she might never again have contact with her former roommates, family or friends. After a honeymoon with Alex, she found herself tucked in a crowded house with five women who had barely finished high school.

"I had a real disdain for people who weren't cultured and intelligent," she says. "The other wives reacted to me fiercely. They were either hostile or else real silly. But I loved Alex so much I maintained my courtesy and waited for things to smooth out."

She was lonely when Alex left home on business trips and wrote about nights when she lay in bed watching her life tick by:

Again I am the little girl, awkward and skinny in junior high. All the futile crushes. New loafers. Math awards. The art history survey paper, the Green Man sculpture. And I am the high school Jonie: the perky haircut and aloof manner. Football games and gymnasium dances. Porch kisses, car kisses. Summernight dates. The coffeehouse: black lights and slow dances. And so short a time since it was Jonie the college girl. Ben Shahn and Henry Moore . . . Warm smiles, intent eyes. And I slipped out of that world. Dropped out of sight. Into the world of Alex Joseph. Alex Joseph's wife.

And she could not help asking herself in those moments, "What the hell kind of marriage is this?"

Jonie worried she would never feel at ease with Alex's wives. But Margaret and Dale were showing her how to cook, and seventeen-year-old Pamela taught her to ride horses and drive a shift truck, and "it happened under my nose—I started falling in love with them."

In November, when Alex went to Montana for a court hearing, Jonie urged him to visit her old roommates. A week later, Jonie was at the door of the trailer when Alex returned in the pickup truck. From a distance, Jonie spotted another figure in the truck. She went running down the steps. Alex climbed out. The figure inside slipped out the far door. Jonie sped around the cab and saw her former roommate Judy, beaming, with her hair in long braids. Jonie grabbed her by the shoulders. "Are you a Joseph?" she asked.

Judy nodded her head yes, happy/sheepish.

Jonie screamed. She was so excited she couldn't contain herself. She slapped Judy on the back and kicked her in the shins. She was crying and she had a reputation for never crying. "Why the tears?" Alex said. Jonie said, "It's the fire, the smoke from the campfire."

She grabbed Judy's arm and ran with her to the creek, still slapping her and kicking and squealing over and over: "Isn't he neat, isn't he neat, isn't he neat!"

The next morning when Jonie saw Judy in the trailer, she said, "I can't believe you're here." Judy whispered, "Oh, Joan, Alex is asleep. Let's go kiss him awake!" And Jonie began to hurt. "I felt so bad," she says. "Judy was so loving and uninhibited. I remember watching her pick up Alex's hand and kiss it. I felt so inadequate, I wanted to go through the floor."

But Judy was in heaven. She laughed. She glowed. She thought she was living with Christ and all the sister wives were angels. Then four months later when Carmen arrived, it was Judy's turn to feel pained. Carmen was her best friend. She had been missing Carmen, longing for her and urging Alex to marry her, "But when he did," she says, "I got tested about how much I wanted Carmen to be there. I saw how crazy Alex was about her and that hurt."

Carmen's arrival nettled Jonie as well. She and Carmen had been intellectual rivals and for six months they knocked against each other and avoided eye contact. Carmen went off to law school, and at Alex's request Jonie visited her and ended up staying months. They would sit on the floor at night and moon over Alex's picture. By the time they rejoined the family in the summer, Jonie recalls: "All us girls started learning to be more loving and demonstrative with each other."

Jonie remembers one night they spent on the ranch Alex bought in Cottonwood Canyon. They had eaten a picnic dinner and shared a jug of wine and were standing around the campfire singing "Blow the Man Down." Ten girls in a line, arms around waists, swaying and smiling and harmonizing. Alex moved down the line and kissed each girl. Later he, Jonie and Judy took a walk through the cottonwoods whose thin leaves shimmered like paper chimes. Jonie says, "We were holding hands and kissing each other and it was just so beautiful! I felt the reality of the union. We both loved this man, he loved both of us and we loved each other and we were just one."

The Book of Joseph

Alex Joseph grew in Modesto, in the flat central valley of California. He was always outspoken, always assumed authority and liked to argue: the sort of person who attracts followers and enemies. He was student body president and captain of the debating team, but high school bored him so he quit to join the Marines. He made sergeant while in his teens. He drank heavily and read paperbacks about religion and murder. After four years he decided the Marines were "a bunch of pansies," so he went back to Modesto and became a cop.

It is hard to get a fix on Alex because he controls what you see and he presents a paradox: scam artist and saint. Shotguns and God. Alex calls himself an "occupational tramp." He has managed a horse ranch, sold cars, been a tax consultant and a fire fighter, taught school, sold health food, set up an underwater gold-mining business and written a column for a singles newspaper. "As soon as I get proficient at something, I lose interest and want to do something else."

He was working at three jobs, living in Sonora with his wife Shirley and their two children, when he converted to the Mormon church in 1965. According to his sister, Diana, it was not long before Alex was "practically running his ward." He preached and studied Scriptures and the life of Joseph Smith, the founder of Mormonism, until he passed everyone by. No one in the local church could answer Alex's questions. On a visit to Salt Lake, he met members of a fundamentalist Mormon sect who practiced polygamy and they answered some of his questions.

The rationale they gave for polygamy, or "celestial marriage," was that it had been revealed to Joseph Smith by God; it had been practiced by the patriarchs in the Old Testament; and it encouraged propagation and survival of the race. But what appealed to Alex was the notion of being a governor, a wise king, "a responsible masculine figure." Alex says, "Polygamy demands that I take on the attributes I've wanted to develop anyway: patience, tolerance, judgment and industry. When women invest confidence in you, you can accomplish four times as much. You're forced to give up ego and expand your capacity for love."

He taught the doctrine to his wife Shirley and to everyone around him, which led the church to excommunicate him in 1969. Trailed by his sister and twenty members of his ward, Alex moved to Pinesdale, Montana, where there was an illicit settlement of polygamists led by an osteopath, Rulon Allred.

The Pinesdale group was one of many that split off from the church in 1890, when Mormon leaders banned polygamy due to pressure from the government and public outrage. The rebel polygamists carried on in secret, even after the State of Utah outlawed polygamy at the turn of the century. To date, the law has rarely been enforced. Authorities estimate there are thirty-five thousand polygamists scattered in the Western states.

As Alex sits at home in Glen Canyon City, he describes the outlaw networks hidden in the mountains from Canada to Mexico. "Whenever you make a practice illegal—whether it's liquor, narcotics or polygamy—you drive it into the hands of gangsters," Alex says. "Atrocities are committed and people have no recourse because they're outside the law, like the Mafia." He spins a tale about settlements where the women wear puritanical clothes and are tried at church court if they appear "too friendly." Men acquire wives by trading daughters or claiming divine revelations. "In one town in Arizona," Alex says, "the high school graduating class is lined up every year and the men take their pick according to rank. I know of two sisters, twelve and thirteen, who were married to a sixty-year-old man. In most of these families the wives live in separate houses and hate each other's guts."

Alex says the groups put forth rival prophets and carry on vicious doctrinaire wars. They publish pamphlets and volumes of books called *Truth*. Men write letters to be sealed until their deaths. Houses are burned. Extortion notes are left on cars. Secret posses train with M-1 carbines equipped with infrared scopes for shooting at night.

As an example, Alex talks about the LeBaron brothers, Ervil and Joel, who started a colony in Baja California called the Church of the First Born in the Fullness of Time. The brothers quarreled and Ervil split off, founding the Church of the First Born of the Lamb of God. In 1972, Joel was murdered. Joel's other brother, Verlin, swore a blood oath against Ervil. "They believe in what they're doing," Alex says, "and they believe they got the right to assassinate anyone who interferes with the building up of God's kingdom."

People who join the sects are asked to turn over all their income. "So when a dispute happens, you got lots of land, ranches, factories and million-dollar combines at stake," Alex says. "For a century, these groups have been killing each other. Now a miracle happens. They've put aside their differences and come together for one purpose—to stop me."

"Why?"

"Because I threaten their structure. I live openly what they do underground. If I were to have polygamy legalized, like I'm trying to do, their financial empire would collapse." He says he's also a threat to the Mormon church because polygamy is still part of their doctrine. "It's against the law so they don't practice it. They believe they got a pass in their hip pocket to go to heaven and it's all punched. Now if, all of a sudden, you tell them they have to get the ticket re-punched, they have to conform to the tenet of plural marriage, you'll have mass desertions. The wives are against it and the men don't want the responsibility."

Alex takes out the gun with the motto, "For Christ's sake." Carmen is idly stacking bullets on the table. "Now you know why I carry this," he says. "The people who're after me know that if they come here, they'll get wasted."

"You could do it single-handedly?"

He smiles and again there is the implicit wink. "It's a bluff game, isn't it?"

When Alex moved from California to Montana, according to his account, he immediately added two wives to his family and lived with them under one roof. Other men in the colony had been foraging for years to get a second wife. They complained that Alex had no business marrying until he could build each girl a house of her own. "He'll pay someday," they said.

Alex fought with the prophet, and the following year Shirley, his first wife, divorced him and took the children. Alex set off again with his remaining brood and followers. He says he discovered the rare herb ginseng growing wild in the desert, went to Hollywood to market it and then bought land in southern Utah.

At this writing, he has been married thirteen times. Three wives have left, so he is living with ten wives who range from sixteen to twenty-nine, five children and two younger sisters of wives. The sisters are pledged to marry Alex when they turn sixteen. The children in the family call their mothers "Mom" and the sister wives "Aunt."

At four in the morning, nearly everyone is up drinking coffee and eating homemade bread while Alex talks. Lorraine, fourteen, is composing a history of the family, with a chapter on Alex's most recent arrest. Alex has never been arrested for polygamy but he was indicted for squatting illegally on public land, stealing a helicopter and selling game fish illegally in his restaurant. He expects trouble from the IRS because he does not pay taxes, and the FDA is investigating his ginseng operation.

"I retailed three million dollars' worth of ginseng last year," he says.

"Who distributes it?"

"None of your business."

"I'm just trying to substantiate this wild claim."

"So is the IRS," Alex says with a laugh.

He asks Margaret to fetch his bank statements. She brings him an envelope filled with canceled checks that bear mauve and pink Arizona desert scenes. Over a sketch of the Grand Canyon is a draft for five thousand dollars. "Large quantities of money pass through me," Alex says, and starts tossing me checks he has written for several thousand dollars each. "This is only one account. I wouldn't tell you about the others."

The week I was in Utah, I did not see Alex engage in any activity that seemed to produce income. The wives worked in the restaurant but business was minimal. When one wife asked if she could be a clerk at the Stop 'n Shop, Alex said he preferred she not work outside the family.

As he riffles through the checks, Jonie and Judy begin singing a John Prine song about moving to the country. Margaret sidles up, kittenish and demure, to kiss Alex good night, and in moments there are six women tucked around his body.

I ask Alex if he has any thoughts about why there have been no historical examples of polyandry—one woman with many husbands. "There would be no purpose," he says. "Our purpose here is enlargement. My family's a bunch of grapes, one stem with twenty-five fruits. To see one fruit with twenty-five stems is grotesque. And it would be destructive. The children wouldn't know who their father was, and I can't imagine ten men who'd submit to one woman and confine themselves to her sexually."

He adds, "If you can do it, I'd really be interested to see it. But let's not play with structures. I got a real structure here. I got three houses, a restaurant, a three-hundred-twenty-acre ranch, a caterpillar, an airplane, horses, automobiles and the family—that unique family you traveled all the way from Los Angeles to see." He pulls off a red white and blue striped headband and twirls it around his finger. "We're here to make a demonstration. And all this conversation isn't worth twenty-four cents."

Exodus

Judy is upset. Her thermometer is broken. We are driving to the ranch, raising clouds of dust, but Judy, in a soft yellow blouse and brown slacks, looks as fresh as if she's just stepped from a bath. "You pray and pray about getting kids, it doesn't happen, and sometimes a month passes and you don't even have a chance to try," she says. "But I'm not going to buy another thermometer. I believe that if you were to psyche yourself up, your body could throw an egg, so it'd be in a position to get fertilized."

When Judy married Alex, her father contacted the FBI and started a campaign to bring his daughter home. In the process, rumors were raised: the Joseph wives were lesbians; the wives were having orgies; the wives were frigid. "None of that is true," Judy says. "Sex is played down a lot in our family." She says Alex doesn't sleep with her as often as he does some of the wives "because he knows he can count on me to be mature. I won't complain about not getting my fair share."

I ask if she ever feels frustrated. Judy pauses. Her blue eyes go distant. "I don't know what it's like to feel horny. I just think about when I can get pregnant."

We turn off the highway into the dun-colored canyon, where the earth is being turned for a new polygamous culture. Alex and his followers have staked out twenty-three homestead sites on public land. The soil looks hard, rocky and ungiving but they intend to prove it can be used for dry farming. Alex is presently involved in a court battle with the Bureau of Land

Management, and if he wins, millions of acres of federal land across the country could be opened up to homesteaders.

Until legal matters are settled, twenty-three families are camping in trailers and army tents. At the Lassen family site, Patsy Lassen is frying tortillas on an open fire. Her husband, Erick, a towering blond, met Alex four years ago and introduced him to Jonie, Judy and Carmen.

Erick was a graduate student in philosophy at Montana when he had a "fateful car accident." He had to buy a new Toyota. The salesman was Alex Joseph. They became friends and for Erick it was a "love-hate attraction. Alex and I used to fight like cats and dogs," he says. "I thought Alex had some really good ideas but some of the stuff he said was wild, off-the-wall shit. Like Christ being a polygamist, I thought that was weird. So I'd go home, go to the library, look up documents and take notes, thinking, 'I'm gonna poke a hole in his balloon.' The next time we met, I'd have all this ammunition but he'd resolve the apparent contradictions and lay some more on me."

As Erick and Patsy became closer to Alex, they started thinking about practicing polygamy themselves. "It was an excruciating decision," Erick recalls. "We had a good marriage and I was looking forward to a beautiful academic life. I didn't want to marry anyone else. I didn't want to plunge into unknown territory." He resolved to do it, finally, because he wanted to follow Alex.

It was Patsy who selected Erick's first plural wife. She started telling her daughter, Amy, who was then four, that a new wife was joining the family but Amy didn't seem too interested.

What Amy recalls of the wedding is this: "I remem-

ber we went to this person's house and my mom was
pregnant. She was crying and my dad looked real
scared. He was standing by this lady, Laurie, getting
married, and I was sitting in a chair watching the
cuckoo clock, waiting for the bird to come out."

Now that is the edge.

"But it all worked out," Patsy says. "We have
three wives now and we'd like a dozen more."

Patsy seems incorrigibly buoyant. She talks, as al
the Joseph wives talk, about the need to stop women
from oppressing men. "Most women follow the ex
amples of their mothers and want to be pushy, to run
a man, domineer him," she says. "In monogamy, the
wife can say, 'If you don't do what I want I'm leav
ing.' And the man is cowed. But in polygamy, if she
tries that, the husband can say, 'Okay, you go, be
cause there are other people here and I have to be
fair.' "

Carmen and Judy nod.

Patsy says, "It's really fun to have a man come
along and say, 'This is gonna be done now.' Not, '
think it should be done,' but 'It's gonna be done.' "

I ask if Erick does this.

"He didn't at first," she says, "it was real hard for
him, but he's learned to be decisive. And he's become
very self-sacrificing. He's a man aspiring to heights
and just being around him is the greatest thing going!'

The Song of Paulette

"I have a hang-up," Paulette says. "I'm too old
fashioned to come right out and ask Alex to sleep with
me." She is sixteen, with Egyptian eyes, a ripe body
and straight black hair. "In the three months I've been

married," she says in a genteel Southern voice, "I've slept with Alex five times and had sex three times. We count 'em."

She takes my hand and leads me across the road to a white trailer where she shares a bed with Melinda, and for the next two hours Paulette tells her story.

It begins in Kentucky. Paulette has won the title of Miss Teenage Kentucky, and at fifteen she is engaged to a boy from Frenchburg. Her brother, Michael, who is "hungry for God," meets a prophet called Joseph who practices celestial marriage. Michael wants Paulette to have a celestial marriage. He takes her to Utah to meet Alex and learn the vows, so she can return to Kentucky and marry for time and eternity.

But Paulette never makes it back to Kentucky. She is sitting in the Red Desert Inn Sunday morning, playing twelve-string guitar and singing "Me and Bobby McGee." Alex stares at her for a solid hour. She wants to impress him. She walks boldly to the booth and sits down with Alex and a guitarist named Richard. They offer her coffee. Richard says, "Paulette, are you and Alex gonna be man and wife?"

Paulette spills her coffee.

"Because if you're not, I want you to marry me."

Paulette looks at Alex. She realizes in that second that he is her husband, the father of her children.

Richard says to Alex, "Are you in love with Paulette?"

"Damn near it," he answers.

"I'm leaving," Richard says.

That night Paulette writes to her fiancé in Kentucky: 'I've made new friends, I've come into Godly contacts and I've decided there's more to the world than getting married at fifteen." Shortly after she turns sixteen, she marries Alex on the ranch. The ceremony

163

is filmed by KUTV in Salt Lake. Paulette wears a white muslin dress and a silver and turquoise wedding band she is paying for on time.

After the ceremony, there is a campfire cookout and singalong. All the sister wives cry and hug and kiss Paulette. Then Judy takes her to the white trailer, changes the sheets, brings out clean towels and turns on the furnace against the chill. Judy kisses her good night and Paulette is alone. She puts on a gift from her mother—a silky white nightgown with little red roses in front. Midnight. Where is her bridegroom? She pulls on woolen knee socks and is sitting up in bed, reading the *Book of Mormon,* when Alex comes in and flops on the bed. "Ya know something? You married a maniac."

He reads her passages from the Scriptures that he says are about him. "Are you afraid of me?" he asks.

"No."

"Do you want to go to bed?"

"Alex," she says. "What a dumb question to ask a girl on her wedding night."

He takes her hand. "I'm gonna go in the bathroom, shave, put on my Brut, brush my teeth and come back and make love to you. Would you like that?"

"Yeah, it's a date."

He turns off the light. A full moon is shining through the trailer window and Paulette is trembling. As she will tell me later, "I feel like I'm about to go to bed with God."

For the first three weeks of her marriage, Paulette sleeps with Judy, who teachers her correct principle until she knows the lines by heart. "I love Judy not only because I love her but because my husband loves her," she says. "My biggest goal is to be a perfect Paulette."

I ask what that means.

She twists her ring.

"I want to have a baby right now, more than anything. But I'm shy about asking Alex. It sounds like I'm horny. I've always been old-fashioned, I think the man should make the advances."

Just a week ago, though, after climbing in bed she called Alex into her room. Her stomach lurched. If the lights hadn't been out, she couldn't have said these words: "Will you be busy tomorrow night? I want a baby, you know." Alex smiled and said, "I was beginning to wonder about you, Paulette. I think you've grown up a lot tonight."

The next evening, Paulette's roommate slept on the couch and Paulette waited for Alex alone in her bed. He never came. In the morning he said there had been a mix-up, he hadn't known where she was sleeping.

"You can imagine how utterly awful I felt," Paulette says. "I expended every ounce of courage in my body to ask him and he didn't come that night or the next. I told myself, I'll never ask him again."

She pats strands of dark hair neatly off her face. "There's no problem in my marriage. I'm in love with Alex and all the wives. What's happening is more or less newlywed growing pains."

Her voice has fallen to a monotone. "I have only one regret about getting married," she says. "I regret that I didn't do it sooner."

Revelations

Today is the day all the Joseph wives are driving to Page, Arizona, to watch themselves on a television special filmed a month before. The white trailer sounds like a dorm on Friday night. "Want to wear my headband?" "Who's got some shampoo?"

The girls laugh and roll on the beds. They try on ribbons, beads and boots. They eat grilled cheese sandwiches and do bust-developing exercises and pass around snapshots of Alex.

Carmen, who is chief of maneuvers, assigns everyone to cars. I end up next to Margaret, who interests me because she was raised in polygamy in Pinesdale, Montana. Her father had seventeen children and two wives, who were "really close," Margaret says, "because they were mother and daughter."

What?

Margaret explains: "My grandmother had my mother by a previous marriage. When my mom was fifteen, she married her stepfather, who became my father. So my mom is really my sister. And I've got brothers and sisters who are my aunts and uncles also."

Margaret speaks in a very high, whispery voice. Slender and quick, she has a heart-shaped face, blue eyes and a Kewpie-doll mouth. She was homecoming queen in high school and had turned down almost every man in Pinesdale when she met Alex. "I was sick of men hounding me," she says. "They wanted to marry me just so they could be in the principle of plural marriage."

When Alex arrived in Pinesdale, he and his wife Shirley requested permission from the prophet to court Margaret, as was the custom. They took her out together, and later Alex visited Margaret alone and proposed. "He looked kind of dippy, wearing baggy pants, but he treated me real nice," Margaret says. "We went for a walk and he told me, 'You're gonna say yes, so why don't you just say it and get it over with?' "

Judy calls from the back seat, "Did he hold your hand?"

"Yes," Margaret says.

"Did he kiss you?"

"Yeah, that decided it."

Carmen squeals, "He's such a good kisser."

Judy laughs and whispers, "Did he French kiss you?"

"Yeah," Margaret says.

All the girls giggle and squirm. Carmen says, "He kisses better than anybody, but it's his most hated thing. He says it's a distraction."

When the laughter subsides, Margaret says, "You know, Sara, if you stay much longer you'll have to stay forever. Us wives do the recruiting."

The Holy Family

It is early evening and Judy is cooking spaghetti. Alex sits in the rocker answering fan mail, writing in pencil on every other line of a spiral notebook. "My finger hurts," says three-year-old Marianne. "Lie down and be peaceful a moment," Alex says. "If it doesn't stop hurting, Daddy will look at it."

Judy brings Alex a plate of spaghetti, then sets the pot on the table. There is a good deal of murmuring among the wives: "You first." "No, please, after you."

Alex finishes eating, holds his plate in the air and two wives reach for it.

Paulette pads up to his chair. "Can I interrupt

you?" She composes herself. "I am being treated unfairly."

"Too bad."

"I think it's important."

"I'm busy now."

Her eyes narrow. "In other words, kiss off and we'll take it up later?"

Alex turns to me. "She's making a play for attention and she's not gonna get it."

"It's not a play," Paulette says.

"I can tell it's petty. You'll live to be sixty, whatever it is."

Paulette stands angrily and as she brushes past Alex, he squeezes her hand.

Later Alex explains: "Because of all the press people we've had here recently, I haven't had the opportunity to be as close to this girl as I would like." He says he's encouraged the media attention because he wants public opinion on his side for his court battles.

He asks who knows the other side of Paulette's problem. Judy says she does. She has just made up a work schedule for the restaurant and left Paulette off. Alex nods. "I want Paulette to work more closely with me. I want her to read my journals and write down her ideas so I can see what her talents are. She thinks it's unfair but actually she's going to get some special attention."

Margaret sits in his lap. "I'd like some special attention, Alex."

He laughs. "Take Margaret off the schedule too."

As they hug and kiss, it occurs to me that I've seen enough. It's possible I have stayed too long. I'm beginning to see how the marriage works for these people, how each wife adds a new dimension to the family. Another reporter, a man from Salt Lake, stayed too long. He was drinking beer with Alex at the restaurant when he blurted: "I'm sitting here taking notes and staring at you, and suddenly *my* life has become absurd."

I ask Alex if there is anyone he looks up to.

"Naw, I wish there was. I suffer a great deal from loneliness. But there's nobody who can show me a better way. What it comes down to is that I'm happy and you're miserable. You're trying to analyze my good health."

What it also comes down to is that neither Alex nor the women could live with one person. So this is the solution. Alex says, "You couldn't extract a monogamous couple from this family. If I pulled out Carmen, Jonie or Margaret, there wouldn't be enough there to make a marriage."

Margaret adds, "And none of us wives could handle living with one man. That's why we live with one man and ten wives."

Alex says, "It's a phenomenon, it's done with mirrors and a plastic head. It's illusion."

The clock strikes 2 A.M. Carmen slips next to Alex and Jonie drapes herself around his feet. Alex strokes Jonie's cheek. Her eyes flutter shut. "When we get the family complete, there'll be only one person. Alex will go away, Margaret will go away." He looks around the room and names each wife. "We'll all go away and there'll be one well-rounded person. One person out in the desert."

1975

5

The Cause

CHILE UNDER ALLENDE:
A Family Chronicle

Note: This piece was written in 1971, two years before Socialist President Salvador Allende was assassinated and the government of Chile siezed by a right-wing military junta. I have made no attempt to update the piece but left it as is—a reflection of the hopes and mood of the country, before it was known what would happen.

Santiago, Chile

In a residential section called Providencia, on a street of pastel houses, each with double doors, metal bars over the windows and locked gates, a family of three generations is sitting down to dinner.

At the head of the table is Alberto, sixty, a short man with a sturdy, peasant frame, a round face and pale blue eyes. Many years ago, at the age of fifteen, he had left his home in Poland, traveled to Genoa and caught a steamer bound for the New World. He had just turned sixteen when he landed at Valparaiso. For the rest of his life he would fend for himself, working tirelessly, traveling by burro across Latin America, saving, investing and gradually building a business network that today includes a farm, small factory, several apartments and stores.

Outwardly, his bearing has always been confident and unflappable, but in the last year, since Salvador Allende Gossens was elected President of Chile, Alberto has lived with a constant fear. His children, who do not share it, are unable to assuage his fear that everything he worked for will be taken from him, that he will be forced to flee the country, that he will be separated from his family or end up "an old man working as an employee of the state."

Across the table, his wife, Luisa, rings a small bell. One of the maids enters with a platter of beefsteaks. It is the beginning of the no-meat period in Chile—twelve days each month when, because of the acute beef shortage, it is prohibited to sell beef in shops or restaurants. The restriction hits people who have little money and must struggle through the period eating such things as horse meat. Luisa, however, can buy large quantities of beef in advance and store it in her freezers until the embargo ends.

Like her husband, Luisa was born in Europe. She came to Chile with her parents when she was thirteen, and, she says, "I always loved Chile. I've been happy here. Life in Chile is *muy dulce*—very sweet."

The word *dulce*, which means not only sweet but pleasant, agreeable, soft, remained fixed in my mind during the weeks I spent in Chile. I found that Chileans—perhaps because they have exiled themselves to an absurdly narrow strip of land at the end of the earth—seem to recognize a shared need to maintain a warm, pleasant, agreeable homeland, where friendships and ties of family are honored above political passions.

Both men and women express physical affection, hugging and kissing on the cheeks when they meet. It is common to find homes in which the parents are at opposite poles politically, but discussions "never become poisonous."

Alberto's older son, Miguel, a striking, thirty-two-year-old professor, is—like his wife, Patricia, and her father, Hugo—an ardent supporter of Allende and his Marxist-dominated Popular Unity Government. Alberto's twenty-six-year-old son, Carlos, and Carlos's fiancée, Iris, voted for Allende, but have reservations about his policies. Alberto and Luisa voted for the right-wing candidate, Jorge Alessandri. Despite their political divisions, parents and children are in constant touch, visit each other, eat together and go out together with a frequency that many Americans might find stifling. "I have no interest in being enemies with my sons," Alberto says. "We encouraged them to develop their own ideas. Now we don't try to convince each other on political matters, because we know it would be a waste of time."

At dinner on this icy winter night in August—the seasons are reversed in Chile—Iris describes the seizure a week earlier by a hundred poor people of a warehouse which her father owns and has been trying to sell. "My father complained to the local governor, who found emergency housing for ten of the families, but then ten more moved in because they thought this was a way to get houses." Alberto and Luisa listen with sad expressions. Miguel and Iris begin to argue about how Allende can solve the housing crisis—one fifth of the people of Chile have no houses and must live in shanties or unoccupied buildings.

Hugo, the white-haired father-in-law, who has been a Communist since his youth, seems to sense what is troubling Alberto and Luisa. "Don't forget," he says, "the important thing here is that we have an opposition, which can speak out and protest. This is why Chile will be like no other socialist country." Alberto and Luisa do not answer; they are thinking, "There may be an opposition now, but for how long?"

The new road to socialism, the ground-breaking experiment that Chile is pursuing with much self-consciousness, is being watched from afar as a test of fundamental concepts of Marxist revolution. In the remaining five years of Allende's term, it will be seen whether it is possible to create a Marxist socialist state through existing political machinery, without a violent break in the system; whether such a socialist state can co-exist with democratic freedoms—specifically, a multiparty system, free speech and free press; whether the ruling classes will give up their privileges without a fight; whether it is possible, as Régis Debray insists it is not, to "vanquish the *bourgeoisie* on its own terrain," and, finally, whether people will voluntarily develop a revolutionary consciousness, voluntarily make sacrifices, struggle to produce more and limit their own purchases in the interests of the state.

There is a tendency, among the foreigners coming to Santiago with hopes of applying what is learned there to other Latin American countries, Italy, France, even the United States, to overlook the fact that the Allende government is a product of Chile's specific political milieu. The country has always had strong leftist parties, which have been integrated in a stable parliamentary democracy. Allende considers his Popular Unity, or U.P., Government, a coalition of six parties, to be the result of a long, steady leftist development.

Because Allende came to office with a plurality of only 1.3 percent, and because the U.P. does not have a majority in Parliament, Allende cannot implement his policies without support from the opposition—primarily the Christian Democrats and Nationalists. Since taking office, he has been able to secure legislation for nationalizing the banks and the copper companies. He has also accelerated the agrarian-reform program initiated by former President Eduardo Frei Montalva, set up new social welfare programs and re-established relations with Cuba and China. He has failed to win support in Parliament for several key measures in the U.P. platform, including the establishment of "neighborhood tribunals," small community courts to administer justice.

It has been reported that Allende is considering calling a plebiscite, asking the country to vote to abolish the two-chamber Parliament in favor of a single house to be elected directly and called the Assembly of the People. If he does not gain a majority in the new assembly, serious questions arise as to how he can continue moving the country in the direction he seeks. Those opposed to his government fear that he will be pressured by the extreme left and the working classes to establish by dictate what he cannot achieve through parliamentary procedure. Andrés Zaldivar, who was Minister of Finance under President Frei, says, "They are going to see that a Marxist socialist system and a democracy are absolutely incompatible." A law student at the Catholic University told me, "When they arrive at the point where they can't advance any more, they will move outside the law. In my heart, I have doubts that there will be another free presidential election. It would be the first time in the world that a Marxist government allowed a country to vote about whether they wanted to continue living under Marxism."

It is interesting that such fears of dictatorship and tyranny are based on examples from other countries, because everyone in Chile—even those who fear Allende most—seems to agree that "no other examples apply." One hears again and again the phrase, "Chile is very special." A union leader says, "No model of socialism in the world has any relevance because in no other country were Marxists elected to power."

This sense of uniqueness carries with it a tremendous burden of uncertainty. Everyone in Chile has the sense of not knowing what will happen in the next days, weeks or months. When politicians are asked what changes they expect, they say they cannot "make prophecies." Businessmen, fearing expropriation or seizure, are afraid to invest more than the minimum to keep operations running. Farmers don't know when or how their land will be redistributed. Students cannot be sure whether the careers they are preparing for will exist when they graduate. Families planning trips are nervous about leaving their homes because, they say, "Everything could change while we are gone." Because of this insecurity, almost all those I spoke with, including politicians, asked not to be quoted by name, fearing retaliation by the present or future governments. A member of the Communist Youth said, "Today everything is fine, and I have nothing to fear. But in six months, there could be a coup or a repression or who knows?"

The uncertainty is beginning to take its toll, but it is all happening beneath the surface. Outwardly, there are few signs of panic, emotionalism or excitement.

But then this, too, is part of the national mystique—
that Chileans are "sober" and "sane."

One of the few ways one gets a sense of a revolution
taking place is from the quantity of propaganda on the
streets. The walls of buildings and private homes are
covered with murals, political symbols and slogans.
Around the Moneda—the presidential palace—giant
banners flutter from Government offices: "We will
cease being poor, thanks to copper," and "Comrades,
give one more hour of work for your country." A
Socialist senator says the walls of Santiago are like a
newspaper. "You can tell what's going on by reading
the walls." Each political party has a painting brigade
which works in the middle of night. In the past, they
have been most active during elections, but since Allende took office they continue nonstop. Each new
Government act spurs a rash of visual comments. On
almost every block, there is a salute to the nationalization of copper, and above the entrance to the Pan
American Bank is scrawled: "Another Bank for
Chile—*Venceremos!*"

Luisa wants to take me shopping, almost from the
moment I arrive. "You are not only a reporter," she
says, "you are a woman. You will see how cheap our
prices are. People come here all the time from Argen-
tina and Peru just to buy." We drive to the boutique
district of Providencia, the only place in Santiago
where one sees young people wearing bell-bottoms
and long hair. They are considered "hippies," but are
actually teen-agers from well-to-do homes who may
have talked about marijuana but have never smoked
it.

Most Chilean men wear dark, shapeless suits and

sweaters. The young women wear pants and ponchos or shawls. They are more interested in South American folk music than North American rock, and they identify with Cubans and other Latin figures.

In many of the stores, supplies are low. One of Allende's first acts was to raise wages and freeze prices in an attempt to redistribute income while curbing inflation. This precipitated a splurge of spending and, within a brief time, shortages of food and manufactured goods, particularly household appliances and automobile parts. Many of the cars in the city are badly in need of repair. Horse-drawn wagons are a common sight. Taxis and buses operate with broken windows, whole sides ripped off or bashed in, engines exposed and coughing fumes. At times, the number of ancient cars creates the illusion of a Forties movie; the loud pops and screeches of backfires are heard constantly in the streets.

The Chilean economy has been in a state of stagnation for years, with industry operating far below capacity, unemployment, and inflation of 35 to 40 percent a year. Because the Chilean escudo loses its value quickly, people who have any surplus earnings use them to buy dollars. A foreigner who brings dollars to Chile will get twenty-eight escudos in a bank, but if he asks in a shop, they will offer him sixty-five, seventy—more escudos each week.

Using the black-market exchange rate, Chilean prices are astonishingly low: a pair of good shoes, two dollars; a cashmere sweater, four dollars; a half-hour taxi ride, fifteen cents; a shampoo and set in a beauty salon, forty cents; a three-bedroom apartment with two terraces and a yard, thirty-five dollars a month. The quality of manufactured products is not high, though. Luisa, nonetheless, cannot resist bargains, and buys toys and sailor suits for her grandchildren.

We return to the house, where Alberto and Carlos, father and son, are waiting. Each has his own car and usually comes home for lunch, the main meal of the day. "Before the new Government, we had an extra car as well," Luisa says. "We sold it so as not to make a show of having money because houses were being occupied." The house in which they have lived for thirty years suggests comfort rather than opulence. It is decorated with Oriental rugs and shelves filled with knickknacks, doilies, crystal and silver. There are fresh flowers in every room, and ubiquitous plates of cookies, fruit and candy. A maid and a cook, who are paid the equivalent of ten dollars a month, share a room in the back. There is a garden with almond and orange trees and a small plot for corn and tomatoes. Surrounding the house, garden and garage is a tall spiked fence with one gate, to which only the maid has the key. When anyone wants to leave or come in, he must call the maid to open it.

Nearly every house, even the most humble, has a similar protective gate. President Allende's wife says she was impressed when she visited the United States by the fact that "you could pass from one house to the next without really noticing because there are no walls, fences or roadways that divide one from the other. It's a marvelous thing, I remember it clearly."

The locks are apparently one of those customs for which, if there once was a reason, no one remembers it exactly. Alberto and Luisa lock their bedroom door when they go to sleep, and lock all their drawers, desks and closets. When I ask why, Luisa says simply, "It is best. The girls are very good, but why should

I test them? This way there is no possibility that they have taken anything."

Such precautions, applied automatically day by day, may help to defend against darker fears. Luisa says, "The situation in Chile is not too bad now. But in a few years, maybe it will be difficult for us. I remember being in Berlin on the first of April, 1933—it was the day of the first Nazi boycott against the Jews. The people did nothing, thinking it wasn't that bad. Five years later, the police were breaking into homes and sending Jews to concentration camps. My experience is that any new, radical political change starts small and gets more and more drastic. It takes about five years to prepare people's minds, to change their way of thinking." I ask if she really thinks such a situation could develop in Chile. Luisa gives her head a quick shake. "I prefer *no pensar*—not to think."

Alberto says, "I always said if there were a Communist government in Chile, I wouldn't stay one more day in the country. Now there is a Communist Government, and I'm still here. Why? Because when it happens, there are other factors. My family all live here, my grandchildren, my friends. My business is here, and I'm not happy if I'm not working." Luisa says more than half of their friends have left, though. "Alberto's cousin closed his store and his house, packed and flew out fifteen days after the election. He was afraid that once Allende took office, no one would be allowed to go."

"Chile is a country with a beautiful climate and lovely, gracious people," Alberto says. "But unfortunately Chile is too politicized." The degree to which Chile is politicized is reflected in the fact that someone is considered "apolitical" if he doesn't work actively for a party. People tell you, for example, that the majority of Chileans are apolitical because only 10 percent belong to parties. But it would be difficult to find anyone in the country who doesn't have strong opinions about the political situation.

Alberto and Luisa, who call themselves apolitical, support Nationalist candidates and always vote against Communists and Socialists. "When we were young, we were leftists," Alberto says. "In 1938, I wanted to go fight in the Spanish Civil War." He pulls from a closet an old scrapbook, and turns to a sepia photograph of a young man with chin thrust forward and a proud, determined stare. "At that time, I felt I could conquer the world," he says. "I was idealistic. Then, over the years, I read about conditions in Eastern Europe. Three years ago, we went back to Poland and visited the only cousin I have there who survived the war. When we were young, we were the closest friends. Forty years later, I met a stranger, a man frightened to talk, frightened to be seen with me because I came from outside the Iron Curtain. This experience, plus everything I've read and heard, convinces me I don't want to live in a Communist state."

Alberto says he was hurt and troubled that his sons voted for Allende. "But what was there to do? I couldn't prohibit them. I was depressed, I'm still depressed, but I believe I must stay calm. If I let myself become nervous, I'll become neurotic and go crazy. I'm watching things carefully, thinking constantly, but I must take it all with patience."

Salvador Allende strides into the dining hall of the Moneda with a jaunty, rocking step. *"Buenos días! I guess there's not much to talk about today."* The group of fifty Chilean and foreign reporters laugh. The copper workers at one of the newly nationalized mines are on strike. There is discord in the countryside over agrarian reform, with reports of armed groups mobilizing. The parties which make up the U.P. coalition are splintering, and a third of the Cabinet members are about to resign. Not much to talk about.

The hall, like the rest of the Moneda, is dark and drafty, with a slightly frayed elegance that suggests the need for restoration. Allende calls for lights, so he can see the reporters, "particularly the women journalists." Then, in sober, deliberate phrases, he says this is the most confused, tangled moment in Chilean politics. While there are actually more forces backing the Government, he says, its base of support is being weakened by internal problems in the U.P. parties. But this reaffirms, he says, that "democratic rights exist, not only with respect to the opposition but within the governing parties as well."

Allende addresses each reporter as *compañero* and in turn is addressed as *Compañero Presidente*. When asked about the strike at the El Salvador mine, where workers are demanding wage increases of 35 percent, Allende says, "The strike cannot continue. It is not easy for the working classes to understand what it means to be part of the Government, to be, in fact, the Government. The copper worker must understand that his problem, however important, is not more important than that of Chile. Copper is the most crucial factor to our economic development. As I've said before, 'Copper is the salary of Chile, and the earth is the bread.' "

Allende says the U.P. Government must change the consciousness of workers and farmers so that they see they are not performing isolated jobs but helping to build up the nation. "I will go to El Salvador to talk with the workers myself, not to reprimand them, for they are exercising a right—the right to strike—which we respect. But I will impose, if I have it, and I believe I do, a moral authority."

On Saturday, as is their custom, Miguel and Patricia have lunch with the rest of the family at Alberto's house. They leave their four-year-old son there for the day and return to their apartment, where they are expecting friends. Virtually all their friends support the Allende government. "I was exposed to leftist politics at school, through my colleagues and the books I read," Miguel says. For a time, he was in conflict with his parents. Then he went to England for four years to do graduate studies, and when he came back, he says, "It didn't matter anymore." With distance, he came to understand that his father's outlook was "completely natural for a self-made man, for someone who had to work as he did to make the life he did. His right-wing ideas are sincere. There's nothing malicious about them."

Miguel had another dilemma to face, however, on his return in 1969. Many of his close friends had turned to the extreme left and joined M.I.R.—the Revolutionary Left Movement. Following Che Guevara and the Cuban model, they had concluded it was not necessary to organize or to educate people, "just put your bodies on the line." Miguel says, "It was traumatic because I couldn't follow my friends into M.I.R. and couldn't find any other place to fit. M.I.R. was assaulting banks and preparing for guerrilla warfare. I was certain that any movement which didn't pass through organizing the working classes couldn't succeed. Also, in general, I find it difficult to join mass movements. I'm very personalist—that's one of the bad features of my class."

Largely because of Allende's victory, Miguel is preparing to enter the Socialist Party, while his wife intends to join the Communists. Patricia says, "It's hard to do political work as an independent. If you want to have responsibility and share in decisions, you must be in a party." She says the Communist Party "may not be perfect, but I think it's the best. The Socialists are more adventurist. The Communists are scientific, theoretical and careful." Miguel disagrees. "The Communists are not as open-minded as they could be and not sufficiently de-Stalinized."

Miguel has an engaging curiosity that extends to almost every person and subject he encounters. He speaks in rapid bursts; he would rather not talk at all than have to speak slowly. Patricia is quieter, sensitive to people's nonverbal messages, but as firm in her ideas as her husband. She was exposed to Communist theory by her father, even though she grew up in a classic bourgeois atmosphere—servants, private schools, vacations in the country. She and her father now have apartments in the same building, a beautiful, modern structure decorated with Danish furniture and rya rugs. They have lunch together every day.

Patricia has her own maid living in, a situation she feels awkward about, but says, "If I didn't have help, I would spend all my time in the house. Things are more difficult in Chile than in other countries—diapers have to be washed by hand, food is more complicated to prepare. I have to consider how I can best contribute to the new government, doing the professional work I prepared for at university or working as a maid. The girl who is with me has four children, her husband is out of work, she needs money and couldn't get any other job. For the moment, she needs me and I need her. But I've always said that the day people can't find servants in Chile is the day we will really be a developed country."

Around six in the evening, several couples with young children arrive and spend the next three hours talking about politics. They are attractive, genial people—*dulce*—who feel hopeful and encouraged about the possibility of seeing in their lifetimes the creation of a country in which workers participate fully in decision-making and there is a decent general standard of living. A lovely green-eyed woman who is a school administrator says she thinks it is the economic sector which will make or break the Government, "because if Allende can't overcome the economic troubles, there will be a great reaction, perhaps a military coup."

Miguel agrees. "That's why they're putting out so much propaganda to encourage workers to raise production. Look, this government is seizing the power of the ruling classes, and they are just standing by. What are they waiting for? An economic collapse. That's why they stopped investing when Allende took office. If it comes to the point where there are no jobs, no food and people have to stand in line with rationing coupons, then the right wing can do something."

The following day, I speak with a man who is indisputably a member of the ruling class. His ancestors have been in Chile since the seventeenth century, have held high posts in government and had streets in Santiago named for them. Raul, as I will call him, is director of a large corporation and has a farm two hours from the city. When I tell him that people on the left believe the ruling classes will not give up what they have without a fight, he says, "They're wrong, or we would never have let Allende become President. As long as he leaves us our liberties, our free press and right of opposition, we are not going to initiate a fight. But if he takes illegal steps, then I think we are morally entitled to oppose him."

Raul is sitting in a beige Barcelona chair on the top floor of a recently built skyscraper. "This business is losing money like hell right now," he says. "Every major corporation in Chile is." He says he is hoping that both his business and farm will escape nationalization because they have good labor relations and are running at full capacity.

Raul says he has no intention of leaving Chile unless the situation becomes extreme. "I don't understand Chileans fleeing at this stage—abandoning ship when they should be maintaining a position and fighting back. Most of the people in my circle see that the struggle isn't over. If Allende can expropriate most of the private sector before his term ends, that will be practically irreversible. But I don't think he can. I think his experiment is failing, and we can be rid of this nightmare in the next election."

Carlos and Iris, who are together constantly, take me to see the *poblaciones*, the shanty towns on the outskirts of Santiago. The sky is overcast, and only the tops of the Andes are visible. It is an eerie sight: the brilliant white peaks seem to float in the middle of the gray sky with no organic relationship to the city below.

The *poblaciones*—crude shacks connected by muddy paths—are plastered with red stars, hammers and sickles and messages. "Finally Chile is wearing long pants," says one. Several clusters have names, "New Havana" and "Red Square." Iris, who is studying architecture, says she is specializing in designing "large communities for poor people, not single houses for the rich." She adds that the rich are not building now anyway because they have no security in Chile.

Carlos plays a cassette of Argentine folk music on the car stereo. Less involved in politics than his brother, Carlos is more playful, social and interested in sports. He is twenty-six, but, as is customary, will continue to live with his parents until he marries. "We are a Spanish-Catholic country, don't forget. There is much repression, and the double standard is still strong." Carlos says he and Iris would like to live together now, "but it would cause such a scandal and crisis in our houses and our circle, it wouldn't be worth it."

Another reason for living at home, he points out, is the financial situation. After Allende's election, Carlos was fired by the company for which he had been working a year. "They cut their staff down to the bare minimum. Then I was out of work for six months, until I finally found a job with the Government. They asked my political views when I applied. I said I support Allende."

Carlos is not sure that, if given the chance, he would vote for Allende again. "I agree with the Government's aims, but with all the propaganda, I think they've aroused in poor people a desire for revenge. Many don't want a real socialism, but to turn society upside down so those who were on the bottom will be on top and vice versa. Allende gives the poor people a sense of authority to do what they want—to occupy houses, take over buses, seize farms. The poor people want everything the upper classes have—nice houses, cars, good jobs—but the Government can't give it to them right away. So they're becoming impatient. I think there will come a time when the Government won't be able to control them."

After work one night, Alberto and Luisa meet two other couples at *Alero de los Ramon,* an elegant Spanish colonial farmhouse that has been converted into a restaurant frequented by the *momias,* or mummies, as the upper classes are called by the left. The dining room is vast, with wood beams, balconies, murals of the farmlands and antique, high-backed chairs. There is no heat, as in many public buildings in Santiago, but the owners have placed open braziers with hot coals throughout the room. By 8 P.M., every table is taken; streams of people are turned away at the door.

Over pisco sours, Elisa, who is Luisa's oldest, dearest friend, says, "We are the ones—the middle classes—who have the most to lose with the new government." Elisa and her husband, Juan, have a small factory where, she says, the workers are steadily demanding more and producing less. "The workers have fought for something, and now they must acquire a conscience. With the copper miners, for example, why are they on strike, when they know the country needs every resource it can put its hands on? I think even Allende is shocked. He never expected people to react this way."

Elisa thinks the Government's policies are "not very wise." She expects an acute food shortage in the months to come, and is storing food in preparation. "Right now the country seems to be split fifty-fifty for and against Allende. But people here are not used to suffering. When they can't get food, they may change their minds about Marxism and socialism."

Sergio, one of Alberto's friends, emigrated from Yugoslavia twenty-three years ago and came to Chile, he says ironically, because it was the farthest place from Russia. "I figured if Communism followed me to Santiago, there would be no escape. Now here it is." Juan smiles for the first time that evening. "This is like the last days of Rome," he says. "It was like this during the war. People thought, 'Who knows what will happen, so let's enjoy while we can.' " Elisa nods. "We used to work very hard and never go out during the week. Now we do it often. And wherever we go, there are crowds of other people doing the same thing."

The stage show begins. A troupe in peasant costumes performs the national folk dance, the *cueca*. The men move with pecking motions, backs arched like a rooster. The guitar rhythms are gentle and *dulce*. A comedian's act follows, and Juan gets up to go to the men's room. He takes a few steps and falls between the tables. He is fifty-six, and has suffered his first heart attack.

A dozen farm workers in black ponchos and hats are standing on the steps of the Ministry of Agriculture, gesturing angrily. They have marched sixty miles to protest that the agrarian reform is proceeding too slowly. The landowners in their district, they complain, are only planting a small portion of the soil. A young woman who is on the staff of Agriculture Minister Jacques Chonchol tells the workers, "I support your seizing the land. It's the only way we'll get things done."

Chonchol, however, in an interview later in his office, says the *campesinos* should take a broader view and try to understand the difficulties of redistributing land while maintaining production levels. "Each peasant wants to see the farm he's next to expropriated immediately because the policy of agrarian reform awakens great expectations. But the peasant must understand we can't do everything in one year."

Chonchol, who studied agronomy in Europe and worked in Cuba on agrarian reform, is one of the most respected figures in Allende's cabinet. He wears thick glasses and V-neck sweaters. When asked a question, he tends to rummage through his papers and rattle off a series of statistics. I ask if he is anticipating a food shortage in March, the end of the agricultural year. He reads figures on seed and fertilizer sales and farm credit. I ask if he is taking any precautions for a shortage. "We're a company to increase production, not plan for shortages," he says with an impatient smile. "Seriously, there is no scientific way to know what the results of this season will be. But I expect production to be about the same as last year. Unless we have bad weather or a natural disaster."

Over the weekend, Miguel, Patricia, their four-year-old son and Patricia's father, Hugo, decide to take a drive to the coast. On the road to Valparaiso, we pass a new collective farm, a jumble of tents and flags, dominated by a banner, "Villa Lenin." The countryside looks as California must have looked in mission days: rolling hills of pink, rocky earth, dotted with cactus and brilliant colored wild flowers. Hugo, who is driving, describes what Chile was like when he arrived from Austria thirty-five years ago. "It was much less settled and less sophisticated. We felt completely cut off from the rest of the world, until the jets and mass media came. On every corner of Santiago you would see drunks sleeping it off. A great many people wore nothing but overalls."

Hugo joined the Chilean Communist Party at about the same time he began building his own business, manufacturing handbags. He now has a factory that employs twenty workers, who are paid partly on an incentive plan. "There is no contradiction between my being a small capitalist and a member of the party," he says. "I've been living in a capitalist society. If I refused to operate a factory, what would I do? Go be a worker myself? That's an individual solution, not a collective one. I worked with the party to change the society against my personal interests."

Hugo has not been politically active for some years, having grown disillusioned with realities in the Soviet bloc. "What happened in Russia is not communism or socialism," he says. "It's a capitalism of the state. The worker participates no more than in a capitalist society, and perhaps his position is worse because he can't strike or protest."

We have reached the coast, and drive north to the resort town of Viña del Mar. A cold sunlight plays on the water, which for long stretches foams over rocks, then washes against smooth pink dunes. Even here, there is no escape from the political slogans—they are painted on the rocks.

We stop for lunch at an oceanfront restaurant and are joined by Carlos and Iris, who have been following in their car. The meal stretches out to three hours, most of it spent dawdling over Chilean wine, waiting for a meandering waiter to bring plates of seafood.

Many of the specialties are found nowhere outside of Chile: *locos*, a succulent, thick abalone; *erizos*, the orange flesh of a spiny sea urchin; and *congrio*, an eel that thrives in the cold Humboldt Current.

Miguel turns the conversation to films and theater. "All the films being made in Chile now are political," he says, and resolves that we should see one that evening.

The film, *Voto Mas Fusil* (Votes Plus Guns), by Helvio Soto, is partly surreal, partly documentary and, from a technical viewpoint, totally clumsy. It traces events in Chile in the period prior to Allende's election, then shows the right wing's abortive attempts to wrest victory from the U.P. Afterward, Carlos says he liked it a great deal. "It captured the constant tension and the fear, which you can still see everywhere you go." Miguel says, "I think the point of the film is that it takes more than votes to bring about change. We must be vigilant against violence from reactionary forces."

Since my arrival in Chile, my requests for an interview with President Allende have been first vaguely, then bluntly refused. At length, the Foreign Office says it will try to set up an interview with Allende's wife, but I must submit questions in advance and I am warned that the interview will be taped to prevent misquoting. Irritated, I give Mrs. Allende's secretary the questions I had intended to ask the President. I arrive, feeling defeated, expecting to hear nothing but small talk.

Instead, Hortensia Bussi de Allende proves to be informed and familiar with the details of her husband's government. She is pleased with the questions, and the interview lasts an hour and a half.

Mrs. Allende says she believes it is difficult for private people to begin functioning collectively. "People talk much about the revolution in theory," she says, "but to build socialism in Chile, we must all become aware that we have to work harder, to produce more, so we can take Chile out of the swamp. We have a very low per-capita income, a high infant mortality rate, illiteracy, unemployment, shortages of housing, hospitals and schools. These are problems we have to solve before we can reach that ideal socialist society where there is only one class, the working class."

She describes efforts the U.P. is making to raise political consciousness. Special courses are being set up for housewives, for workers, farmers and the illiterate poor in which political education will be combined with the teaching of technical skills. The Government is also starting a network of free child-care centers, which will feed children three months to six years old, give them medical care, preschool education and their first lessons in government; their mothers will be freed to work outside the home.

Mrs. Allende is convinced that women's rights will be more easily attained in a socialist than a capitalist society. "I've seen it with my own eyes—in the European socialist countries, the men and women share in child-raising. You don't find the *machismo* we have in Latin America, where the man expects to be served. He sits down at the table and, if there is no servant in the house, waits for his wife to bring his food. The wife washes his clothes, irons, sews. It doesn't occur to him that he could press his own pants or pick up a broom. This is what I would like to see in Chile: a greater co-operation between man and woman."

Mrs. Allende and her husband have always co-operated as a political team. She is an attractive brunette with flawless skin, who is partial to pearl earrings and dresses which fall discreetly below the knee. She was a supporter of the left before meeting her husband, she says, but was influenced by his ideas.

I ask if she thinks the transformation from capitalist to socialist state can be achieved without violence. "I'm not a seer. I can't say this won't happen. But we believe, at the moment, that we can make the changes within the democratic legal process." She says she believes the U.P. Government will be so successful that Chile will never go back to a government of the right or the center. "But I want to emphasize that what we have now is a government of transition, a nationalist government, committed to recovering our national wealth. This is a step toward socialism, but we won't be able to do everything that a socialist government can do. Another government will continue all the way."

The night before I leave Chile, Alberto's family gathers at Miguel and Patricia's house to say goodbye, bringing presents, records and candy. Alberto gives me a long hug and apologizes for leaving early. In the morning, he must take Luisa to the airport. She is going to Mexico to see her parents, and fears it may be the last visit. "It's becoming so expensive for us to travel now, and what if the Government won't let us go?"

Carlos and Iris are sitting in a corner, their arms around each other. Miguel, Patricia and Hugo are talking about the Government's ultimate goals. Hugo says he feels there are grounds for fear that eventually Chile will be completely socialized. "The Government says they won't nationalize middle-sized and small enterprises, but I know small factories that have been taken." Patricia protests, "They were plants that were functioning below capacity or not at all."

Miguel says, "I personally hope Chile won't be completely socialized, because I've been in Russia. I've seen that putting small industries and crafts in the state's hands doesn't work, and there's no need for them to be in the state's hands. If the U.P. were to change their policy on this point, I think a lot of people who are backing them would withdraw their support."

Hugo asks, "What kind of society are we going to have, then?" Miguel: "Millions of people are going to be educated who never were before. Thousands will become small landowners or administrators of worker-owned factories. What kind of mentality will they have? This is the real revolution—the way the country works is changing. Social ties are changing. It's impossible to predict what will be the end result."

Hugo suggests there may be a military government before there is a socialist state. Carlos says, "I have a different opinion. I think any violence will come from the extreme left, who want a total upheaval, not a gradual transformation." Miguel shakes his head. "For the moment," Miguel says, "the Government has enough popular support to prevent any attempt from the left or right to precipitate a conflict. And everyone knows this."

Hugo smiles. "I think you are right, for the *moment*."

The moment, finally, is all anyone can maintain a grasp on during what Allende calls "the most confused" time in Chile's history. In addition to the doubts, however, there is a sense of binding national strength, an understanding that somehow people will bear up and endure.

At the end of the evening, Miguel, Patricia, Carlos,

Iris, Hugo and I walk outside and stand for a moment on the damp grass. The sky has cleared, and the Andes are fully visible to the east. We admire the full moon and the stars. The elements seem to hint, prematurely and perhaps deceptively, that the raw Chilean winter is coming to an end.

1971

NOTES FROM
THE LAND
OF THE COBRA

In the fall of 1973, I returned to live in Berkeley, California, after a nine-year absence. I found my old friends who had been activists in the Sixties preparing to go back to school or work. The kiosks in town were covered with ads for psychic healing, acupuncture, meditation, kung fu, red-pepper cures, sex therapy and dream control. Former S.D.S. members were talking about building a new Communist Party. "We've rediscovered the Old Left," one said. "We've rediscovered communism and socialism."

Men were baking bread, women were sawing wood. Almost all those I knew were tending gardens and raising children with names like Circle, Lorca, Fidel and Butterfly. They were, in short, settling in for the winter, for the long, slow road to revolution, when on a still November night, the Oakland Superintendent of Schools, Marcus Foster, was shot and killed.

In rapid sequence, a terrorist band called the Symbionese Liberation Army claimed responsibility for killing Foster; the group kidnapped Patricia Hearst, granddaughter of William Randolph Hearst; Patty

Hearst announced she was joining the band and appeared with them in a robbery of a San Francisco bank. Then on May 17, a bungalow in Los Angeles where the S.L.A. was ambushed by police erupted in flames, killing all known members except Patty and Bill and Emily Harris.

The acting head of the S.L.A. was a black ex-convict, Donald DeFreeze, known as General Field Marshal Cinque. The leading soldiers and theoreticians were young white women. The youngest was Patty, twenty, who took the name Tania and in a voice with the same refined, airy softness as that of Jacqueline Kennedy Onassis, vowed to fight for the "freedom of all oppressed people."

The unfolding of the S.L.A.-Hearst drama shocked me out of two-year stupor, an indifference to the news that even Watergate could not disturb. The affair seemed to set off in me and everyone I encountered powerful fantasies and fears. It was a screen which reflected our private plots, and it was a screen on which the movie was always changing, the images constantly reversing themselves.

Because I could see myself in Patricia, Mizmoon, Randolph Hearst, in all the characters, I spent weeks prowling around the settings, looking in windows and talking to strangers. What I have come up with are fragments, shards of pathos and humor, and a suspicion that the symbols in this drama may be more potent and meaningful than the reality.

It is noon at Sproul Plaza, the University of California. No card tables, no speakers, no leaflets are to be seen. No major demonstration has occurred in three years. In the sun by the fountain, students are playing music. A grinning fat man is blowing bubbles from a jar, and a quartet of girls in gym shorts leap by.

At the edge of campus near Telegraph Avenue, wooden booths are set up each morning to sell fruit juices, Chinese food, falafel and donuts. In the Fruity Rudy stand, painted orange with a green awning, Nancy Ling Perry, who liked to be called Ling, worked for a year and a half.

Everyone in the community must have bought juice from Ling. I know that I did. She was the most visible and accessible of those who have been identified as S.L.A. soldiers. With Ling, as with everyone in this story, there is no detail to be culled from her past that explains what sent her over the edge. She is described by people who were intimate with her as a kind, honest person with strong humanist convictions, "not the type to be violent."

Ling was twenty-six, and like the other S.L.A. women, over-qualified for the work she did. Ling held a degree in English from Berkeley and took graduate courses in chemistry. But she saw her profession as a revolutionary, which meant not taking the first steps up a bourgeois career ladder. It meant working at marginal jobs. (Mizmoon Soltysik was a janitor; Emily Harris, a clerk-typist.) It meant living in a dingy rooming house in Oakland, wearing clothes scavenged from free boxes on the street and hitchhiking for transportation.

Ling was four feet eleven inches, wiry and fast. She would squeeze juice for hours and never gossip or flirt with customers. She had been through a period of experimenting with drugs and once painted her fingernails green. Noel McCloud, who worked with her at Rudy's, says she did not like exchanging small talk with people who weren't "political." She also scorned leftist "oldtimers from the Sixties," whom she viewed as lame and dissipated.

Ling had a strong attraction to blacks. She lived among them, spoke their language and for six years was married to a jazz musician. It was a stormy relationship with periodic separations, and after the last, in early 1973, Ling looked for an outlet for her political passions.

She began visiting inmates at Soledad, San Quentin and Vacaville. By the summer, she had connected with an odd karass of desperadoes and dreamers—Cinque, Mizmoon, Camilla Hall, Russell Little, Willie Wolfe, Joe Remiro, Angela Atwood, Bill and Emily Harris—who with a few others were training for guerrilla combat. Two of them, Remiro and Harris, had been taught to kill by the U.S. Army in Vietnam.

The group adopted code names, rented hideouts, stole ammunition, collected wigs and practiced shooting with BB guns. They formed security rules such as "Keep your handgun with you" and "Always know where your shoes are." They wrote reams of propaganda and drafted a constitution for a grand Symbionese Federation.

In October, Ling rented a ranch house in Concord which the S.L.A. used as a base until January 10, the night Remiro and Little were picked up by police and charged with murdering Foster. Ling herself set fire to the house "to melt away fingerprints."

Soon afterward, she disclosed her identity to the world: "My name was Nancy Ling Perry, but my true name is Fahizah." Her tone was exalted, her faith in her own rhetoric absolute. "I have learned that what one really believes in is what will come to pass."

When Rudy Henderson, proprietor of Fruity Rudy, first saw Ling's picture on the front pages, he says,

"It didn't surprise me. She talked a lot about prisoners and the poor people, but she never mentioned guns."

Ling and Rudy had grown close during the time she worked for him. Ling told her friends she was in love with Rudy. He is a tall black man of forty-seven with close-cropped silvery hair, known as an eccentric who can be snappish and surly. He operates four Fruity Rudy stands, teaches tennis and lives a block from campus in a hotel with stained carpets and strange odors.

Rudy used to play drums and would take Ling to jazz clubs. "Ling liked me and I didn't sort of care for her," Rudy says. "One time she shouted in the street, 'Don't you know I love you!' " He shakes his head. "She was trying to rush me into something and I was a cold fish."

Ling knew Rudy wanted a color TV set, so she tried to find a scam—some way for him to acquire one cheaply. When two men picked her up hitchhiking and offered her a stolen set, Ling ran to find Rudy on the tennis court. He paid the men $150 in cash and triumphantly carried the box to his hotel room. When he and Ling opened it, they found wood and bricks inside. "See what you brought me!" Rudy said. Ling cried.

Noel McCloud recalls, "Ling felt so guilty about it that she told me, 'Maybe I'll go in the city and turn a few tricks.' She wanted to make the money to pay Rudy back." Noel, a twenty-one-year-old who studies communication and public policy, adds, "This shows me Ling had a conscience."

Ling did repay Rudy with money borrowed from relatives. When people asked why he accepted the money, Rudy grumbled, "She's like a sister to me but she has to learn."

Thinking back, Rudy says he feels badly about the way he treated her. "I liked her more after she made her move," Rudy says. "You get to know a person better after a thing like this. I know she was serious about revolution, about helping the poor. She was not playing games. She was an out-of-sight girl." Rudy folds his arms across his chest. "I tell you, I love the girl now."

We will never know what happened during the final hours in that yellow house in Los Angeles, but it is clear that the six inside had passed through some alchemical psychic process and come out ready to die. They strapped bandoliers across their chests, stationed machine guns in the living room and slipped knives into special pockets sewn in their jeans.

They did not sleep for days before the shoot-out, and lived on soft drinks and beer, cheap white bread sandwiches and cigarettes. Up to the end, they were trying to recruit "strong brothers and sisters" for the revolution. When they found themselves absurdly outnumbered, they gave no thought to surrender. They took the offensive and fired.

"You are witnessing the biggest gunfight in the history of the West," one of the news correspondents shouted into his beeper phone. Could the battle have been staged for the evening news? The shooting began at 5:50 P.M., Pacific standard time, and the fire erupted at 6:30 P.M. The camera crews had been given two hours' notice to prepare for live color coverage.

All the players were speaking lines from B movies. The FBI called Patricia a "fugitive" who was "armed and extremely dangerous." James Johnson, eighteen, says Patty told him, "They'll have to kill me before I go back." Another witness told police the S.L.A. "lived by night," and Randolph Hearst's own San

Francisco *Examiner* came out with this headline: "They Died By Fire."

In California, the S.L.A. shoot-out seemed an event almost as gripping as a presidential assassination. People stopped strangers on the street to ask if Patty was all right, and called friends to tell them to turn on the television. At the Student Union in Berkeley, groups gathered around monitors, staring at the incongruity of palm trees and flame.

When I stepped outside my door after the news, I expected to see shotguns and fire, but the sky was clear and my neighbors were pruning roses. I thought of Tom Matthews, the eighteen-year-old from Lynwood High School, who was kidnapped by Patty, Bill and Emily Harris before the shoot-out. After spending the night with these three people that the entire state law-enforcement apparatus was seeking, he drove home to play in a championship baseball game. I imagined what he was thinking all that night, crouched under a blanket, cursing his luck and hoping he'd get out of this in time to make the game. He did, and they won, 2–0.

When the fire was extinguished and the body count final—six of the nine known members dead—the FBI said they believed the S.L.A. had been "decimated." Charles Bates, head of the San Francisco bureau, said, "Anything can change from day to day on this, but we feel the death of six people has taken its toll on the organization."

Others, however, worried that it was not the end, that new terrorist groups would surface in the future. Joe Remiro had said in prison on Easter Sunday: "The S.L.A. ain't nothing, man. The revolution is on with or without the S.L.A. . . . if the entire S.L.A. and everybody who relates to the S.L.A. would be killed tomorrow, the next day they'd have to kill a lot more."

As I drive down Telegraph Avenue, I stop for a little girl in a sailor dress standing in the street with her thumb out. She is six years old. "You're the youngest hitchhiker I've ever seen," I tell her.

"That's the way it goes," she says. "I've been hitching since I was three. My mom taught me."

I am on my way to see Michael Rossman. He is thirty-four and something of a Berkeley fixture: leader of the Free Speech Movement, crusader for educational reform, and, at the moment, he says, "I'm working with kids, writing and doing sex therapy." Michael greets me with a bear hug, notes that my shoulders are tight and shows me an exercise to unlock tension.

Michael says he never knew anyone connected with the S.L.A. "In one sense, it's ten or twenty isolated people, but in another sense it's ten or twenty million people, because that's us there! We contributed the energy the S.L.A. is running on. It's clear where those ideas come from: women's liberation, lesbianism, the black struggle, the Vietnam veterans, prison reform, the Black Panther food program."

I ask how the S.L.A. makes him feel. "Crazy and confused," he says. "The S.L.A. says to me: where are you with your passions of the Sixties? Remember bygone days when you marched for the downtrodden, the poor, the blacks? Well, look around, buddy, the war isn't over. All the problems in America are still there and you, buddy, what are you doing?"

He mimics the answer: "Oh, I'm sitting on my cushion meditating, studying acupuncture and teaching kids to stay open. I've grown mature. I know how

long things take. I've learned revolution is complicated, that it's not a simple matter of good guys and
bad guys."

Michael slams his hand on a chair.

"There's still a part of me that feels the need to do
something right now."

Russell Little, who is twenty-four, has written his
autobiography for the underground *San Francisco
Phoenix*. Every other sentence ends with an excla-
mation point. ("My father grew up in Alabama!") In
hit-and-run prose, Russell describes his working class,
Southern cracker background, his political awakening
at the University of Florida and his transformation to
a "long-haired, pissed-off radical!"

By accident of birth, Russell missed out on the Sixties and came of age just when the New Left hit a
slump. Russell describes what happened when he
drove across country to Berkeley in 1971. "I expected
things to blow up all over California but they didn't
. . . The era of riots and demonstrations had passed
. . . People started talking about educating the people
again. Bullshit to that. What about all the people who
had been educated in the Sixties?"

Russell decided the only revolutionaries "who didn't
die or go underground by the Seventies" were in
prison. He joined the Black Cultural Association
(B.C.A.) at Vacaville, a group set up to give convicts
pride and prepare them to re-enter society. There he
met Cinque and a number of young white visitors who
reinforced each other's urges and frustration. Russell
says, "We grew tired of waiting . . . we decided to
seize the moment." They would form a guerrilla army
and fire the first shots, because "revolutionary violence is necessary, is practical—it works!"

The American left, in its entire spectrum, disputes Russell Little on this point. Angela Davis, Cesar Chavez, Jane Fonda, Tom Hayden, Huey Newton, the Black Panthers, the Communist Party and the Maoist Venceremos organization have denounced the tactics of the S.L.A.

Dan Siegel, a radical lawyer, tells me he sees the S.L.A. as a "threat and a setback. The S.L.A. gives a picture of the left as wanton, crazy killers, and we're at a time now—because of the economic crisis, the energy crisis and Watergate—that radical-left ideas could flourish. The S.L.A. was trying to be a guerrilla army without having any mass base. They took actions that people couldn't support or even understand, and the result was they were murdered."

The killing of Foster caused almost universal anguish. Members of the S.L.A. claim they assassinated Foster because he supported a plan to introduce identification cards and guards in the schools. What they do not mention is that Foster, with the backing of community groups, withdrew the plan from the School Board agenda on October 9, almost a month before he was shot.

The S.L.A. has not justified the Foster killing to anyone outside its ranks. Carolyn Craven, a black reporter who grew up in the Movement, says, "Black folks have never been given enough power in this country to be No. 1 on anybody's hit list. Why Foster? Why not the head of Standard Oil of California, or Union Oil or Bank of America? By what standards do you kill one of the few black superintendents of schools in the country? You go down on East Fourteenth Street in Oakland and explain it to the people, because the S.L.A. hasn't bothered!"

Carolyn's feeling is echoed by Popeye Jackson, who

has spent twenty of his forty-four years in prison and heads the United Prisoners Union, a group working to change the penal system.

Popeye wears a black leather jacket and black straw hat and speaks in a muffled volley. "If I were in the S.L.A., there's no way in hell I would have shot Foster or kidnapped Hearst," he says. "If they'd kidnapped the head of the California Adult Authority, that would have been different. They could have gotten all the prisoners out of jail."

Popeye knows most of the identified S.L.A. members. He worked on an educational film strip with Mizmoon and Camilla Hall and saw them as "two regular sisters," no different from hundreds who volunteer to tutor prisoners. There are five women to every man in the prison movement, he says, "and they're not interested in the problems of women prisoners. They're only interested in the men. Most of them get involved in a romantic trip. When they talk about violent revolution, they're living in a dream world! We don't have no nuclear weapons, we don't have no jets. We can't buy one tank. How we gonna have a revolution? We have to educate the people first."

After he watched the "incineration" in Los Angeles, Popeye said he was furious. "The pigs burned them alive and that was not called for. They murdered the S.L.A. because they didn't want the S.L.A. to come forward and talk about *why*."

What happened to Patricia Hearst, and why? If she had been able to return home to Hillsborough, what would she have gone back to?

To a white, twenty-two-room house with Greek columns and pots of orchids always in bloom. To Etruscan vases, Persian carpets, candelabra and burnished mahogany. To quiet, opulent Santa Ynez Avenue, where nothing happens outside all day except that in the afternoon, ladies with pearl necklaces may drive by in their Country Squire wagons.

Perhaps the Hearsts would have taken her to rest at San Simeon. The Hearst castle there is a state museum, but hidden behind it in a vale swarming with butterflies is a Gothic house the family still uses. Or they might have sent her north to Wintoon, the baroque alpine estate overlooking the McCloud River which Phoebe Apperson Hearst had built by craftsmen brought here from Bavaria.

What would Patricia say to her parents and they to her? A young man who is a close friend of the family describes dinners he would have with them before the kidnapping. "It was relaxed and cordial, but there were subjects everyone tacitly agreed not to bring up. Sooner or later, Mrs. Hearst would voice some absurd opinion like, 'We've got to stop nudity.' She had seen a nude ballet and was terribly upset. Among the young people, it got to be a game: Who in the room would flinch, or be the first to change the subject?"

Patricia, he says, had a rebellious edge and caused a minor family scandal when she moved into an apartment with her boyfriend, Steven Weed. It was from this apartment on February 4 that she was kidnapped—an act which so violated the genteel, insouciant pattern of her life that such order might never be restored.

There are numerous clues about the process of Patty's conversion to the S.L.A. The tapes she made suggest that Patty came to believe her parents betrayed her, let her down, sacrificed her for the sake of money. This impression may have been planted by the S.L.A., but toward the end, Patty believed it.

In the first tape, February 12, Patty said: "I just want to get out of here and see everyone again and be back with Steve . . . I just hope that you'll do what they say, Dad, and just do it quickly."

The S.L.A. was asking Hearst to give seventy dollars' worth of food to every poor person in the state. Hearst protested this would cost hundreds of millions. In her second tape, February 16, Patty told her father the S.L.A. was not trying to make unreasonable demands. "They have every intention that you should be able to meet their demands . . . so whatever you come up with basically is O.K. Just do it as fast as you can . . . Take care of Steve and hurry."

Hearst offered to put up two million dollars for the poor. The S.L.A. demanded four million more. Hearst threw up his hands. This was beyond his financial capability, he could negotiate no further. Later, however, the Hearst Corporation was able to produce the additional four million, to be held in escrow until Patty's return.

Hearst's withdrawal from negotiation must have been a bitter blow to Patty. Surely she felt that her father, with his influence and connections, could have raised any sum he wanted.

Weeks went by. In her third tape in mid-March, Patty said: "I don't think you're doing everything you can, everything in your power. I don't believe that you're doing anything at all. You said it was out of your hands; what you should have said was that you wash your hands of it. . . . If it it had been you, Mom, or you, Dad, who had been kidnapped instead of me, I know that I and the rest of the family would have done anything to get you back. . . . I'm starting to think no one is concerned about me anymore."

In her fourth tape, on April 3, announcing her decision to "stay and fight," Patty turned on her parents with stinging words. She accused them of playing games all along, "stalling for time—time which the FBI was using in their attempts to assassinate me. . . . Your actions have taught me a great lesson, and in a strange kind of way I'm grateful to you."

I have no doubt that the Hearst family believes they did everything they could to get Patty back. But it is also easy to see how Patty could have been vulnerable to believing they did not.

From the date of the kidnapping, there have been sexual innuendos surrounding the case. People speculated that Cinque was a figure like Charles Manson who kept the women around him in a sexual trance. During call-in shows to a black radio station, people predicted Patty would become involved with Cinque. One woman said, "Some black dude has kidnapped a rich white girl. What else is gonna be going on! And Cinque is a *handsome* black dude."

In Berkeley, it was known that Cinque was sleeping with Mizmoon, Ling and Emily Harris. Emily wrote to her father in Illinois on January 30, describing her affair with Cinque: "A beautiful black man has conveyed to me the torture of being black in this country and being poor." Emily said she and Bill had opened their marriage, "so that it no longer confines us, and I am enjoying relationships with other men. I am in love with the black man . . . and that love is very beautiful and fulfilling."

The bank robbery, however, reversed the illusion.

Four women marched ahead of Cinque into the bank while men waited in the getaway car. People who had known Cinque at Vacaville, such as David Inua, one of the founders of the Black Cultural Association, said, "Cinque is not a bright man. He has no ability as a teacher or a leader. Those were not his phrases on the S.L.A. tapes—that's not the way he talks." Now it seemed the S.L.A. might be a regiment of women—two of whom were known to be lovers—using Cinque as a figurehead to carry out their plans.

When I first learned of the kidnapping, I remembered that as a young girl I often had dreams of being kidnapped and falling in love with one of my captors. I also remembered Temple Drake, the heroine of William Faulkner's *Sanctuary*, who chose to live with her abductor, a hood named Popeye, in a Memphis whorehouse before being "saved" and returned to a decaying social order.

The possibilities for speculation are endless, but it is realistic to assume that some relationship developed between Patty and the S.L.A. Patty celebrated her twentieth birthday among the S.L.A. They gave her books to read, like George Jackson's writings from prison. They exposed her to conditions of blacks, Chicanos and the poor, and initiated her into knowledge of the evils of American foreign policy. They nursed her when she came down with a cold, showed her karate and taught her to shoot a gun. They offered her a heroic name, a rebirth.

I have known many women who came to Berkeley from conservative, moneyed families and almost overnight took new identities. Anne Weills, thirty-two, was a child of wealthy parents in Marin County. She met and married a New Left leader, Robert Scheer, became a radical feminist, separated from Scheer and is at present working to build a revolutionary organization in the working classes.

Anne says she understands the leap Patty seems to have made. "Once you see the way poor people and racial minorities live, you feel terribly privileged, and if you have any social conscience, you feel guilty," Anne says. "What can you do to make up? If you're surrounded by blacks who are furious and want retribution, and by strong, committed women, you can get a lot of energy. You become alienated from your family because you see yourself as so special, so different and morally right."

When you're young, she adds, you also feel invulnerable.

In Patty's case, when the time was right, the S.L.A. gave her a choice: Go back to your own kind (who've already abandoned you) or join us.

In her good-by tape, Patty said she had discovered a new kind of love. She told Steven Weed: "I've changed, grown. I've become conscious and can never go back to the life we led." (In how many homes across the country recently has a woman delivered that message?)

After the FBI had labeled her a criminal, people continued to pray for Patty. She has proven to be a transcendently sympathetic figure, like certain actresses whom the audience always roots for even when they are cast in unattractive roles. In her tape, Patty said: "Love doesn't mean the same thing to me anymore. My love has expanded as a result of my experiences to embrace all people."

Colston Westbrook has been marked by the S.L.A. as an enemy to be "shot on sight." He was outside co-ordinator of the Black Cultural Association and teaches linguistics at Berkeley. The S.L.A. claims he is an FBI informer and worked as a "torturer" for the CIA in Vietnam.

It is 10 P.M., and I am meeting Westbrook outside a Japanese restaurant on San Pablo Avenue. He pulls up in a blue Volkswagen with the license plate NGOMBE, parks and watches me from the rear-view mirror.

When he gets out, he says we're not going to the restaurant but an office next door. It is a small store-front with peeling plaster and flurorescent lights. We sit on folding chairs in the debris. He makes two phone calls to two "sets of police," then takes an electronic device from his pocket and speaks into it: "Machine, I'm at M.C.'s."

Breathing hard, Westbrook takes a beer from a brown paper bag. He is a burly man wearing a black and white knit cap with a tassel. He seems to thrive on publicity, on playing verbal chess with reporters and drawing a cloak of suspicion about him. He speaks six languages and will receive a master's this June in black English dialectology. "It's a brand new field, my own field, I made it up," he says.

I ask why he went to Vietnam. "Money, why else. I was told by the American Embassy in Tokyo I could make ten thousand dollars working in Vietnam. They said it pays to be black in Nam." He smiles. "I've never been a torturer. But I know how to do it. I know how to cut a cat's throat."

Westbrook was teaching at Berkeley in 1971 when he was asked to work with the B.C.A. They ran classes for inmates in everything from Swahili and nation-building to astrology. On Friday nights there were cultural meetings, which several hundred outsiders attended. They opened with a flag ceremony: the tri-color of the Republic of New Africa was paraded on stage accompanied by music and black-power salutes. There were speeches, poetry readings, plays and de-bates. It was at these meetings that Cinque met most of those who were to form the S.L.A.

Westbrook worked with Cinque and says he never had trouble with him. "It's the white women in the S.L.A. who were against me. They accused me of taking lewd pictures and sexy-looking black women wearing high miniskirts into the prison. Sure I took some foxes, some of my prime stock in there. And I took *Jet* calendar pictures. Because if you want to dangle a carrot in front of the inmates to get 'em to learn and come to meetings, you don't dangle com-munism. You dangle fine-looking chicks they'll think maybe they can get next to.

"The S.L.A. women say I tortured the inmates by taking in chicks they couldn't do anything to. That's why those lesbians were mad at me."

I ask if he feels out of danger now.

"No! Nothing's changed until they find out who's controlling this. There are people who haven't come out of the woodwork yet. I know—that's why they want me dead."

Who does he think is controlling the S.L.A.?

He gives me a hard stare. "You really want to get me in trouble, huh?"

Is it a man, I ask.

"As far as I know."

Someone known to the public?

"Yes." He finishes his beer. "At the right time, you expose your hand." He waits a beat. "There's a theory that *I'm* No. 1, because I haven't been killed."

I tell him I'm no good at these games.

"Are you really a reporter?" he asks. I'm wondering myself.

"How would you like to join the CIA? You'd be a natural."

As I'm leaving, he suggests I visit a psychic he knows. "You might break the story. Find the head of the S.L.A."

If I did, I'm not sure what I would do.

"Tell me!"

No, I wouldn't tell you.

He leans forward, eyes wide, and whispers, "How do you know I don't already know?"

The names, word play and coincidences in this drama have sent writers and conspiracy buffs into reverie. DeFreeze takes the name Cinque, but calls himself Comrade Cin, undoubtedly aware this will sound the same as Sin. "Devoto" runs through the S.L.A. web. Members often use it as an alias.

Tania, in whose name Patty steps forward, was a German woman in love with Che Guevara. She fought and died with his guerrilla band but was suspected of being a spy for the Soviet establishment. Joe Remiro claims he is related to Joseph Alioto, Mayor of San Francisco, "in the grandparents somewhere." Alioto claims the S.L.A. attempted to kidnap four of his grandchildren.

The seven stated aims of the S.L.A. are identical to the seven principles of conduct set forth years ago by Ron Karenga, founder of US—United Slaves. Karenga sits in jail in San Luis Obispo for the shooting of two Black Panthers at U.C.L.A., but two of Karenga's men, George and Larry Stiner, happened to escape from San Quentin this past March. The Panthers have a feud with both US and the S.L.A. They assert that DeFreeze was a Government agent paid to foment trouble and create an atmosphere of terror.

Patty Hearst's use of the word "ageist" brought a moment of comic relief. After Patty called her fiancé, Steven Weed, a "sexist, ageist pig," the San Francisco *Chronicle* ran a box headlined: "The Latest Word. Webster's Third New International Dictionary defines 'agist' as a verb meaning 'to take in (livestock) for feeding or grazing and to collect the amount due therefore.' "

The metaphor seemed strained. Was Patty the livestock? Was Steven grazing her for money? The next day, the *Chronicle* corrected itself. "Ageist," they had learned, is the latest Bay Area political insult, applied to someone who discriminates against any age group, particularly the old.

"Gay Power"
"Kid Power"
"Love Yourself"
"Eat the Rich"

The words are painted on Channing Way, just below Shattuck. This block has a mystique in radical circles, and until recently was the home of a ten-foot-high, red, papier-mâché fist. People who live here in decrepit Victorian houses crawling with wisteria and rhododendrons feel it is a special place. They've built a bulletin board and installed chairs on the sidewalk. There's a coffeehouse in someone's spare room and a free box on the street with clothes and cast-off items.

Until the S.L.A. brought police to the block, life was easy on Channing Way. Few people worked, because they could get by on almost nothing. In the summer, they would plant vegetables and sunbathe nude in overgrown backyards. On warm nights there might be a block party where everyone would take Quaaludes and dream about the coming of the revolution.

Camilla Hall and Mizmoon Soltysik both lived on Channing Way. I am talking about them with Kate Coleman, an outspoken woman who has been in Berkeley on and off since 1960.

"I think I understand their motivation," Kate says. "It's frustration, it's failure, we all feel failure whether we've failed or not. Do you realize how many people who went to college with us are out in the woods, croaking on their communes because the revolution didn't happen and they can't get back in the economy because they've been out so long?"

Kate says many women she knows who are political have "nothing happening in their lives. The left is fragmented, dying, and the S.L.A. women probably felt they had to do something to set people on fire. It's the nihilist blaze of glory: you start the revolution with six people and don't worry about organizing the masses. You must live the revolution even if you're before your time. The appeal is very powerful."

Kate says she could never join an underground group because "my nature is so up-front and flamboyant. But the S.L.A. loved the secrecy and the plotting. They knew they weren't infiltrated because they didn't have a broad-based organization. But that was also their downfall. Because if they survived, how could they grow? They could only build up myth."

All over Berkeley, political families are closing up apartments and loading their cars. Some will drift to the country until the heat is off. Some will continue working on small contained projects like a home-birth center or a school election. Some will do what Dan

Siegel has done—move into neighborhoods like East Oakland to connect with working people.

Siegel is twenty-eight, an attractive, modest-looking young man in a sports shirt and slacks. In 1969, when he was student-body president at Berkeley, he gave a speech that sent thousands surging down Telegraph Avenue to reclaim People's Park. Bob Dylan was singing from speaker vans: "You can have your cake and eat it too." Marvin Garson was writing: "That high feeling—when you're relating to each other as brothers and sisters—that's the revolution! That's what's worth living for and dying for."

Siegel is sitting this morning in the smoggy sun near the Oakland Superior Courthouse. "I don't think you'll ever see thousands marching in support of the S.L.A.," he says. "I imagine the S.L.A. believed it was doing real revolutionary acts that threatened the existence of the state. But the people in it were inexperienced, naïve and idealistic."

He muses: "I remember how arrogant we used to be. I remember thinking how great it was that we didn't need ideology, strategy or the working class. Young people would be the revolutionary force in America. Then the New Left fell apart, and it was probably good for us."

Siegel says he no longer has "the illusion that revolution will be easy or that a few gallant people can do it. Winning the hearts and minds of tens of thousands of people—that's what making revolution is about."

He walks toward the courthouse, where he is preparing a test case in which the community is suing the district attorney, and he says that it's funny but in some ways, he feels old.

1974

THE FIRST
ADVANCE WOMAN

It was a wet February night, with a full moon shining on the lakes and sleepy ranch houses of Winter Haven, Florida. A twenty-eight-year-old man, Bryon Hileman, whose credentials are impressive—professor of political science, husband, father, founder of a dozen political action groups—was standing on the balcony of the Holiday Inn, sighing and swabbing his forehead with a handkerchief.

He shuddered and turned to his friend. "Well," he said, "come on in and meet the Tiger Lady."

The second man hung back. He bent in to look in the window of the motel room and saw a dark-haired young woman in jeans, sitting on the bed with a telephone at her ear.

"She's talking."

"That figures," Byron said. "Rose tells me so many things to do that when I leave her room, my head is spinning. I took two tranquilizers tonight for the first time in nine years. I've gained five pounds in the past two days because I'm a compulsive eater when I'm nervous. And my wife cried yesterday and the day before."

The friend slapped his leg and whispered: "Is that right!"

Through the window, they saw Rose hang up the phone and walk quickly to the door. Byron moaned. "Here goes. Lambs to the slaughter."

In the two days that Rose Economou, advance woman for Senator Edmund Muskie, had been in Winter Haven to prepare for a thirty-minute rally at the train station the next weekend, she had given Byron Hileman, her only "local contact," responsibility for the following: getting out a crowd; moving people in buses; setting up a phone bank; recruiting volunteers; calling all churches, clubs, and schools; inviting bands, black leaders, unions and politicians; buying refreshments; and sending literature to all registered Democrats.

So far, Byron had not done one of those things. He had no helpers. There was no one but him, solitary and quaking, taking Rose's orders. By the end of the week, a total of ten people were to be drawn into the effort. Most of them wanted to help Muskie be elected President of the United States. But by Friday, what they wanted more than that was to see Rose Economou leave town.

The advance man has been a character in American politics for as long as anyone knows. He arrives on location from two to ten days before the candidate, and attends to every detail: the choice of VIPs to ride in a motorcade; the eruption of a "spontaneous" demonstration; the packing of a hall with excitable, photogenic bodies. He is rarely paid, and has little to go on but his wits and nerve and other people's needs and gullibility.

The job did not have a name until 1959, when Jerry

Bruno built advance work into a science for John F. Kennedy's presidential campaign. In 1972, the presidential candidates opened the field to women. The Muskie organization received a windfall of publicity by introducing the first two advance persons: Marsha Pinkstaff, a former Miss Indiana; and Rose Economou, a social planner from Chicago. The women have functioned no more and no less effectively than the men, for it turns out that sex counts less in advance work than age. Nobody could do this job much after thirty. It requires one to travel constantly, to have no private life and to need no income other than living expenses on the road. The advance man will never be sent back to the same town or to his home state, because he is expected to make enemies and to take the blame for anything that angers local supporters. Advance work is called, by one veteran, "the absolute lowest level of politics. The goal is serious, but the exercise is silly. Politics becomes an effort at making things look good."

The effort to make Muskie look good on a two-day train trip down the central gut of Florida had its origins last December. Muskie's chief advance man, Michael Casey, sold the whistle-stop to campaign strategists on the grounds that it would generate "a media explosion. Because of the nostalgia element, we'll make all three nets." Casey did not worry about details until February 2. Then he ran into so many problems trying to lease railroad equipment that the dates had to be changed three times. "I'm starting to sweat," Casey said, "and I'm a calm guy."

On February 10, he closed a rental agreement with Amtrak for $5,800, pronounced the train "go" for February 18 and 19 and assigned advance people to each of the eight towns on the route from Jacksonville to Miami. Rose Economou (the name is Greek; it's pronounced like economy but with a "moo" at the end) was deployed from New Hampshire to Winter Haven. "Rose is really something in a small town," Casey said. "She's twenty-five, she's been advancing for four months and we've gotten a dozen letters from people who want her back."

I met up with Rose at the Tampa airport at two in the morning, Saturday, February 12. She had not slept in several days, but words were spilling from her in a whisper-jet voice, easy on the ear but persistent. "I have one contact here, and our organization tells me they're having trouble with him. I thought, uh oh, another dictator."

Rose was wearing aviator glasses and a white coat lined with fake fur. She is slim, long-legged, with a wide face and strong jaw. "I feel so awkward coming into Florida," she said. "But I can visualize just how I want this stop: old-fashioney, with lots of bunting, little kids with flags and high-school bands. Just one big party. Won't that be fun!"

We slept four hours at an airport motel, then drove sixty miles inland, past groves of orange trees and flat, lime-green fields with cows grazing. When we reached what seemed to be the center of Winter Haven—an intersection with four corners of parking lots and a banner announcing a Guy Lombardo concert—Rose said, "This is it? Oh, I'm starting to feel sick inside."

She checked into the Holiday Inn, which was in the midst of welcoming the Boston Red Sox to their winter quarters, and called up her local contact. An hour later, he walked through the door: a short, slightly overweight man wearing a brown suit with a Kiwanis pin in the lapel. He gave her his card:

THE CAUSE

Byron P. Hileman
Professor Political Science
Polk Community College

She asked him to take her to see the train station. They had lunch at a drive-in called Andy's Igloo and while waiting for hamburgers and pineapple milk shakes, Rose asked Byron about the town. He ran down the statistics: twenty-five thousand people in the city, fifty thousand in the area. Democrats outnumber Republicans three to one. Main industries: agriculture and tourism (because of Cypress Gardens). "The county went to Wallace in '68, but things are changing. The fact that I myself am involved in local politics is evidence. I'm considered 'wildly liberal.' I am to Winter Haven what Jerry Rubin would be to New York City."

Byron said he had worked for McCarthy in '68, but then became "terribly disillusioned with the phoniness of the so-called New Consciousness. To me, Muskie represents the antithesis of this phoniness, while he has the right position on the issues. I volunteered to help out in his campaign, but there were no other volunteers in the area so they dumped the chairmanship in my lap."

As he drove Rose back to the motel, he said, "When they told me you were coming, I thought, that's the strangest name I've ever heard. But it grabs you." He laughed merrily. "Once you get the hang of it, you can't get it out of your head."

When Byron left, Rose said, "I don't think he's so horrible. I'm going to have him call a meeting tomorrow." She began thumbing through the phone book. "Wouldn't it be great if we could draw two thousand people? We could outcrowd Miami. Wouldn't that be out of sight?" She bounced on the bed in excitement.

The phone rang. "Rose, I'm here!" It was Rich Evans, the chief advance man in Florida, who was driving up the route of the train, checking every stop. When he walked into Rose's room, he was, as is his custom, grinning. "I think the secret to good advance work is a big smile on your face. It throws people off." Rich, a tall, hale blond, used to organize singles clubs across the country before he became an advance man. "Everybody likes Rich," Rose said.

Rich suggested they go to a reception celebrating the start of the annual Florida Citrus Showcase. They found the hall packed with red-faced men and ladies wearing chiffon dresses, platinum hair, orange plastic shoes and lavender eye shadow. Rich introduced himself to everyone he saw. One man stepped back aghast. "Is Muskie coming here? I'll tell you, whatever he's for, I'm not."

SUNDAY. Byron was nervously eating a piece of Danish pastry in the coffee shop. Rose asked about volunteers. "Can we get ten people for chairmanships?"

Byron's face reddened. "Let me explain something to you. I'm not enthusiastic about this visit at all—it's come too late. I've been sitting here the past two months screaming bloody murder because nothing was getting done. Then last Friday, out of the blue, I get two calls, one telling me to open two headquarters next week, and the other telling me about the train. After that, I had one of my infrequent fits. I tore a newspaper in half, cussed everybody out, called the state office and told them to go to hell. When I got over the fit, I figured, oh, what the hell. Now I'll help you all I can to do this job, but your plans are overdrawn. I don't have any organization. I just have one helper—Charles Davis. I've got classes to teach and my family to take care of. Things aren't gonna work out the way you think.''

Rose stayed in her room the rest of the day, washing her hair, making calls and humming "The Swanee River.'' She spoke to the head of the Muskie office in Tampa and asked if he could send busloads to the rally. The man complained that no one in the state had been consulted about doing a whistle-stop. "No Floridian would have recommended it.''

Rose hung up calmly. "What he doesn't understand is that this is being done primarily for the media. It will also give our supporters a feeling of momentum, but the effect on the general public will be slight. It always is, except through the media.''

The Muskie staff is "media sensitive,'' partly out of an awareness that in 1968, according to a series of Gallup polls, less than 6 percent of the people saw any one of the presidential candidates in person. Yet Muskie's schedulers continue sending him to shake hands at factories and shopping centers, asking for votes one at a time. A partnership between the media and the candidates seems to keep politicians locked in this ritual dance. The candidates say they must stage crowd events and "visuals'' like the train because the press demands them; the press complains about "contrived routines,'' yet continues to reward "visuals'' with extra coverage and to judge a candidate's merit by the crowds he draws. The press even helps subsidize such campaigning. The Muskie organization, for example, made back half the cost of renting the Florida train by charging each reporter sixty dollars to ride it.

*   *   *

MONDAY. I spent the day driving to other towns along the train route; when I returned to Winter Haven at sundown, Rose was pacing in her room, swearing. "I've had a terrible day. The local newspaper printed the wrong information because Washington sent them the old schedule. I have no leaflets. No people to give out leaflets. And I can't get phones installed—it takes two weeks." She stamped her foot.

"I'm goddamned pissed! I've never been part of anything as bad as what's going on in this town. And it's all my fault, because I trusted these people."

The phone rang—it was Byron. "We're gonna mail cards to everyone on the Democratic voter list," Rose said. "We've got to get twenty-five volunteers to address twenty-four hundred envelopes. I don't care how." She hung up. "I said that just to make him nervous." She laughed. "I got four hours sleep last night. That's why I'm acting this way."

That night, Byron drove to Lakeland, the largest town in Polk County, for a meeting called by former Mayor Joe Ruthven to organize the Muskie operation in the region. Byron had taken two tranquilizers and was just calming down. "Rose has scared me out of my wits all day. I figured she's the professional, right? If she's cracking up, it must really be bad. I couldn't believe the language she used, right in a store!"

I asked why he didn't give up. "There's too much of the Protestant ethic in me. I feel like I can't let this poor girl down."

When Byron walked into the meeting at the OK Tire Store in Lakeland, Mayor Ruthven asked, "Well, you all set to open the headquarters?"

Byron fidgeted. "We had planned to do it this week, but we've been having a problem with this, uh, advance work. Senator Muskie's coming to Winter

Haven Friday, and we've got Rose Economou in town. (He pronounced it Econo-mew.) She's the lady advance man, and she says we have to send out twenty-four hundred invitations. Could you loan us some volunteers?" Ruthven told him to bring the cards to Lakeland and they would address as many as they could.

Byron walked out euphoric. "The weight has been lifted. I thought I'd have to address twenty-four hundred envelopes myself, stay up seventy-two hours and die of a cardiac when Muskie steps off the train." Byron said he had never been this upset, "not even over my oral exams. But I'm not suited for this work. I'm an academic. I can write speeches like nothing, but when Rose hands me this broad organizational task, I feel like it's a problem in calculus." There were three passengers in the back seat, and all were howling with laughter at Byron's style of exaggerated self-pity and terror. "And I like Rose," Byron said. "If she'd take off her tiger suit she's be a real nice girl."

Byron had the effervescence knocked out of him when he stepped into Rose's room. "Good news," he said. "I bear glad tidings. The Mayor's people will address those envelopes. Okay? All right? Rose, you don't seem very positive."

Rose did not look up. "What else did the Mayor say?"

"You answer me first. You're not gonna send them out, are you?"

"No."

"Why?" Byron asked weakly.

"I called Tampa. They have an offset machine and professional secretaries. If we get the list there in the morning, they can do it in a few hours."

She began rattling off the things to be done the next

229

day. Byron perched on the edge of the bed, struggling not to slip off, smoking and trying to write down what she was saying. "Honey, wait, please wait. We can't do ninety-two things at once."

"I'm gonna do more than I did today, goddamn it!"

TUESDAY. Rose woke up to heavy rain—a bad omen. Crowds shrink from rain. In the afternoon, a box was delivered with five thousand handbills printed in antique script: "Picnic at the Station, Meet Ed Muskie."

"Oh, super," Rose said. "Aren't they beautiful?"

Byron nodded grimly. "I was happy for a moment, then I thought, What am I happy for? They all have to be handed out."

He picked up the phone to order roses for his wife Becky. "She screamed and broke four dishes this morning," Byron said. "She's too young to take this kind of tension. We've only been married six months, and she thinks she hardly ever sees me because of politics."

Rose suggested bringing her along. An hour later, Byron returned with Becky and his two children by a previous marriage, a five-year-boy and a six-year-old girl. The kids watched television and took to following Rose around, chanting her name. Becky, a blue-eyed, warm-spirited girl of nineteen, found herself gradually sucked into the chaotic process. She recruited her friends to work in the evening, ran errands, typed, sewed and even made phone calls saying she was on Senator Muskie's staff. "That's a laugh," she said. "I'm probably voting for Wallace."

Rose instructed Byron to find a school band to perform. "Tell them the band will get to be on television, in *Life* magazine and all the big newspapers." Byron tried every school in the county to no avail. Before he went home, Rose gave him the evening's plan: "Put two people on the phones, calling clergymen and asking them to tell everybody they know. Have the other volunteers leaflet at shopping centers and all the clubs that meet tonight, especially the Knights of Columbus. They're a sure winner for us."

When Charles Davis came by, Rose told him, "Hit the high-school basketball game. Pass out handbills and recruit too. Go up to everybody and say, 'Do you wanna help us with Senator Muskie's trip?' "

Charles scratched his head. "I don't feel right asking strangers to work. This is the first time we're having a big-time campaign in Florida. The kids are kinda apathetic."

"We have to change things," Rose said.

Charles, who is twenty-three and teaches geography in junior high, picked up his fifteen-year-old sister Carole. She wore braces and saddle shoes with pompons tied on the back, and carried a comb for her hair, which was wet from swimming practice. "Now, Carole, we're supposed to ask anybody and everybody that wants to and will, to work with us on this train trip. The boss says to just ask people cold."

Carole stood at the entrance to the gym, and most of the students who passed her looked at the handbill and said something on the order of "Ick." She forgot about recruiting. Charles fared no better. They drove back to Byron's and announced, "We bombed." There were three college students in the dining room, and one said. "So did we. The shopping center was dead. The American Legion wouldn't let us in, and the Knights of Columbus didn't even meet. I wonder how Byron's doing at the Coin Club." Becky rolled her head back and laughed. "I'm in a good mood now. I think this is fun that it's all bombing."

Byron came home and asked Becky to get him a tranquilizer. He swallowed it and called Rose. "Things are a mess. The clubs are not accepting us so far." Rose told him to call the Grand Knight of Columbus at his home. When Byron did, the Knight told him he couldn't make an announcement to his group because they don't take political stands. Byron said, "Being as Muskie is a Catholic, we were kind of depending on the Knights . . ." He slammed down the phone. "What incredible goddamned stupid people we have in this county! Who's asking for a political stand?"

Becky said, "You wanna call some ministers?"

"Preachers?" Carole said.

"It was *Rose's* brilliant idea."

"Who is this mysterious Rose?"

"She's the boss, and you should see her," Becky said. "She doesn't eat, she doesn't sleep. She's gonna kill herself. And she doesn't get paid. I think Rose is crazy. Why else would she drive herself like that?"

WEDNESDAY. "There's a jinx," Rose said. She and Becky drove around town, shopping for supplies, and could not find one person who knew about the train.

The motel room was becoming a disaster zone. Every surface was obscured by stacks of paper, posters, bits of lumber, fliers, buckets of plastic American flags (made in Japan), cases of beer, bunting, old sheets, crepe-paper streamers and Styrofoam fake-straw hats. The motel was close enough to the station so that whenever a train passed, there was a faint whistling. The sound grew progressively more ominous.

Rose said she was on a "downer. I have no band.

I need more people and not Byron at the top. I just don't feel I'm being effective with Byron."

At six that night, there was supposed to be a sign-painting party at Byron's house. Rose got there at eight. Seven people were sitting on the floor, still working on their first sign. They were measuring with rulers, outlining in pencil and laboriously coloring in spaces. George Harrison was singing "Wah Wah" on the stereo. Rose took a brush and started painting directly on cardboard: "The sun shines on Senator Muskie." Byron returned from his night class in a sweat. "Where is she? Rose, where were you at six? We had seven people here sitting on their asses for two hours."

Rose said, "They still are," and walked off to the back room.

Byron, startled, turned to the seven limp forms. "Look, we gotta have some organization. All fifty signs have to be done. Don't measure. Just eyeball 'em."

The group groaned and came to life; they began scrawling on the signs: "Ed," "We like Muskie," "Super Ed." Rose, alone in the back room, was making a master banner out of three bedsheets. Byron sat at the phone, calling everyone he could think of and begging them to help decorate the station. He made a list of people who could work. "Rose, we're making progress," he called.

Rose yelled: "Tell them to bring hammers, stepladders, rope, tables."

"Damnation," Byron said. "Hey, Rose, I'm gonna assign all my classes to come. That'll be a small crowd."

Silence.

Byron: "I never get any reaction from that woman."

He opened his third cigarette pack of the day. "This whole thing has put me in a real personal quandary. I have a desire myself to run for office. I can see myself on the floor of the State Capitol being some classy legislator. It's appealing. But if I had to live under this tension . . ."

Everyone was leaving now, and one young man got in his car, started the motor and smashed right into Rose's car. "I didn't see it," the young man said. "I just didn't see it."

THURSDAY. Rain again. But at last, a story about the train appeared on the front page of the *Winter Haven News-Chief*. Rose asked Tom Skinner, a round-faced, slow-moving young man, to find a place to buy popcorn and rent Early American costumes. "Rent one for me, Becky, and Byron." Byron said, "I will *not* be in costume." Everyone laughed.

Rich Evans called up for a report. Rose said, "Oh, baby, I have no music, no VIP guests. What's my program? The band that we don't have will be playing when the train pulls in, and we'll have two hundred wet people, because it's raining. If it rains hard we'll be lucky to get fifty."

Four hours later, a local rock band was talked into playing for free. Tom got a friend who works in a dime store in Lakeland to promise to pop four sacks of corn, as a special favor. And Byron arranged for the Florida Citrus Queen to present Muskie with a glass of orange juice.

At four-thirty, Byron, Tom and Becky's teen-age brother Jim tied a rented speaker onto Rose's car and took off to cruise. Byron picked up the microphone. "Senator Edmund Muskie . . ." Jim laughed and scrunched down. "I hate to be stared at." Tom said, "Me too."

One old man on the street booed.

Tom said, "I'm waiting for a bullet to hit the windshield."

They pulled up to a canning plant just as the workers were getting off. Byron began his pitch, and the mike went dead. "What next, what the hell next! Jim, can you fix it?"

Jim was jiggling the wires. "It's just like my amplifiers. But I have no confidence in myself." He held the wires at an angle and the power came back. By this time, the workers had disappeared.

They drove to the Northgate Shopping Center, which, to their joy, was teeming with traffic. Byron started to speak, but now the mike switch wouldn't work. He began to laugh, groan and pound his head on the upholstery. "Every goddamned thing I touch turns to shit! I want to go home. I want my mama is what I want. Tell Rose I died. Tell the Senator tomorrow I'm indisposed, I'm being driven to the hospital."

Jim was using a can opener to take the microphone apart. Tom hit the brakes suddenly, and all the tiny wires, screws and microscopic curlicues spilled down the cracks in the floorboard. Everyone collapsed with manic laughter. Recovering, Byron said, "They call Rose the ten-percenter because she turns out ten percent of the population in some towns. Winter Haven is gonna lower her average severely."

Back at the motel, Rose told Tom and another student to get something to eat and charge it to her room. "Go on, you've been working hard." Byron said lightly, "You've never offered to buy me dinner."

Rose: "You haven't done any work."

Byron did a double take. He stalked out to the restaurant with the others, ordered a hamburger and paid for it himself. He was so furious he could hardly swallow. "I've been abused once too often. When this is over I'm resigning. It's never enough, no matter how hard you try, and I've tried to the best of my ability. Rose has never said I've done a good job—not one word of praise or thanks. If she had, I'd have felt a lot better about things."

Tom was staring sadly at his plate. "I think Rose should apologize to you." Byron shook his head. "She doesn't care about people's feelings. She just used me as an instrument. If she'd been a man, I'd have punched her in the mouth."

When Rose heard later that Byron was angry, she said, "Is that the royal screw. If the stop goes well, Byron will get all the Godblessed glory and I'll disappear. I don't mind it if people hate me. But when Byron gives everyone this defeatist attitude, they end up hating politics."

FRIDAY. Miraculously, the day began with clear sunlight. Byron had stayed up most of the night writing Rose a twelve-page letter explaining why he was hurt. He dropped it at the front desk and left to teach his classes. Rose put the letter in her purse without opening it. Seconds later she had forgotten it. Her mind was fixed on a single point—3:55 P.M.

Through the morning, she ran nervously around the train station in jeans and a yellow sweater. She threw bits of crepe paper on the palm trees and cactus, while others wrapped streamers around poles, hung bunting and attached pairs of American flags to the walls.

At noon, she went back to the motel to pack. Byron

arrived at the station, missing her by minutes; after checking the scene, he went home to change. When Rose returned, dressed in a suede miniskirt and high-heeled sandals, the station was deserted. She started blowing up balloons. She had a dozen on strings when she suddenly remembered something. "Where's Byron?" She stood still, blinking, as if the lighting had just been altered. "I wonder why he wasn't here?"

Without warning, a gritty wind came up, tearing the crepe paper from the walls. Tom asked Rose who would be picking up the popcorn from Lakeland. "No one," she said. "I decided to get hamburgers from McDonald's instead." Tom flushed. "My friend got up at six this morning to fix that popcorn."

At one-thirty, the first official crowd members arrived. They were mostly senior citizens, who lined up their cars facing the tracks and just sat in them, waiting. At three, the buses from Tampa delivered one hundred fifty students, and the grounds took on a festive air. The students danced in the parking lot, drank beer and tossed Frisbees. Byron drove up with his family and started furiously passing out buttons. The handmade signs popped up above the crowd, hovered a few minutes and then all but three went under. "They're hard to hold in the wind," one girl said.

At three fifty-five, the crowd pressed toward the platform. By my estimate, there were at most four hundred. Rose said, "Let's sing 'God Bless America!'" No one did, so she started cheering loudly by herself: "We want Muskie!"

At four-ten, a whistle floated in from the north, followed by a black engine. Byron turned his eyes heavenward. Rose was jumping up and down screaming, "Muskie! Muskie!" The train chugged through with Rich Evans hanging over the side, Roosevelt

Grier singing "Aquarius," girls waving, flags flying, TV cameras poking out, and, lo, why, there was Ed Muskie! Right there on the back platform, in a bright blue shirt, smiling and reaching for hands.

After Byron introduced him, the first thing Muskie said was how much fun it was to do a whistle-stop. Muskie knew—all the candidates know—what went on in Winter Haven, in all the towns, in preparation for his arrival.

Muskie spoke about "pollution of the human environment." He described the pollution due to "unkindness, fear and hatred," and said the goal of Americans should be to reach "not the moon but each other's hearts."

"A-a-a-men," Rosie Grier sang. The train started off; the crowd waded up the tracks until Muskie was only a blue spot with arms. Five minutes later, the station was empty.

There was no celebrating, no after-party for the volunteers. When the decorations were ripped down, everyone went off in the hissing wind. Charles Davis said, "I think it was worth it. I think Muskie got a lot of publicity, and I had some fun." Becky was leading her two exhausted children by the arms. "Peace," she whispered. Tom Skinner said he would do it all again, "with somebody other than Rose. I don't think you oughta step on people like she did." Byron sighed. "Maybe in two weeks I'll be glad I went through it. Maybe."

Rose herself was disappointed at the crowd. "But for here, I think it was a success. And I only got three people angry at me. That's not so bad. That's the nature of my job. There are so many forces pulling you in every direction, you just can't leave everybody happy. That's why women haven't done it before. No one thought they could be tough enough."

In the car driving off, she read Byron's letter. When she finished, she said, "I had to be brutal with these people because they didn't realize the magnitude of the thing." She said she had known the day she arrived that it would be "criminal" to rely on Byron. "But I was dependent on him. He was the only one who had information, and contact with Muskie sympathizers. I think by the end of the week, he reached a much greater capacity to do this work than he thought he was capable of. And I don't think he'll quit, because he'll find out he likes it."

At midnight, Rose got on a Greyhound bus headed for Miami. She planned to sleep in the airport until she could get a plane north, where she had two days to advance a labor rally in New Hampshire. While in transit, she would write her report on Winter Haven, and perhaps work on a needlepoint pillowcase for her mother.

At the depot, she stood in her coat in the milk-warm night, her skin still winter pale. "I feel just full of energy," she said. "Even though I know I didn't do a good job here, I feel at peace. It's as if I haven't been working." She picked up her suitcase, spun around abruptly and waved. "I can't wait for the next advance to start."

1972

6

Forever Young

THE ROAD

Once I knew a famous man who had a famous wife and four gifted children—a famous family. When the children turned twenty-one, they each inherited a quarter of a million dollars.

The first child invested the money.

The second child spent in on psychoanalysis.

The third spent the money on dresses, and the fourth bought land for a commune.

I remember a time, in the early 1970s, when I was certain the fourth was the wise child. There was a consensus, among people I knew, that the only task worthwhile in life was seeking answers to unanswerable questions. This process was known, variously, as "working on yourself," "seeking God," "dropping out," "getting back to the garden," aspiring to "higher consciousness." There were a hundred paths to the realms beyond—through music, meditating, living in the wilderness—and the pursuit of any and all was felt to be, in the words of Ram Dass, "the only dance there is."

For many years, I went out on the road, bringing back reports of the New World. This was before *Time* and *Newsweek* had run cover stories on the "consciousness movement" and Tom Wolfe had labeled the Seventies the "Me Decade." In the period of innocence, we thought of ourselves as explorers, like the Victorians who trekked across Africa looking for the true source of the Nile.

In 1973, two of my close friends were Buddhists. Three were Sufis, two practiced Hindu meditation and all were vegetarians but me. I had been on diets since the age of sixteen and had never managed to lose the unwanted five pounds. A new set of eating restrictions was more than I could take, higher consciousness or not.

A state of grace was considered more valuable than money, although, curiously, it often required money to attain. One mystic school charged fifteen hundred dollars for a three-month course, during which participants could not work at outside jobs. It was not uncommon for people to quit their careers and disappear entirely into movements, ashrams, and yet, just a few years later, almost all of them were back to eating meat.

The road trip was over. "We've been given the tools," one friend said. "Now we have to make them work in the world." We stopped meditating and taking so many psychedelic drugs. We became more serious. Culturally, we did not adapt. We failed to learn disco dancing and could not even recognize the names of stars headlining at the Roxy. In a sense it was a just fate, for we had ridiculed those who had not adapted to our ways. Now it was our turn: the music we liked was no longer popular; it was obsolete.

I think this understanding became unavoidable when I was watching *The Last Waltz*, Martin Scorsese's film about the final tour of the Band. The musicians who appeared in the film—Bob Dylan, Robbie

Robertson, Neil Young—had become stars in their twenties and now, they had gray in their sideburns.

"They look like middle-aged men," I said to my friend Ron Koslow, who is the author of *Lifeguard*.

"Come on, they're not middle-aged!" Ron said. "If they are, that means I am too."

Watching them play, I began to feel happy. Their music is a signal code that unlocks a memory of a time of passion, wildness, wonder, living by impulses. I am certain I'll still respond this way when the musicians have white hair, long white hair, and hobble out to play their electric guitars with arthritic fingers. And I imagine Ron will keep insisting, "They're not old."

At the end of the film, Bob Dylan sang "May you stay forever young." Robbie Robertson of the Band explained why he believed it was time to quit. "We've been on the road for sixteen years. The numbers scare me." Clearly, sobriety had set in. "We've learned a lot from the road, we've had our share, but I'm superstitious."

"How do you mean?" Scorsese asked.

"Don't press your luck," Robbie said. "The road has taken a lot of them. Buddy Holly, Jim Morrison, Otis Redding, Jimi Hendrix, Janis, Elvis." He shook his head. "It's a goddamned impossible way of life."

1979

RHINOCEROS

Rock 'n' roll, amplified so loud it approaches the pain threshold, seeps out the walls and through the closed doors of the Gray Manse in Lake Mahopac, New York. On week-nights, carloads of teen-agers from sleepy towns in upstate Putnam County follow the road around the lake and park in the driveway, drinking beer and listening. Some of them get up the nerve to walk past the white marble columns into the three-story mansion, and come bolting out, amazed at what they have seen.

The Gray Manse, once the summer estate of a marine welding executive, is home and rehearsal hall for Rhinoceros, a year-old rock group that consists of seven musicians, two equipment managers, a road manager, a rotating pool of women and a friend called Lan, a young man who makes clothes, cuts hair and cooks.

On a snowy Thursday in February, two of the band members are rehearsing in the basement. The rest of the house, at five in in the evening, is waking up and having breakfast. John Finley, a short, toothy figure with blond hair that makes two or three waves before dropping to his shoulders, rides down the grand stair-

case in a moving chair. The rooms on the bottom floor
are high-ceilinged, lavish period settings from the
nineteenth century, like an antique suite at the Met-
ropolitan Museum with the velvet ropes down. John,
in sky-blue pants and a purple poncho, is swallowed
up by the colors and textures: Oriental carpets, gold-
encrusted statues, stuffed elk, Victorian furniture and
candelabra.

On the upper floors, the rock group has been able
to impose its own style: candles, frankincense, psychedelic posters and Indian silks thrown over the
fluted lampshades. There are stereo and television sets
in every room, all playing at top volume. In the front
bedroom, Alan Gerber, twenty-one, is lying on a pink
silk spread listening to Thelonious Monk.

When John comes upstairs with a bowl of cereal, he
puts on a gospel record, "Run, Sinner, Run," by the
Davis sisters. "Nothing moves me as much as gospel
music," he says.

Across the hall, Danny and Steve Weis, brothers,
are watching *Land of the Giants* on television and
listening to Judy Collins on the stereo. Danny,
twenty, is the key sexual presence of the group. He is
tall and haughty, with ice-blue eyes, a pouting mouth
and a head of long, flaxen hair that is layered, teased,
permanent-waved, ratted and sprayed until it has acquired the consistency of cat's fur. Steve, seventeen,
is dark-haired and so thin—110 pounds on a six-foot,
one-inch frame—that when he stands on stage in skin-
tight black pants, he looks like a *Vogue* model photographed with a distorting lens.

Organ chords rise from the basement, drowning out
all the records and television sets. Michael Fonfara
has turned his amplifier all the way up and is jamming
on the keyboard in the high register. Danny says to

his brother, "Let's go down and join him." Billy Mundi and Doug Hastings, who are married and don't live in the main house, have arrived, and the band is soon assembled.

Danny, on lead guitar, starts a new song and moves around the room, pulling after him the red umbilical cord that ties him to the amplifier. He stands in front of Doug, and they stare into each other's eyes, moving and nodding in unison until they are playing in sync. Danny turns to his brother, Steve, on bass guitar, pulling him into the rhythm—sync. Then he walks to Billy on the drums, catching his eyes and matching up with him—sync. Then Michael on organ, Alan on piano, John singing at the microphone, until everyone in the room is moving the same way and the air is steaming with this communion.

At this moment, which the musicians call "magic" or "holy," they experience intimations of transcendence. Alan describes it: "When we're really getting it together, we're all at peace. You're not even you anymore, you're part of something that seven people are feeling." John says, "You cease to be. You're a vessel, the instrument of your soul." The group works for that transcendence every time they play. They reach it for moments, during certain songs, but the complete experience is rare. "When we play a set that has it throughout, everybody walks off like this." John folds his hands in prayer. "It makes us happier than anything in life."

Rhinoceros, a group of musicians who have served their time in different bands, is past the scuffling stage that young rock groups go through—playing at college dances, auditioning on off-nights at coffeehouses, dragging demonstration tapes from record company to record company. With an album out on Elektra, Rhinoceros is able to demand enough money for performances to keep the ten man entourage living high in Mahopac. They rehearse during the week, travel and play on weekends, and, if popularity grows, will make a new album every eight to nine months.

While the band rehearses until the early hours of the morning, the current groupies, who go by names like Cleo, Pandora and Honey, have the run of the Gray Manse. They gather on the second-floor landing, trade scarves, blouses, hair rollers and fish stories about the rock stars they have slept with.

Honey claims to be the ex-girlfriend of Jimi Hendrix. She is telling the other girls, "Mick Jagger is sending me a ticket to London . . ." Pandora, a rougey blonde wearing a feather and sequin costume, has just been hired as a Playboy bunny. Smiling, empty-eyed, she says, "They want me for centerfold."

The groupies dress each other up in see-through blouses, golden chains and furs, and descend the stairs to the basement. No one in the band acknowledges their entrance. They leave after a half hour and take a two-hour communal bath. Like a mini-harem, the girls amuse each other and stay apart from the band, until it's time to go to sleep. They raid the downstairs kitchen, find nothing but Wonder bread, cereal, giant jars of peanut butter and jelly and king-size cartons of milk. Once in a while, someone in the house will make soup or a stew, but the normal diet is cereal and sandwiches. The girls settle for Puffed Rice with powdered sugar, and decide to explore the glassed-in sun porch of the mansion. Among the wicker and chintz furniture is an old Victrola with a cabinet full of 78 records.

Honey takes one out, cranks up the machine and places the heavy, cylindrical needle down. As the pounding of Rhinoceros rattles all the glass, George M. Cohan begins to sing in a scratchy, distant voice: "My girl May, she meets me every day, in fact we used to go to school together . . ."

One of Howard Johnson's orange and blue installations comes into focus on the New Jersey Turnpike, halfway between New York and Philadelphia. Four of the Rhinoceros walk across the parking lot in their colored silks, leathers, tassels and flying hair. They are greeted by whistles and catcalls from a group of truck drivers. Alan turns to John, who is wearing a neon-orange T-shirt, his blond curls bouncing and his eyes puffed up and pink from sleep. "You look like a depraved chick."

The band drives in two rented cars, collecting recepits at every tollbooth, gas station and diner. Danny Hannagan and Burt Schraeder, the equipment men, drive the instruments and amplifiers, together worth more than ten thousand dollars, in a rented Avis truck with giant Rhino posters on the sides. When they fly, they call a special airline service that packs the equipment and moves it through terminals. With luck, the baggage, Danny and Burt arrive at the concert hall several hours ahead of the group, so that when the band walks in, everything is set up to play.

In Philadelphia, the first car stops at a gas station for directions. Doug rolls down the window to talk to the attendants, but before he can open his mouth, one of the mechanics yells, "Naaaaaa," and gives them the finger with his grease-blackened hand.

Every time it happens, the group is suprised. "What's with that guy? Jee-sus. I wish we had a long stick with a boxing glove at the end of it, so we could just let him have it."

It is the hair, of course. The hair brands them—outsider. Playing rock is a means of living out a definition of the good life that defies the American dream: never have a steady job, keep crazy hours, get stoned, play music, draw constant attention, and, if you do all these things well, make lots of money. The band members look at ads in the magazines—see the gray-haired couple in the rowboat, the wife is handing her happy husband a worm for his fishing rod. If you squirrel away now for the future, you can retire at sixty and have a cottage on a lake. The reasoning behind this scene—years of working, saving, sacrificing—has no meaning to musicians. They know people their own age who have bypassed the daily grind and are living at the rainbow's end of the work ethic. If twenty-year-olds can live high in Big Sur, or Florida, or the Catskills without saving for forty years, what does this mean to people who have gone the other way? It means, to some of them, that perhaps what they did was unnecessary. Is it surprising that the gas station attendant is moved to rage when he sees John Finley with his long curls?

None of the band members, who range from seventeen to twenty-six, has ever had a regular job. With the exception of Billy, who is an ex-Hell's Angel from East Los Angeles, they all come from middle-class families. Their fathers are insurance salesmen, engineers, shoe retailers.

Each Tuesday, the band members get seventy dollars in cash. Their manager pays the rent on the house in Mahopac, and also pays for car rentals, musical equipment and expenses on the road. As the band's album *Rhinoceros* climbs the charts, they can demand higher prices for performing. But it is difficult for the album to catch on until the band travels around the country, stirring up interest.

From inside the Rhino car, Philadelphia looks gray. The people on the streets seem bloodless At the Franklin Motor Inn, "the boys," as they are called, pair off, two to a room. The television sets come on instantly and stay on until the band checks out.

At 8 P.M., after eating steaks and shrimp, both the consistency of rubber, in the motel restaurant, the boys drive to the Electric Factory. The place is a psychedelic barn with a circus theme—swings, slides, funny-house mirrors, Dayglo-painted benches and a hot-dog stand. In the dressing room, John starts to write the set, deciding what numbers to play in what order. Everyone is stoned, pacing, anxious to get on stage. They file out past benches of teen-agers in shetland sweaters and respectable haircuts, tune up and are on.

Danny's costume is a black leather jacket and a black bowler hat. With his pale skin and yellow hair sticking out in points from under the hat, he looks like a spook—one of those skeletons in top hat and tails that dance through children's cartoons. Danny bends at the knees, and starts the band into "Apricot Brandy."

The sound of Rhinoceros is hard white rhythm 'n' blues. When the group first made recordings, John says, "We listened to the tapes and they sounded like a rhinoceros. The bass and drums sounded lumbering and fat." He hits his fists on his knees. "Choonka, choonka, choonka." Rhinoceros never plays a song the same way twice; the performance varies with the group's emotions. On stage, Danny moves around to each player, yelling, "Oh yeah, go!" Alan pitches forward over the piano, and when he sings, his soft features pinch up around his aquiline nose, giving him the look of an ascetic Jew. Doug, with his happy face and ringlets of brown hair, arches his body against the guitar. Michael plays the organ half-standing against a high stool. He wears pink goggles and an Indian mirror cloth shirt unbuttoned to show his olive skin. John directs the show, talking to the audience, banging on a cowbell.

John is soaking when he comes off stage. He pulls off his shirt, and a blonde wearing a skirt that barely covers her plump bottom starts massaging his shoulders. Girls are fluttering about the dressing room, and a student from Temple University is interviewing the band with a cassette recorder.

During the second set, the band begins to feel magic rising. Everyone is synced together, drawing out songs with improvisations. At the end of a walloping chorus, Danny is jumping off the floor, guitar and all. John is bouncing, knees apart, head thrown back. The frenzy reaches the audience, making them wriggle and squirm. Song spills into song, until they arrive at "Monster." It begins with strange, whirring noises that build to a kind of electronic doomsday. John and Alan sway, their chins up, bodies dangling. Strobe lights flicker, faster and faster. When the music explodes, John is frozen in attitude, his head all the way back, his hands flayed apart in the air. It is as if he is suspended in a wind machine, at the still point, and the entire band is there.

It is snowing outside, at 1:30 A.M. The band hurries back to the hotel with a newly acquired set of groupies. There is a lot of knocking on doors, tromping from room to room, smoking, drinking from a flask of

Seagram's apricot brandy and watching television until the last station in Philadelphia goes dark at 4:30 A.M. Many of the groupies encourage musicians to add whipping to their sexual encounters. One groupie called Ruby, a blonde with hooded black eyes on a vacant, moon-shaped face, gave a young musician two sleeping pills, and the next thing he knew, he was tied with scarves to the four corners of the bed. Ruby, wearing black boots, was hitting him, just enough to sting, with the edge of a belt. "I flashed on it," the musician said later. "I thought I'd take the trip, see what it was like." The next day he tied Ruby up, "and she seemed to dig it." That night he threw her out. "Groupies love to be treated like dirt."

Michael says, "Most of the girls we've been meeting lately are interested in getting into whipping. You know, you take off your belt and kind of tease them with it, and then you start doing it harder." John laughs. "Whipping and bondage are symbols of the mental games that go on between us anyway—the possessiveness, the emotional sadism. There's some of that in all of us."

There is some of the groupie in almost every woman who watches a rock singer in leather pants, snapping his body and making a sound so loud it is near pain. A San Francisco groupie made her compulsion explicit by having a gold ring put in her nose. The band members claim to dislike groupies, and pass them around like cigarettes, but groupies flourish in all the large cities because rock stars need them. They don't bring wives or girlfriends on the road, because, they say, "the chick and the band end up fighting for the guy's attention."

In Philadelphia, Billy and Roger Di Fiori, the road manager, pass up the girls for a Roy Rogers movie and the wrestling matches. They sit in their room all day, flipping the dials and gabbing at each other in *Mad* magazine talk. Billy is twenty-six, the oldest in the band, and has taken on the role of group therapist and policeman. He came to Rhinoceros from the Mothers of Invention, which was the last stop on a train of rock groups: Buffalo Springfield, Thor 'n' Shield, The Elysium Senate, Skip 'n' Flip, The Medallions, and Ross Dietrick and the Four Peppers.

Most people are frightened when they first see Billy—a round, grizzly-haired figure with a big stomach and bird legs. During a month on the road, Billy never wore anything but a pair of purple and blue striped pants with calico patches, a T-shirt and a green cap, which no one is allowed to touch. When he climbs on stage, the T-shirt rides up and the pants slip down, showing the cleavage of his behind.

Billy is the only one of Rhinoceros who finished college—a B.A. in music from U.C.L.A. He learned bass drum in high school, when he still had other interests, like riding with the Hell's Angels. "I still have to get in a fight once in a while. When I joined this band they were afraid I'd either punch them in the mouth or light them on fire. I use that to keep them in line."

Billy complains that Rhinoceros has the problems common to every band with teen-agers in it. "All the kids have the mentality of a sixteen-year-old. They left home to make good and impress their parents that they were doing something." Billy bawls out the band for yelling foul words in the hotel corridors, for belching into the microphones on stage, for setting off firecrackers in the parking lot and for fighting over petty matters and ruining performances. "I'm willing to put as much time into this band as everybody else," he says. "But after it's all over, I want to go to Juilliard, to finish what I need for a master's degree so I can teach music in high school."

Over the door to the Electric Factory, Ben Franklin, who started it all with his kite and key, looks down his cardboard nose through pre-hippie wire-frame glasses. Saturday night, the second night in Philadelphia, John has written a set that Danny doesn't like. John wants to sing a number they haven't done in a while, "because if we really get it on, we'll kill the audience, and we'll get it on us too."

Danny says the song needs work. "Why can't we do 'You're My Girl'?"

John says, "I'm sick of it."

"Look, man, I play a lot of songs I'm tired of."

"Yeah, but I'm the one that's gotta get the song on vocally."

Mike and Steve side with Danny. Doug and Alan are with John. Danny's face is twitching. "I can see everybody getting uptight. Let's stop it right here." He cuts the air with his hand.

John walks out, slamming the door. Steve throws a cigarette pack after him. Outside, John crumples the paper on which he wrote the set. He hurls a record against the wall, then walks back in. "I don't know what to do. I don't know how to write the set."

Danny says, "It's your uptightness that's the root of the problem."

"Okay, I'm uptight. Leave me alone."

They are ten minutes late for the stage call. The set begins—the same songs as the night before, but they are dead. When it is over, the band walks off solemnly, straight back to the dressing room, no chatting or fooling with the chickies. The feeling between them is tangible, sexual, as between lovers who have seen a quarrel blow up over nothing and burn out, leaving them close and bittersweet.

Billy speaks first. "What went wrong is that we had a teen-age quarrel."

Danny sighs. "I just wanna forget about it." His stomach is cramped, and he wants to get the paregoric out of the car.

"You shouldn't let John bug you," Billy says. "John digs bugging people, isn't that right?" John nods. Billy says, "When John gets uptight, let him tear his hair—when he does that, he's getting rid of it. He sits in here writing a song, or a poem, because that's what a set is, and you guys say you don't wanna play it. He's hurt, and I don't blame him. I'd be pissed too."

The door swings open. Two freckled boys wearing Western hats and kerchiefs announced, in pubescent voices, "We're from the *Free Press*. Can we talk to you?" Half the band walks out, and the two boys sit down. "What are your names?" Silence. "I'm Alan." "I'm John." And then this grizzly man who has ridden with the Hell's Angels says, sweetly, "I'm Billy."

"Any good group that can stick together can make it." Paul Rothchild, a producer at Elektra Records, noticed in the fall of 1967 that a number of groups were breaking up. He began wondering what would happen if he took one from this group, one from that, and put the best musicians together.

Rothchild called every available musician he knew and invited him to Los Angeles. His vision was of a supergroup of superstars, who would hammer a new approach to white rhythm 'n' blues. He sent plane tickets to thirty, and on November 30, they began showing up at his house in Laurel Canyon. Alan Gerber flew out from Chicago. John Finley, who had recently quit John and Lee and the Checkmates, then the top group in Canada, came from Toronto. John walked into the oversized living room, looked around at fifteen people he had never seen before and thought, "We're gonna be a group?" John sat in a corner and didn't say a word. Neither did Doug Hastings, who had come down from Seattle where he was playing with the Daily Flash. Rothchild passed a guitar to a young man from Oklahoma and said, "Play." Alan recalls, "It was great. Then he passed it to another guy, and he was great too. I was so spaced out that when they passed it to me, I said groovy, and sang my songs."

The boys stayed for several months at the Sandy Koufax Tropicana Motel, rehearsing at a rented theater. "We would jam in shifts," John recalls. "It was dog eat dog." Rothchild listened to the sessions, discouraged some people, brought in others, including Danny Weis and Jerry Penrod from the Iron Butterfly, Michael Fonfara from the Electric Flag and Billy Mundi from the Mothers of Invention. By March, Rothchild decided the group was complete at seven members.

They went into a recording studio for eight days and made an album. Most rock groups spend close to a month in the studio, recording a few parts at a time and then dubbing voice and additional parts over that. The way Rhinoceros wanted to record was live, all together, standing in a circle and playing into a cluster of mikes—one feeding back to them, the others recording.

Before the album was made, Elektra had spent $50,000 on the group, paying their room, board and transportation, equipment rentals, rehearsal costs, and then buying out old contracts for three of them. The expense of making, promoting and distributing the album raised the total to $80,000. A few months after its release, Rhinoceros had sold 100,000 albums. Not until it sells a quarter of a million will the band have written off its debt to Elektra and begin to earn money from the record.

In the fall of 1968, the band decided to move to New York to build their reputation; there were more playing opportunities for the group there than in any other part of the country. They lived in the decaying Chelsea Hotel in New York for a few months, then found the house in Mahopac. About that time, Jerry, who was playing bass, started having fits of despair. One night in a town on Long Island, the band had a blowup before going on stage. When it was time to play, Jerry had disappeared. From information that has trickled back, the band says, Jerry "went straight—cut his hair, went back to art school in California and moved back with his parents." Danny's brother, Steve, who had been working as equipment manager and had casually learned Jerry's parts, was asked to take his place.

If no one else quits, Rhinoceros will be an unusual case. Even the most successful groups have been unable to hold together beyond a few years: the Mamas and Papas, Cream, Big Brother and the Holding Company, the Lovin' Spoonful, Love, Traffic, the Byrds, the Buffalo Springfield. The list of casualties runs on, and the cause of death is almost always personal squabbles. Danny Weis quit the Iron Butterfly because of a falling out with the organist. "I can't even remember the reason now," Danny says. "Oh yes, he resented me playing leads more often than him."

After that Danny gathered a group that was to be called Nirvana, but before they could get off the ground, Danny fought with the bass player and the group disintegrated. The musicians wander, forming new groups, or becoming studio musicians, producers or single artists.

Jac Holzman, President of Elektra, says it is difficult for a group to stay together more than a year after a record is released unless they see a steady increase in popularity. "The group hangs together by a string. It's one gigantic holding action until the miracle happens."

Friday morning at eleven o'clock, when the band is due to leave Mahopac, is the time everyone decides to do laundry. Alan discovers another rip in the only pair of jeans he wears. "Lan, could you do a fast patch job? If I don't have my pants, I'll feel insecure."

Danny bounds up the stairs. "Cunnilingus, everyone."

"Cunnilingus," John calls from his room.

John has finished packing, and is staring out the window at the snowbound road. He broods, "Why haven't I ever been able to make it with a chick?" John is twenty-four, and the longest relationship he has had lasted three weeks. He drives the sixty miles to New York with the band every Sunday to go to The Scene, a rock club where groupies hang out, but rarely brings the girls back to Mahopac. "I don't want to have to deal with them the next day."

John is not the only one in the group who is, as they put it, "going through changes." Danny has been forced to look at himself more closely. Since he joined his first rock group at twelve, Danny has always been the star. With Rhinoceros, the stress was on playing together, rather than separately to the fans. Danny was criticized, and made to realize, he says, "that I'd been on an ego trip for eighteen years, and that I didn't really want to be the fancy lead guitar player whom all the chicks drooled over. When that happened, I stopped wearing all my satin clothes. I started listening to others in the band."

Danny, like the others, learned music when he was young. His father, John Weis, was a country-western guitarist who played at churches and naval training bases around San Diego. Danny was an honor student in high school, but left home at seventeen when his group, the Iron Butterfly, was offered a chance to play at a club in Hollywood. "We got forty dollars a week and lived in a room above the club that had no bed, no heat and smelled awful." He met a girl, twenty-five, who was a trapeze artist and stunt woman, moved in with her and got married at eighteen. The marriage ended two years later.

"Being married to a musician is tough on a chick," Danny says. "You sit at home every night by yourself while your husband is surrounded by chicks who throw themselves at him. I learned from being married that you have to get all the sex thing out of your system, because the music is so tied up with sex that it's a real struggle, even if you're married, not to go after it."

The language of rock is rooted in sexuality. The instrument is your "ax." What you play on it are "licks" and "chops." If two players get into competition, they "fight each other with their axes." A band gets on stage to "get it on." If you "dig" something, you "flash on it," "turn on," "get into it."

The communication between band and audience is as physical as it is aural. Steve says, "I know certain lines on the guitar that, if I'm interested in a chick, I can look straight at her and do it to her. This one line starts high on the neck of the guitar and goes down to the lowest part, fast. It's like a slap in the crotch." When Mike works on the organ, he is thinking of making love. "The beat does it to me." And Danny says he gets so sexually and emotionally excited that, "I've come on stage lots of times, just from the music, and it's unbelievable. Sometimes I fall off the stage, and other times, I cry, right up there." Jimi Hendrix, feeling the same currents, set fire to his guitar. Jim Morrison of the Doors sang "Touch Me" and then exposed himself on a Florida stage.

After a set, the band waits for girls to approach them. "You've made the first move by playing. It's up to them to take you up on it." Steve, at seventeen, has had more experience with sex, drugs and alcohol than many men have in a lifetime. He started sniffing glue at eleven and, by fifteen, had tried marijuana, speed, LSD, barbiturates, mescaline, opium and hashish. He had also had groupies in twos and threes. Steve's father had died when the boy was fourteen, and Steve was shunted from school to school as a problem child. He was stoned almost every day he went to class. At sixteen, he convinced his mother to let him go to Hollywood to live with his brother Danny and his wife. Danny, then eighteen, became Steve's legal guardian.

All of the band members believe they will have to get out of the atmosphere of drugs and sex someday. But Danny says he will play guitar the rest of his life. He watched his father, who was "the best guitar player there was," become an insurance salesman to support his family. "It killed him. I saw him die from it. He wanted to play music and he had to sell insurance. I knew I could never do that. I said to myself, fuck it, I don't care if I starve. I'm gonna play music until I die."

Friday night in Schenectady, the marquee in front of the Holiday Inn says, "Happy Birthday Peggy." Watching television in his room, Danny picks up the electric guitar and tries to get Michael's attention. The guitar is barely audible when not plugged in, but after several minutes of crazy picking by Danny, Michael turns his head away from *The High Chaparral* and drawls, "You're insaaaaaane."

When the guitar is plugged into an electric amplifier, it works like this: the musician plucks the strings, causing them to vibrate. The vibrations are picked up by a set of small magnets under the strings and sent as electric impulses through a cord to the amplifier. The amplifier magnifies the impulses, converts them back to musical sounds and feeds them out a speaker. Each guitarist uses a separate amplifier, and will use two or three in a large hall to make the sound louder and fuller. Michael's Hammond organ needs a special Leslie organ amplifier and several mikes in front of it. Alan plays a Rocky Mountain Instruments electric piano which has its own amplifier. The vocal parts and drums are not amplified, but carried directly over a public-address system. Most bands amplify themselves up to the point of distortion. It is always different to hear a group live than to hear them on records, because the volume transforms the experience. Even between numbers, there is a constant electric buzz. "It's security," John says. "The louder you are, the more confident you feel, especially in a strange place."

Schenectady, a depressed industrial town in central

New York, is not only strange but grim. The job is at the Aerodrome, a warehouse converted into a seedy psychedelic nightclub. Girls with troubled complexions, wearing cheap hairpieces and elephant pants, flail about by themselves on the dance floor.

The sets at the Aerodrome go well. John is exhilarated when he comes off stage, but Alan is depressed. "This is the kind of place that makes me hate playing rock 'n' roll." Danny is sitting still. "It's weird out there." John says, "Maybe I was wrong. I felt great singing, but since I've been off . . ." He goes out to the bar, and a shrill-voiced girl says to him, "I'm not very pretty but I'm fun to watch," and starts twitching her pasty face. "Shit."

Boston is better from the start. "The whole thing feels special," Alan says, halfway along the Massachusetts Turnpike. No one in the band knows exactly how to get to Boston. On the itinerary handed them that morning, there are no directions, no time listed for sound checks or performance, and the hotel is misspelled, "Sheriton Boston." Even if they had directions, they would probably lose them. They lose everything—letters, tickets, keys, money, phone numbers. The Boston Pop Festival, the itinerary says, is at the Boston Armory. When they find the armory, it is boarded up and dark. The festival, they learn after driving around for several hours, is at the Boston Arena. No one in the car is worried or nervous. They are soaring.

Danny describes the perfect gig: "A good gig is going there, being happy in the car and feeling well healthwise. I usually ache all over, have a headache or a backache and very little energy, mainly because I don't exercise. All I do is sit, sleep and eat. The next thing is getting real smashed before the gig, playing a magic set, meeting really pretty chicks and having a groovy thing at a Holiday Inn, or some other hotel that has good, hard double beds, so they're good for my back. That's a good gig.''

For John a good gig is building up emotional power over the audience. "To do that, you have to live the music, not perform it. If you sound sad, you have to feel sad and be sad. If the spirit and emotion is there, you can make people jump out of their seats, cry and scream. One gig we did, there was a killing while we were on. I don't know what that means, but it happened. It was, well, curious.''

The Sheraton Boston has fountains, suspended staircases and Peggy Lee singing "Fever" over the Muzak. The band doesn't usually stay in hotels like this. They prefer motels that are easy to get in and out of. The first carload walks into the lobby and the lobby turns, as if the hundred or so people milling about are one body.

Steve is the most conspicuous. He is all in black, with a black satin shirt open to the waist, a large cross bumping against his concave chest, and black, crushed-velvet pants. Over his pale face is a black desperado hat. Alan is wearing a blue flowered satin shirt with puffed sleeves. His silky brown hair hangs over his eyes and, together with his sideburns and mustache, dominates his appearance.

The hotel manager refuses to give the group rooms until they pay in advance. They try to eat dinner, and are turned away from all four restaurants in the hotel for lack of coat and tie. They drive to a restaurant called the Red Fez in Roxbury, frequented by students from Harvard. A waitress comes at them holding out her arms. "I'm sorry, we're closing." A sign

in the window says, "Open until 3:00 A.M." The waitress is glaring at Danny with his white, cat's fur hair
and Steve in his black satins and desperado hat.
"Yeah, we understand," John says.

The band doesn't press trouble. This is the dues
they pay. No one in the group owns a tie. "It comes
down to which one you want more, your freedom or
their approval," John says. "I enjoy dressing and
being who I am. I don't need them. They're the cre-
tins."

Giving up on dinner, they drive to the Boston
Arena, an old roller rink, filled with mildewed air and
dirt. "It looks terrible," Steve says, as they fight
through a jam-up in the parking lot. The policeman at
the gate doesn't believe they are Rhinoceros, and
holds them aside until an official is summoned. The
group still hasn't found out what time they're going to
play, and it's too late now for a sound check. They
are escorted to their dressing room, a musty green cell
with a bank of toilets, showers and dirty sinks, in
which a dozen Cokes have been placed. "Aaaaggh,
it's a latrine," Steve yells. It is 9 P.M., they are to play
in thirty minutes, and half the band hasn't shown up.
"Let's not get worked up over it," John says. "We'll
just upset ourselves."

The other carload walks in with ten minutes to go.
They had been stopped in Connecticut for speeding,
taken to the police station and arraigned, then had
gotten lost on the way into Boston and driven right
through the city and out for ten miles before they realized it.

Rhinoceros is third on the program, after Daddy
Warbucks and the Grass Roots. They will be followed
by the Colwell-Winfield Blues Band and Canned Heat.
The Arena, they discover, is an "echo bomb." The

bleachers are half filled—about a thousand people huddled in coats against the drafts. The vast spaces in the building make it impersonal.

The whole band knows, though, that they're going to have a good time. In the first number, they throw back their heads, laugh and call to each other. Danny starts his rounds, moving up to John and getting into rhythm with him. Then he faces Steve, who nods his wilting head at Danny, "Mmmmmmm, yeah." John begins to lose himself in "Top of the Ladder," jumping, skipping, snapping his body in half with the downbeat of the drums. When the song ends, he wipes himself with a towel, then grabs the mike. "Hey, wanna catch some ass, wanna get it on?" Laughs, and a few jokers yell, "Yeah." John says, "Let's catch some ass," and Danny starts "Apricot Brandy."

There are boos when John says, "We've only got five minutes left. But we'd like to go out stomping." Everyone in the band except Billy stands up now and pounds the floor, Thwack! Thwack! clapping their hands and waving tambourines. They keep up a rhythm, two minutes, then Danny waves at Billy, "One, two, three, go!"

Through the song, "You're My Girl," the band is jumping, waving their free arms, grabbing anything to shake—sticks, bells. Michael is playing the organ standing up. The kids in the front rows are on their feet screaming. Even the policemen in front of the stage are nodding, their white caps moving, ever so slightly, up and down.

When the band finishes, dripping wet, people rush at them and grab their hands. They make their way to the dressing room, sigh and collapse.

Alan: "I had such a good time!"

Mike: "Oh, fuck, it was so good."

Steve: "We kiiiiiiilled 'em!"

John: "It feels so great to crack a challenge like that. Those people didn't wanna move, and we made 'em wiggle asses. We really had to work at it."

They close the door, and sit together in the musty room with its urinal smell. Their bodies are limp, their eyes fixed on the ceiling. They smile, and blink, and every now and then make this sound, a soft, airy sigh, which is the beginning of a laugh: "Aaaaaaaaaahhh."

1969

OPEN LAND

Wheeler Ranch: free land—live-in, drop-in.

—Commune Directory.

The idea of open land was introduced in California by Lou Gottlieb, a singer with the popular folk group The Limelighters. In 1962, Gottlieb bought a thirty-two-acre piece of real estate in Sonoma County, north of San Francisco, and called it Morning Star. Gottlieb and a friend, Ramon Sender, decided to start a community at Morning Star with one governing precept: access to the land would be denied to no one. With no rules, no leaders, they felt, hostilities would not arise and people could be reborn by living in harmony with the earth.

Gottlieb deeded the land to God; shortly, a woman sued God because her home had been struck by lightning. "Now that God owns property," her lawyer argued, "he can be sued for natural disasters."

Things were relatively quiet at Morning Star until 1967, when hippies began to patronize open land. "From the first," Gottlieb said, "the land selected the people. Those who couldn't work hard didn't survive. When the land got crowded, people split." Gottlieb pointed to the sky. "With open land, *he* is the casting director."

What would happen, I asked, if someone behaved violently or destructively? Gottlieb, who was wearing nothing but a blanket and a safety pin, frowned. "There have been a few cases where we've had to ask people to go, but it's at terrible, terrible cost to everyone's soul. When the land begins to throw off people, everyone suffers." He shook his body, as if he were the land rejecting a germ. "Open land has no historical precedent. When you give free land, not free food or money, you pull the carpet out from under the capitalist system."

A mile north of Gottlieb's land was another ranch, 320 acres, ten times the size of Morning Star. It was owned by Bill Wheeler, who had come West from Connecticut looking for a farmhouse where he could paint. Bill is tall, gaunt, with deep-set blue eyes, a full beard and long hair streaked yellow by the sun. His voice is gentle, yet conveys stubborn determination and, in other moods, a sense of delight in mischievous fun.

Bill Wheeler and Lou Gottlieb became close friends. In the winter of '67, when Sonoma County officials tried to close Morning Star by bulldozing all the dwellings except Gottlieb's house, Bill Wheeler declared his land open. Many of the Morning Star people moved to Wheeler's. Others traveled to New Mexico, where they founded Morning Star East on a mesa near Taos owned by another wealthy hippie. Within a year, the Southwest, particularly New Mexico and Colorado, was dotted with more pieces of open land than any other region. The communes became crowded. More land was opened in California, Oregon and

Washington, and Gottlieb planned to buy land and deed it to God in Holland, Sweden and Spain.

"The hippies should get the Nobel Prize for developing this simple idea," Gottlieb said. "Why did no one think of it before the hippies? Because hippies don't work, so they have time to dream up truly creative ideas."

When I visited Wheeler Ranch in 1970, I was surprised to hear people refer to themselves as "hippies." I thought the term had been rendered meaningless by overuse. American culture had absorbed so much of the style of hip—clothes, hair, language, drugs, music—that it had obscured the substance of the movement, with which people at Wheeler's still identified. Being a hippie, to them, meant dropping out completely and finding another way to survive. It meant saying no to careers, no to consumption of technology's products, no to political systems and elections. Lou Gottlieb, who was once a Communist Party member, said, "The entire Left is a dead end. The hippie alternative is to turn inward and reach backward for roots, simplicity and the tribal experience."

In the first phase of the movement, hippies settled in slums, where housing would be cheap and many things could be obtained free: food scraps from restaurants; secondhand clothes; health services from free clinics. But the slums proved inhospitable. The hippies were preyed upon by criminals, pushers and the desperate.

In 1967, they began moving to rural land where there would be fewer people and life would be hard. They took up what Ramon Sender called "voluntary primitivism," building their own houses out of mud

and trees, planting crops by hand, rolling loose to-
bacco into cigarettes, grinding their own wheat, canning vegetables, delivering their own babies and educating their own children. They gave up electricity,
the telephone, running water, gas stoves, even rock
music. They started to sing and play their own—folky
and quiet.

My first view of Wheeler Ranch comes at dawn. I
am rain-soaked and bad-tempered from spending the
night in the car, unable to find the place. In the morning light, however, the way becomes clear and I am
awed by the lambent beauty of this nineteenth-century
pastoral tableau. As far as the eye can see, there are
no houses, no traffic, nothing but verdant hills, pine
trees, cows, yellow wild flowers and the ocean with
whitecaps rising in the distance. Women in long skirts
and shawls, men in lace-up boots and overalls are sitting in the grass playing banjos, guitars, lyres, wood
flutes and dulcimers. Children who look, male and female, like Tom Sawyer are scampering through the
garden playing tag.

Only four-wheel drive vehicles can maneuver across
the ranch, and ultimately Bill wants all cars banned.
"We would rather live without machines," he says.
"The fact that we have no good roads protects us from
tourists. People are car-bound; even the police would
never come in here without their vehicles."

Although it rains a good part of the year, most of
the dwellings do not have any source of heat and are
not waterproof. They look like shacks out of Dog-
patch—old boards nailed unevenly together, rough
poles and odd pieces of plastic strung across the poles
to make wobbly igloos. "Houses shouldn't be de-

signed to keep out the weather," Bill says. "We want to get in touch with it."

Bill installed six chemical toilets on the ranch to comply with county sanitation requirements, but, he says, "I wouldn't go in one of those toilets if you paid me. It's very important for us to be able to use the ground, because we are completing a cycle, returning to Mother Earth what she's given us."

Because of the haphazard sanitation system, the water at Wheeler's is contaminated and until people adjust to it, they suffer dysentery, just as tourists do who drink the water in Mexico. There are periodic waves of hepatitis, clap, crabs, scabies and streptococcic throat infections. No one brushes his teeth more than once a week, and then they often use "organic toothpaste," made from eggplant cooked in tinfoil. They are experimenting with herbs and Indian healing remedies to become free of manufactured medicinal drugs, but see no contradiction in continuing to swallow mind-altering chemicals.

People at Wheeler Ranch have rejected communal living; they live alone or in monogamous units, cook for themselves and build their own houses and gardens. "There should not be a main lodge, because you get too many people trying to live under one roof and it doesn't work," Bill says.

With couples, the double standard is an unwritten rule: the men can roam but the women must be faithful. There are many more men than women, and when a new girl arrives, she is pounced upon. Mary Cordelia Stevens, or Corky, a handsome eighteen-year-old from a Chicago suburb, hiked into the ranch one afternoon in October and sat down by the front gate to eat a can of Spam. The first young man who came by invited her to a party where everyone took PCP, a tranquilizer for horses. It was a strange trip—people rolling around the floor of the tipi, moaning, retching, laughing, hallucinating. Corky went home with one young man and stayed with him for three weeks, during which time she was almost constantly stoned. "You sort of have to be stoned to get through the first days here," she says. "Then you know the trip."

Corky is a strapping, well-proportioned girl with a milkmaid's face and long blond hair. She talks softly, with many giggles: "I love to go around naked. There's so much sexual energy here, it's great. Everybody's turned on to each other's bodies." Corky left the ranch to go home for Christmas and to officially drop out of Antioch College; she hitchhiked back, built her own house and chicken coop, learned to plant, do laundry in a tin tub with a washboard and milk the cows. "I love dealing with things that are simple and direct."

Bill Wheeler admires Corky for making it on her own, which few of the women do. Bill is torn between his desire to be the benefactor-protector and his intolerance of people who aren't self-reliant. "I'm contemptuous of people who can't pull their own weight," he says. Yet he constantly worries about the welfare of others. He also feels conflict between wanting a tribe, indeed wanting to be chieftain, and wanting privacy.

Because of the fluidity of the community, it is almost impossible for it to become economically self-sufficient. None of the communes has been able to survive entirely off the land. Most are unwilling to go into cash crops or light industry because in an open community with no rules, there are not enough people who can be counted on to work. The women with children receive welfare, some of the men collect unemployment and food stamps, and others get money from home. They spend very little—perhaps six hundred dollars a year per person. "We're not up here to make money," Bill says, "or to live like country squires."

When darkness falls, the ranch becomes eerily quiet. No one uses flashlights. Those who have lived there some time can feel their way along the paths by memory. Around 7 P.M., people gather at the barn with bottles for the late milking. During the week, the night milking is the main social event. Corky says, "It's the only time you know you're going to see people. Otherwise you could wander around for days and not see anyone." A girl from Holland and two boys have gathered mussels at a nearby beach during the day, and invite everyone to their tipi to eat them. We sit in silence, watching the mussels steam open in a pot over the grate. A boy with glassy blue eyes whose lids seem weighted down starts to pick out the orange flesh with his dirt-caked hands and drop them in a pan greased with Spry. A mangy cat snaps every third mussel out of the pan. No one shoos the cat away.

Nancy Johnson, in her shack about a mile from the tipi, is fixing a green stew of onions, cabbage, kale, leeks and potatoes; she calls to three people who live nearby to come share it. Nancy has a seventeen-year-old, all-American-girl face on a plump, saggy-stomached mother's body. She has been married twice, gone to graduate school, worked as a social worker and a prostitute. Her children have been on more acid trips than most adults at the ranch. "They get very quiet on acid," she says. "The experience is less staggering for kids than for adults, because acid returns you to the consciousness of childhood."

Nancy says the children have not been sick since they moved to Wheeler's two years ago. "I can see divine guidance leading us here. This place has been touched by God." She had a vision of planting trees on the land, and ordered fifty of exotic variety, including strawberry guava, camellia and loquat. Stirring the green stew, she smiles vacuously. "I feel anticipant of a very happy future."

With morning comes a hailstorm, and Bill Wheeler must go to court in Santa Rosa for trial on charges of assaulting a policeman when a squad came to the ranch looking for juvenile runaways. Bill, his wife Gay, Gay's brother Peter, Nancy and Corky spread out through the courthouse, peeling off mildewed clothes and piling them on benches. Peter, a gigantic, muscular fellow of twenty-three, rips his pants all the way up the back, and, like most people at Wheeler's, he is not wearing underwear. Gay changes her infant daughter Raspberry's diapers on the floor of the ladies' room. Nancy takes off her rain-soaked long johns and leaves them in one of the stalls.

It is a tedious day. Witnesses give conflicting testimony, but all corroborate that one of the officers struck Wheeler first, leading to a shoving, running, tackling, pot-throwing skirmish which also involved Peter. The defendants spend the night in a motel, going over testimony with their lawyer. Bill and Corky drive to a supermarket to buy dinner, and wheel down the aisles, checking labels for chemicals, opening jars to take a taste with the finger, ummm, laughing at the "obsolete consciousness" of the place. They buy greens, Roquefort dressing, peanut butter, organic honey and two Sara Lee cakes.

The next morning, Nancy says she couldn't sleep because of the radiator and all the trucks. Gay says,

"I had a dream in which I saw death. It was a blond man with no facial hair." Bill, outside, staring at the motel swimming pool: "I dreamed last night that Gay and I got separated somehow and I was stuck with Raspberry." He shudders. "You know, I feel love for other people, but Gay is the only one I want to spend my life with."

The jury goes out at 3 P.M. and deliberates until 9. In the courtroom, a mottled group in pioneer clothes, mud-spattered and frizzy-wet, are chanting, "Om." The jury cannot agree on four counts, and finds Bill and Peter not guilty on three counts. The judge declares a mistrial. The county fathers are not finished, though. They are still attempting to close the access road to Wheeler's and to get an injunction to raze all buildings on the ranch as health hazards. Bill Wheeler is not worried, nor are his charges, climbing in the jeep and singing, "Any day now . . ." God will provide.

Roads across the eastern half of Washington State are flat and ruler-straight, snowbound for long months, turning arid and dusty in the summer. At an empty crossing in a poor, wheat-growing county, the road suddenly dips and winds down to a valley filled with tall pines and primitive log cabins. The community hidden in this natural canyon is Tolstoy Farm, founded in 1963. It is one of the oldest communes to be started on open land. The residents—about twenty-four adults and almost as many children—are serious, straightforward people who, with calculated bluntness, say they are social misfits, unable or unwilling to cope with the world "outside." The community has no rules, except that no one can be asked to leave. Because it predates the hippie movement, there is an absence of mystical jargon. Only a few are vegetarians. Members do not want the location of the farm published for fear of being inundated with "psychedelic beggars."

I drive to the canyon in the morning and, seeing the condition of the ground, leave my car at the top and walk down the steep, icy road. The farm is divided into two parts—eighty acres at the north end of the canyon and a hundred and twenty acres at the south. The families live separately, as they do at Wheeler's, but their homes are more elaborate.

The first house in the north end is a hexagonal log cabin built by Huw Williams, who started the farm when he was nineteen. Huw is slight, soft-spoken, with a wispy blond beard. When I arrive, he is cutting out pieces of leather, wearing a lumberman's shirt and a knife strapped to his waist. His wife Sylvia is nursing their youngest son, while their two-year-old, Sennett, wearing nothing but a T-shirt, is playing on the floor with a half-breed Norwegian elkhound.

I ask Huw how the community has stayed together for seven years. He says, deadpan, "The secret is not to try. We've got a lot of rugged individualists here, and everyone is into a different thing. In reflection, it feels good that we survived. A lot of us were from wealthy backgrounds, and the idea of giving it all up and living off the land was a challenge."

Huw grew up on a ranch forty miles from the canyon. "I had everything. When I was fourteen, I had my own car, a half-dozen cows and six hundred dollars in the bank." When he was fifteen, his house burned down and he saw his elaborate collections—stamps, models, books—disappear. He vowed not to become attached to possessions after that and took to sleeping outdoors. He remembers being terrified of violence, and idolized Gandhi, Christ and Tolstoy. At seventeen, he became a conscientious objector and began to work in draft resistance. While on a peace walk from New Hampshire to Washington, D.C., he decided to drop out of the University of Washington and start a nonviolent training center, a community where people could live by sharing rather than competing. He persuaded his mother to give him eighty acres in the canyon for the project, rented a house, called the Hart House, and advertised in peace papers for people to come and share it with him.

The first summer, more than fifty came and went and they all lived in the Hart House. One of the visitors was Sylvia, a fair-skinned girl with long chestnut hair and warm wistful eyes that hint of sadness. They were married, and Huw stopped talking about a peace center and started studying intentional communities. He decided he wanted a community that would be open to anyone, flexible, with no prescribed rules to live by. Work would get done, Huw felt, because people would want to do it to achieve certain ends. "It's a Western idea. You inspire people by giving them a goal, making it seem important; then they'll do anything to get there." If people did not want to work, Huw felt, forcing them would not be the answer.

The results were chaotic. "Emotional crises, fights over everything. A constant battle to get things done. A typical scene would be for one guy to spend two hours fixing a meal. He had to make three separate dishes—one for vegetarians, one for nonvegetarians and one for people who wouldn't eat government-surplus food. He would put them on the table, everybody would grab and if you stood back you got nothing. When people live that close together, they become less sensitive and manners go right out the window.

It was educational, but we knew it wasn't suitable for raising children.''

The group pooled resources and bought another hundred and twenty acres two miles away. Huw and Sylvia built their own cabin and moved out of the Hart House; another couple followed. Then around 1966, the farm was swamped with runaways, addicts and hippies. A schism grew between the permanent people and the transients. The transients thought the permanents were uptight and stingy. The permanents said the transients were abusing the land. When most of the permanents had built their own cabins, they began talking about burning down the Hart House. I heard many versions of the incident. Some said a man named George burned it. Some said everyone did it. Some said they watched and were against it but felt they should not stop it. Afterwards, most of the transients left, and the farm settled into its present pattern of families living by themselves.

The only communal rituals are Thanksgiving at the schoolhouse and the corn dance, held on the first full moon of May. Huw devised the corn dance from a Hopi Indian ceremony, and each year it gets more elaborate. Huw builds a drum, and at sundown everyone gathers on a hillside with food, wine, the children in costumes, animals and musical instruments. They take turns beating the drum but must keep it beating until dawn. They roast potatoes, and sometimes a kid, a pig, or a turkey, get stoned, dance, sing and drop to sleep. "But that's only once a year," one of the men says. "We could have one every month, and it would hold the community together."

Not everyone wants this solidarity, however. Some have staked out corners of the canyon where they want to be left alone. The families who live nearby get together for dinners, chores and babysitting. At the north end, the Williamses, the Swansons and the Goldens visit constantly. On the day I arrive, they are having a garden meeting at the Swansons' to decide what to order for spring planting.

The Swansons, who have three young children, moved into the canyon this year after buying, for a thousand dollars, the two-story house a man called Steve had built for his own family. Steve had had a falling out with Huw and wanted to move to the south acres. The Swansons needed a place they could move into right away. The house has the best equipment at the farm, with a flush toilet (sectioned off by a blanket hung from the ceiling), running water and electricity that drives a stove, refrigerator and freezer.

Jack Swanson, an outgoing, ruddy-faced man of thirty-five, with short hair and a mustache, works on a newspaper a hundred and fifty miles away and commutes to the farm for weekends. His wife, Barbara, twenty-four, looks like a Midwestern college girl: jeans cut off to Bermuda length, blouses with Peter Pan collars and a daisy-printed scarf around her short brown hair. But Barbara is not what she seems. "I've always been a black sheep," she says. "I hate supermarkets—everything's been chemically preserved. You might as well be in a morgue."

Barbara is gifted at baking, pickling and canning, and wants to raise sheep to weave and dye the wool herself. She and Jack tried living in various cities, then a suburb, then a farm in Idaho, where they found they lacked the skills to make it work. "We were so ill-equipped by society to live off the earth," Jack says. "We thought about moving to Tolstoy Farm for three or four years, but when times were good, we put it off."

Last year their third child was born with a lung disease which required months of hospitalization and left them in debt. Moving to the farm seemed a way out. "If we had stayed in the suburbs, we found we were spending everything we made, with rent and car payments, and could never pay off the debts. I had to make more and more just to stay even." Jack says, "Here, because I don't pay rent and because we can raise food ourselves, I don't have to make as much money. We get help in farming, and have good company. In two or three months, this house is all mine—no interest, no taxes. Outside it would cost me twenty thousand dollars and eight percent interest."

A rainstorm hits at midnight and by morning the snow has washed off the canyon walls, the stream has flooded over and the roads are slushy mud ruts. Sylvia saddles two horses and we ride down to the south 120. There are seven cabins on the valley floor, and three hidden by trees on the cliff. Outside one of the houses, Steve is feeding his rabbits; the mute, wiggling animals cluster around the cage doors. Steve breeds the rabbits to sell to a processor and hopes to earn a hundred dollars a month from the business. He also kills them to eat. "It's tough to do," he says, "but if people are going to eat meat, they should be willing to kill the animal."

While Steve is building his new house, he has moved with his wife and four children into the cabin of a couple I shall call George and Liz Snow. George is a hefty, porcine man of thirty-nine, a drifter who earned a doctorate in statistics, headed an advertising agency, ran guns to Cuba, worked as a civil servant, a mason, a dishwasher and rode the freights. He has had three wives, and does not want his name known because "there are a lot of people I don't want to find me."

Steve, a hard-lived thirty-four, has a past that rivals George's for tumult: nine years as an Army engineer, AWOL, running a coffeehouse in El Paso, six months in a Mexican jail on a marijuana charge, working nine-to-five as chief engineer in a fire-alarm factory in New Haven, Connecticut, then cross-country to Spokane. Steve's abrasive style inevitably led to friction in every situation, until, tired of bucking the system, he moved to the farm. "I liked the structure of this community," he says. "Up there, I can get along with one out of a thousand people. Here I make it with one out of two."

Several times a week, Steve, his daughter Laura and Stash, a man who lives alone at the farm, drive to the small town nearby to buy supplies, visit a friend, and, if the hot water holds out, take showers. They stop at Joe's Bar for beer and hamburgers—forty cents "with all the trimmings." Laura, a slender, quiet girl, walks across the deserted street to buy *Mad* magazine and look at rock record albums.

There are three teen-agers at the farm—all girls—and all have tried running away to the city. One was arrested for shoplifting, another was picked up in a crash pad with seven men. Steve says, "We have just as much trouble with our kids as middle-class parents do. I'd like to talk to people in other communities and find out how they handle their teen-agers. Maybe we could send ours there." Stash says, "Or bring teen-age boys here."

The women at the farm have started to joke uneasily that their sons will become businessmen and their daughters will be suburban housewives. The history of utopian communities in this country has been that the second generation leaves.

In theory, the farm is an expanded family, and children can move around and live with different people. When I visited, all the children except one were staying in their parents' houses. Tension seemed to be running through the community, with Steve and Huw Williams at opposite poles. Steve's wife, Ann, told me, "We don't go along with Huw's philosophy of anarchy. We don't think it works. You need some authority and discipline in any social situation." Huw says, "The thing about anarchy is that I'm willing to do a job myself, if I have to, rather than start imposing rules on others. Steve and George want things to be done efficiently with someone giving orders, like the Army."

At dinner when the sun goes down, Steve and George's house throbs with festivity. The cabin, like most at the farm, is not divided into separate rooms. All nine people—Steve, Ann and their four children, the Snows and their baby—sleep on the upstairs level, while the downstairs serves as kitchen, dining and living room. "The teen-agers wish there was more privacy," Steve says, "but for us and the younger children, it feels really close." Most couples at the farm are untroubled about making love in front of the children. "We don't make a point of it," one man says, "but if they happen to see it, and it's done in love, they won't be afraid or embarrassed."

While Ann and Liz cook *hasenpfeffer*, Steve's daughters, Laura and Karen, ten, improvise making gingerbread with vinegar and brown sugar as a substitute for molasses. A blue jay chatters in a cage hung from the ceiling. Geese honk outside, and five dogs chase each other around the room. Steve plays the guitar and sings. The *hasenpfeffer* is superb. The rabbits have been pickled for two days, cooked in red wine, herbs and sour cream. There are large bowls of beets, potatoes, Jell-O and the gingerbread, which tastes perfect, with homemade applesauce. Afterwards, we all get toothpicks.

Liz, an uninhibited, roly-poly girl of twenty-three, is describing how she hitchhiked to the farm, met George, stayed and got married. "I like it here," she says, pursing her lips, "because I can stand nude on my front porch and yell, fuck! Also, I think I like it here because I'm fat, and there aren't many mirrors around. Clothes don't matter, and people don't judge you by your appearance like they do out there."

Huw has assumed the job of teacher for the four children of school age. Huw believes school should be anarchic, and that the students should set their own learning programs. Suddenly given this freedom, the children, who were accustomed to public school, said they wanted to play and ride the horses. Huw finally told them they must be at the schoolhouse every day for at least one hour. They wander in and out, and Huw stays half the day. He walks home for lunch and passes Karen and another girl on the road. Karen taunts him, "Did you see the mess we made at the school?"

"Yes," Huw says.

"Did you see our note?"

Huw walks on, staring at the ground. "It makes me feel you don't have much respect for the tools or the school."

She laughs. "Course we don't have any respect!"

"Well, it's your school," Huw says softly.

Karen shouts, "You said it was your school the other day. You're an Indian giver."

Huw: "I never said it was my school. Your parents

said that." Aside to me, he says, "They're getting better at arguing every day. Still not very good, though." I tell Huw they seem to enjoy tormenting him. "I know. I'm the only adult around here they can do that to without getting clobbered. It gives them a sense of power. It's ironic, because I keep saying they're mature and responsible, and their parents say they need strict authority and discipline. So who do they rebel against? Me. I'm going to call a school meeting tonight. Maybe we can talk some of this out."

In the evening, ten parents and five children show up at the school, a one-room house built with eighteen sides, so that a geodesic dome can be constructed on top. Sylvia is sitting on a stool in the center nursing her son. Two boys in yellow pajamas are running in circles, squealing, "Ba-ba-ba." Karen is drawing on the blackboard—of all things, a city skyscape. Rico is doing a yoga headstand.

Steve and Huw begin arguing about whether the children should have to come to the school every day. Steve says, in a booming voice, "I think the whole canyon should be a learning community. If you want to teach them, why don't you come to our house?" Huw, standing with a clipboard against his hip, says, "They have to come here to satisfy the county school superintendent. But it seems futile when they come in and say I'm not qualified to teach them. Where do they get that?"

Steve says, "From me. I don't think you're qualified." Huw: "Well I'm prepared to quit and give you the option of doing something else, or sending them to public school."

Steve says, "Don't quit. I know your motives are pure as the driven snow . . ."

Huw says, "I'm doing it for myself as well, to prove I can do it. But it all fits together."

They reach an understanding without speaking further.

Steve says, "I'd like to propose that we go door-to-door in this community and get everyone enthused about the school as a center for adult learning and cultural activity first, and for the kiddies second. Because when you turn on the adults, the kids will follow. The school building needs finishing—the dome should be built this summer. Unless there's more enthusiasm in this community, I'm not going to contribute a thing. But if we get everybody to boost this, by God I'll be the first one out to dig."

Huw says, "You don't think the people who took the time to come tonight is enough interest? I may be cynical, but I think the only way to get some of the others here would be to have dope."

Steve: "Get them interested in the idea of guest speakers, musicians, from India, all over. We can build bunk dorms to accomodate them."

Huw: "Okay. I think we should get together every Sunday night to discuss ideas, hash things over. In the meantime, why don't we buy materials to finish the building?"

On the morning I leave, sunlight washes down the valley from a cloudless sky. Huw, in his green lumberman's shirt, walks with me to the top road. "My dream is to see this canyon filled with families who live here all the time, with lots of children." He continues in a lulling rhythm: "We could export some kind of food or product. The school is very important—children from all over could come to work and live with different families. I'd also like to have doctors here and a clinic where people could be healed naturally. Eventually there should be a ham radio system set up between all the communities in the country, and a blimp, so we could make field trips back and forth. I don't think one community is enough to meet our needs. We need a world culture."

Huw stands, with hands on hips, the weight set back on his heels—a small figure against the umber field. "Someday I'm going to inherit six hundred more acres down there, and it'll all be free. Land should be available for anybody to use, like it was with the Indians." He smiles. "The Indians could no more understand owning land than they could owning the sky."

1970

BABA RAM DASS
The Metamorphic Journey
of Richard Alpert

A forty-one-year-old man with long, graying hair emerged from the Boston International Arrivals Terminal carrying a suitcase full of Indian silks and an unwieldy, bowl-shaped instrument called a tamboura. Tall and light of step, he wore a sweater and bell-bottom slacks, and his face shone with healthy color. He hesitated at the door to the waiting room, for he imagined that when he passed through the door, he would be swallowed by a mob of white-robed bodies, strangled by hugs and suffocated by a hail of flowers. For the man was Baba Ram Dass, formerly Dr. Richard Alpert, returning to the United States after a year and a half in India, his second journey to the East.

During his absence from this country, a book he had written, *Be Here Now*, had been published and sold two hundred thousand copies. That is twice the trade most best-sellers do, although the book was not promoted and never acknowledged by any national publication. Tapes of his lectures had been played on radio stations, and transcripts were printed in underground papers and scholarly journals. For a year, Ram

Dass had been receiving about a hundred letters a week.

Shortly after his return, Ram Dass said, "I was afraid of the karma I had brought on myself with that book, afraid of the numbers that were going to overwhelm me. So I put off coming home, and hung around England for six weeks. I felt I wasn't ready to wrestle with fame and power." Finally he cabled his father that he was on his way to Boston. "I got to the airport all prepared for some Frank Sinatra hysteria scene, and there was nobody there. Nobody! My father was out of town and didn't get the cable." Ram Dass took a bus into the city, checked his tamboura and wandered around "really digging this total reversal of my expectations."

Had he sent a few more cables, there indeed would have been people at the airport, and I might have been among them. I had read *Be Here Now* in 1971. Although I had had many opportunities to see the folly of this impulse, there, nevertheless, it was: if I could just talk to Ram Dass, get near enough and ask the right questions, certain mysteries and doubts might be resolved.

The concepts Ram Dass expressed matched suspicions I had held but never fully trusted. What struck me was his assertion that one could hold all the keys to the kingdom—money, power, beauty, achievement—and still have an unsatisfied gnawing in the gut: "It's not enough." You might want success in a project, or a trip to France, or a house in the country, and as soon as you get it, you find yourself wanting something else.

Most of us, he said, spend the first part of our lives living in the future and the rest living in the past. In order to live in the moment, he said, one must be free of attachment to those unending desires. We have all had tastes of the here and now experience: sailing on a perfect summer day, or sitting with a group of especially close friends, when there is an absence of wanting, of needing anything more. For a moment, we're not worrying about past troubles, or planning what to do when the boat docks or the friends leave. We are, briefly, outside time, outside desire. And by "working on yourself," Ram Dass said, one can progress toward inhabiting that state more frequently.

I made inquiries about inerviewing Ram Dass. He was back in India, and when I met him a year later, his thinking had changed. He was headed for the gap across which lies sainthood, or psychosis—a state beyond the range of perceiving we consensually call normality.

One of the first things he said was, "I'm living in a totally psychotic space now, because in my universe there's only one other being besides me and it's God. And all day long I'm constantly talking to him." He said he sensed in India the profundity of the surrender required, "the power of the death, the true death of the ego. I had figured I could go through the whole transformation without ever missing a step. But you can't take any personality baggage with you. Whatever is left of the old separate being has to die. It feels as if something irrevocable has happened and my faith is not quite shakable anymore. My relationship to my guru and through him feels somewhat beyond the pale."

Because of this faith, he no longer needs to wear white garments and holy beads, or set up a little altar wherever he goes with his books, candles and pictures of saints. "I don't need the physical reminders for fear I'll go under." Neither does he need to persuade or teach anyone. He will avoid public activities, speaking to large groups and "playing the holy man so much. I'm just going to be another guy and hang out."

So once again, the master metamorphosist has pulled his disappearing trick. Ram Dass said, "I see my value at this moment as symbolic: somebody who was a psychology professor, was a drug person, and is still all but primarily none of those anymore; somebody who was an Indian student but is not primarily that now either. By changing form, I can help people get the essence of the thing without getting caught in the form. That's really the fun, because they'll say, 'I thought you were————!' And I'll say, who was that? You were focusing on the wrong thing, it's just that I was wearing a brown jacket yesterday." He laughs. "When expectations are broken, people grow."

Ram Dass once said he felt "blessed by having been given everything that Western society could offer:" affluence, lots of love, the best education, and the fruits of advanced technology, including drugs, the best drugs. "All that was part of my preparation to now know something else." The affluence came from his father, George, a dignified, Republican financier-philanthropist, who was president of the New Haven Railroad and helped found Brandeis University.

When Ram Dass talks about Richard Alpert, he tends to paint him, often hilariously, as a tormented, miserable wretch. But those who knew him as a student and later at Millbrook, say he was always warm and charismatic, with an infectious sense of humor. David McClelland, a psychology professor for whom Alpert worked at Harvard, says he was an excellent and ambitious scholar, who gained rank with unusual speed. "No one observing him would have known about the inner anxiety, and he didn't talk about it."

At Harvard, Alpert taught psychology and practiced psychotherapy. He flew his own plane, collected antiques, cars, a sailboat and scuba-diving equipment. Although he had spent five years in psychoanalysis, he says, he was tense and suffered diarrhea every time he lectured. He drank heavily, was a compulsive eater and a closet homosexual, "living with a man and a woman at the same time in two different parts of the city—a nightmare of hypocrisy." He looked at his colleagues on the A team at Harvard and saw that none seemed fulfilled. He feared he himself would wake up forty years later no less neurotic or more wise, and he panicked. "I thought, the best thing I can do is go back into psychoanalysis. But then I started to have doubts about the analyst. Is his life enough? Whose life is? Who's saying, right, it's enough?"

He was, at this time, an atheist, and had difficulty even pronouncing "spiritual." But on March 5, 1961, a tab of psilocybin was to blow out all the old pegs. One of his faculty drinking buddies, Timothy Leary, had started a research project with mind-altering drugs, allegedly to explore their potential benefit for criminals, addicts and sick people. Alpert was brought in as the steadying influence, to control Leary's wild flights and keep the research within respectable scientific bounds. But the first time Alpert took psilocybin with Leary, he discovered a place inside himself where an "I" existed, an essence deeper than his social and physical identity. And this "I" was all-knowing.

The more drug trips he took, the more he trusted the inner voice, and the less reinforcement he needed from the environment. In 1963, when he and Leary were forced to resign from Harvard in a ritual of public exorcism, they barely broke stride; moving to Millbrook, New York, they set up the Castalia Foundation to study the mystic aspects of drugs. They created the word "psychedelic"—mind revealing—and for seven years, used their bodies as test chambers to discover a permanent route to higher consciousness. They took new drugs as fast as they were invented, but each seemed to have built into it a crash back to the everyday emotional swamp.

They turned for help to ancient texts; when Leary found the *Tibetan Book of the Dead,* he interpreted it as a metaphor for psychological death and rebirth, rather than a guide for actual death and reincarnation. They experimented with meditation, diet, hypnosis, but nothing was as intense as LSD and nothing stuck.

By 1967, Alpert was in a state of despair. the dimensions of which must have been truly hideous. He had cut all his lifelines and was adrift in the midst of nowhere. He could not go back to the academic world, and after hundreds of acid visions, neither he nor anyone else knew how to make constructive use of the experience. He didn't even want to take acid anymore. "What for? It was going to show me the garden again, and then I would be cast out."

His mother died early in the year, and when a friend invited him to travel across India, he accepted, not in hope of learning anything but because, oh well, what else? He watched the countryside go by and the depression never lifted. Then in Katmandu, a chance encounter with a six-foot-six, blond, twenty-three-year-old American boy—Bhagwan Dass—led him to an ashram in the Himalayas where he met his guru, Maharaji (a title meaning Great King).

For each person, it probably takes a different kind of jolt to break the shackles of faith in the rational mind. For Alpert, it was meeting a twinkly, fat old man wrapped in a blanket, who immediately told him exactly how his mother had died and indicated that he knew everything in Alpert's head. At first, Alpert says, his mind raced to come up with an explanation. Then, like a computer fed an insoluble problem, "my mind just gave up. It burned out its circuitry." There was a wrenching in his chest and an outpouring of tears. "All I could say was it felt like I was home. The journey was over."

I have heard many rumors about Ram Dass and they all center on "what really happened" in India. According to various, comically murky sources: Alpert was on morphine; Bhagwan Dass was on heroin; Alpert followed Bhagwan Dass because he was sexually attracted to him; Alpert never went barefoot; Alpert spoke constantly about his mother and it would have been no feat for the guru to pick up the information. The need for these rumors is puzzling, because *something* happened in India and Alpert came back changed.

In his book, he describes studying yoga in the Temple of Hanuman, the Hindu monkey God who exemplifies the perfect servant. Dass means servant, so Ram Dass, the name Alpert was given, means servant of Ram, or God, as Ram was one of the incarnations of the God Vishnu, the preserver. Baba means father, and is a term of endearment and respect.

Alpert followed a ritual of study, meditation, a cold bath at 4 A.M., vegetarian diet, exercise, breathing and cleansing practices. He vowed sexual continence, and for six months he was silent, using a chalk and slate to communicate. As a result of not speaking or expending sexual energy, when he returned to this country, he was like a spring uncoiling. He met with Tim

Leary in San Francisco, who suggested he simply hadn't finished with his sexual trip. "If you're turning all of your energies into your own being, it becomes autoerotic."

Alpert laughed, and later told an interviewer, "I haven't cured my neurosis, I just got bored with it. For fifteen years I was basically homosexual. Psycho-analysis improved my relations with women but it didn't wipe out the homosexual desires. Drugs did a lot more, because with drugs it was obvious that, bi-ologically, this was not the way God meant it. So I became sort of even, bisexual. When the spiritual trip took over, the importance of the whole issue started to fall away. The new dimensions made it irrelevant."

In India, the spiritual community in which Alpert lived was bhakti in orientation. Bhakti is that branch of yoga where the heart is the vehicle for transcend-ence. One approaches God through expressions of love, by singing songs to God, by seeing God in others and serving them. The seeker is to God as lover to beloved. "At first the Hindu thing offended me," he says. "It was so gauche, maudlin and mushy. I was more attracted to jnana yoga, the yoga of the mind, but once I allowed myself to lead with my heart, I got so high it was fantastic."

He picked up several clues about the meaning of LSD. One of his teachers said that because America is a highly materialistic country, "God has shown his avatar there in the form of LSD, a material. The peo-ple needed a material for approaching God, and they received it in LSD." One morning Maharaji sent for Ram Dass and asked for LSD. He swallowed 915 micrograms, a dose large enough for four men; Ram Dass watched him all day and nothing happened.

"Seeing that freed me from confusing my method of getting to the light with the light itself."

In 1968, Maharaji told Ram Dass to return to the United States for a brief time. Ram Dass arrived in Boston barefoot, all in white, with beads and a beard. His father told him to get in the car quick, "before anybody sees you." His father listened to the stories about India, and liked to have Ram Dass perform for his friends. On cue, he would say, "I don't understand a word of it, but if he's doing it, it's o.k. with me." Ironically, he saw the holy man rountine as a harmless relief after his son's plunge into drugs. He took to calling him Rum Dum, while his oldest son, a stockbroker, referred to the "aging hippie" as Rammed Ass.

Ram Dass moved into a cabin behind the main house on his father's estate in New Hampshire. He fixed his rice and tea, read and meditated. The first time he drove into town for groceries, he passed two young men with long hair. Feeling and high and devine, he waved. When they didn't wave back, he thought, "See. Here you are, filled with loving thoughts and thinking everybody must love you in return. That's another kind of ego trip. Those kids think you're crazy. So cool it out, Ram Dass."

When he emerged from the store, the two young men and three others were waiting. One approached hesitantly, and Ram Dass said to himself, "Ah, I shouldn't have doubted. Of course he saw the love." Then he waited, reverently, for the boy's opening words.

"Um, are you the new connection?"

Recalling the incident later, Ram Dass said, "I saw it all—a strange man with a beard, driving a Cadillac.

What else could I be? I waited in the peace within for the answer to arise. At length it came. I said: 'I am not that kind of connection.' "

The next day, the five young people appeared outside Ram Dass's cabin. They brought friends who brought friends, and by the end of the summer, there were more than two hundred. Ram Dass said he was a beginner on the path and not a model for others, but kids found that after sitting with him for an hour, they felt stoned. They concluded, "If I just do whatever this guy does I can get what he has." So Ram Dass taught them mantras, holy songs, how to meditate, how to set up a puja table or altar in their home and how to develop a witness, an observing mechanism in the mind that watches everything go by without judging. The young people began using the Indian greeting, *Namaste*, which means, I salute the light within you.

In the fall, Ram Dass gave a four-hour talk called "The Transformation of a Man" at the Bucks County, Pennsylvania, Seminar House. The Pacifica Radio network broadcast a tape of it, and Ram Dass hit the lecture circuit. He drove from town to town in a yellow Mustang, sitting in half lotus, chanting mantras. He spoke at churches, medical schools, growth centers and colleges, and was at a Rotary Club luncheon the day Leary was sentenced to jail in California for possession of marijuana. Occasionally he took planes, ordering ahead for a vegetarian meal, and favored staying at Ramada Inns because "they give you more stuff than Holiday Inns." He told a friend he did not have to live in poverty because in India, "I was walking barefoot, sleeping on the ground, and I realized a deeper contentment than I'd ever known. Once I knew I could be perfectly content with that little, then it was all right to stay in groovy hotels and have credit cards, because I'm not attached."

For his evening appearances, he wore white Indian clothes. Sitting on a stage, surrounded by flowers and incense, he would play the tamboura and sing to Ram; then he would speak. His message was ever so gentle. He would run down Buddha's Four Noble Truths and have the audience laughing all the way. The first truth, he said, is that all life is suffering, because it's in time. "Birth, death, not getting what you want, even getting what you want means suffering because you're going to lose it, in time."

The second truth is that the cause of suffering is desire, or attachment. "If you don't try to hold on, you don't suffer over the loss. If you're not attached to life, you don't fear death. We're dying at this moment. It's a downhill trip all the way. So the third noble truth is: give up attachment, give up desire, you end the suffering, you end the whole thing that keeps you stuck."

The fourth truth is Buddha's eightfold method for giving up attachment, which Ram Dass summarizes in the phrase: work on yourself. And what a felicitous phrase for American ears. It echoes the ideals we've been urged to believe in all our lives: the virtue of self-improvement; the wisdom of doing what the syndicated lady problem-solvers tell their readers to do, no matter what the trouble—"Look to yourself." But those who listened closely to Ram Dass sensed that he meant something quite different from Dear Abby, for his kind of self-work leads ultimately to the end of the self as we know it—the ego.

The notion of destroying the ego is troubling because we tend to think that if there is no ego, there is nobody to be conscious of anything, and so we no longer exist. But if you can conceive of yourself as an essence which is being expressed through your thoughts, feelings, body and behavior but is not seated in any of those, you are open to what Ram Dass suggests: "a complete perceptual reorganization of who I am. I am without form, without limits, beyond space and time. I am light, love, consciousness, energy. It's a hard one. I'm still doing it."

In this framework, the ego is only a surface casing; all the emotions which seem to lie deep within you are but twitches in the outermost crust. "It's interesting, because as a psychologist I always treated the personality as real and terribly serious. That's what the whole growth movement, the encounter thing, all of Western psychology does. But it's not real, it's all just stuff. Pain, pleasure, anger, guilt—they're only mind moments, and there's always a new moment."

Even the mind is not really you. "*Cogito ergo sum* is a lie. *We* exist behind our thinking." Ram Dass says there are other ways of knowing besides through the senses and the mind, and quotes Albert Einstein: "I did not arrive at my scientific discoveries through my rational mind." The other way of knowing is intuitive, and requires transcending the mind, which works in time, and can only think with an object.

"The place we're aiming for—Heliopolis, highsville—is outside time, and there is no subject-object. There is no knower who knows a thing, no experiencer having an experience. The knower *is* the knowledge, the experiencer is one with the experience. That's why they say LSD is a false samadhi, because there's still an experiencer. The drug doesn't kill the ego. If it were a real samadhi, *you* wouldn't come back."

At the end of his talks, Ram Dass always told people that whatever course they were following was perfect, because "it's all predetermined anyway. The very moment you wake up is determined. There are no accidents in this business. So you don't have to do anything. The guru is inside you, you don't have to go to India. The next message you need is always right where you are."

Ram Dass returned to India in November of 1970. *Be Here Now* was being hand-lettered at the Lama Foundation, a spiritual commune in New Mexico, to which Ram Dass had assigned all rights and royalties.

There were also, by this time, more than a hundred and sixty hours of Ram Dass tapes in circulation. WBAI in New York played them through 1971, and that summer, a group of listeners formed a meditation group in which Hilda Charlton, a grandmotherly woman who had been seeking God all her life, became the spiritual leader. Meanwhile, rumors flew back from India: Ram Dass was coming home in December, January, February, never. His "head was changing." He would not teach or give interviews anymore. I decided to write him, telling him about myself and my interest in an interview.

To my surprise, he answered shortly, saying he would be in America soon and we might "share a moment." If writing an article brings you closer to God, he said, "it is good sadhana [spirtual work], which is all there really is. You can keep contact through Marty Malles in Brooklyn."

I called Marty Malles, and we had a strange conversation in which I spent the first half stammering and the second half laughing with him. He said he was thirty-four, a salesman of ladies' underwear, and had just been to India with his wife and two children on his annual three-week vacation. He had been following Ram Dass since 1969, and Maharaji was now his guru. "You're calling because Maharaji sent you to us. Maharaji shines through Ram Dass. Maharaji wrote that book, and if it touches you it's because Maharaji loves you."

I let all this roll off me, but accepted an invitation to come to the meditation group. I walked into the apartment on Riverside Drive, found the usual jumble of shoes by the door and about seventy people sitting in darkness reciting "Affirmations": "I am God's perfect child, I am free, I am free." They chanted "Sri Ram, Jai Ram"—hail to Ram, victory to Ram. Marty led a meditation, there was more singing and when the lights came on, everyone was in each other's arms.

I began to spend time with Marty and others in the satsang, as a spiritual community is called. Marty wore regular clothes on his rounds selling underwear, then he would change into white or saffron shirts, white Indian pants and sandals. He is short, with a mane of blond hair and a pear-shaped body that people find huggable.

Marty told me stories, in a thick Brooklyn accent, about his trip to India to see Maharaji. The guru had first spoken to him one morning when the Americans were told to come to the temple at nine. Marty arrived at seven, and watched the women bathe Maharaji. The water they use to wash his feet is later doled out to devotees to drink. It is believed that the power of a saint comes out his feet, so if a seeker is prepared, if his conduits are open, just a sip could throw him into samadhi. "One of the guys was given a cup the first day he got there, and after he drank it, he asked what it was. When he found out it was Maharaji's wash water, he freaked out. He put a water purification tablet in his mouth and swallowed it."

On Tuesday nights, Marty invited people to his apartment in Brooklyn to worship Hanuman. Marty's wife, Pauline, cooked Indian food, and Marty played the tamboura Ram Dass had lent him. There was a puja table in the living room, and on the walls were shiny pictures of Hindu legends in which the male Gods have effeminate, blue-gray bodies. It was bizarre, but the combination of singing and dancing and smiling and hugging never failed to make everyone high.

For long periods, I forgot that I had originally called Marty on business—to get to Ram Dass. I was not sure, anymore, why I was so compelled to reach him. Then one Monday in May, a publisher called and said he might send me to India to interview Ram Dass. I cursed my luck. Ram Dass had left India by now and was last seen in London. I tried to trace him, but it was like that infernal children's game where every clue to the treasure leads only to another clue. Marty, curiously, was of no help. The one person who knew Ram Dass's phone number in London visited Marty on Tuesday night, but Marty forgot to ask for it. On Thursday, I reached a man in London who said Ram Dass had gone to Scotland with R. D. Laing, and nobody knew where they were staying. At this I gave up, and was partly relieved.

On Friday, Marty came to pick me up for the meditation. As we were walking out the door, I said casually, "I bet he's in Boston right now." Marty went to the phone and dialed George Alpert's number. Ram Dass answered the phone.

The next morning, I was on the first shuttle flight to Boston. It was pouring rain when the taxi dropped me at the brick town house near Beacon Hill. I pressed the buzzer and shouted through the intercom, "Is Ram Dass there?" I heard muffled voices: "Oh what, Sara, New York, groan—just a minute." Phyllis Alpert, George's second wife, answered the door in a pink housecoat. It was just after nine, a Saturday morning, and I had woken everybody up. I sat alone in the living room. After some time Ram Dass appeared, put his hands in the temple pose and nodded. I said, "I thought if I didn't get here twenty minutes after we spoke . . . I feel like an idiot."

He said lightly, "There's no reason either of us should feel like an idiot." He went to the kitchen to brew Indian tea. "How does it feel to be back?" I said. "I can only think about the tea now, unless you want a superficial answer." He began to sing softly, "*Sri Ram, Jai Ram.*" It was eerie, seeing the original after the copies.

Ram Dass brought out the tea on a silver tray and took me to the back room. "This is where I hang out." It was a cozy study, with an Oriental rug, dark bookcases, a white fireplace with fluted columns and cherubs, and a gold velvet convertible sofa on which the bedclothes were left unmade. We sat on cushions on the floor. There was a chill, and Ram Dass, wearing thin white pants and tunic, put on a jaunty, plaid, Scottish wool cap and wrapped himself in a mohair blanket. He was much taller than I had envisioned—six foot two. His crown is bald, but from the sides and back of his head, hair sprouts in a capricious assortment of lengths. His blue eyes, fixed on me, were open so wide they seemed more vertical than horizontal.

He picked up the tamboura, closed his eyes and sang "*Sri Ram.*" After a silence, he opened his eyes; I turned on the tape recorder. I asked what being with

Maharaji this time had meant to him. "Wow. I'm speechless." He shook his head. "I went back to India with the fantasy that I would be going back in, that I had been out in the world, the marketplace, and now I was going back to the cave to recharge." He laughed softly. "Maharaji knocked that into a cocked hat. In a year and a half in India, he allowed me exactly eleven days when I was not surrounded by Westerners, doing the same thing I do in America.

"You see, when I was speaking and running ashrams in New Hampshire, all the people who gathered wanted me to help them with their trips. So for like nineteen hours a day, I was rushing around being there for everybody, and I started to feel starved to death because nobody wanted *me*. They wanted *it* but not me, and I was starving and I rebelled. I got to hate them all because they were my murderers. So I went to India thinking, Now I'm going to get away from them all, and preserve my ego in a cave." He laughed, "Can you hear that inversion? But every time I tried to be alone, Maharaji would send huge numbers of Westerners after me—'Go be with Ram Dass. Ram Dass is your guru, he'll help you.' Like, kill him, kill him faster!

"It was an incredible period, the longest I've ever gone through with no conceptual understanding of what's happening to me. Because I'm so good at describing things, but Maharaji's so far out I can't even find him. At moments he seems like a bungling old fool. Other times he's a wizard, he's divine, or he's just a nice teacher. Every time I label him he immediately destroys the label."

On his first visit to India, he said, the guru had been a remote, loving presence; this time he did more direct teaching. "He took me through fierce trips about anger, jealousy, sex, greed and attachment to the physical body. I saw that my bonds to him were much deeper than I had planned them to be. It was as if I had surrendered more, so the next level of operation could take place.''

Maharaji asked Ram Dass why he had come back to India. Ram Dass said because he was not pure enough. "I asked him for only one thing, one boon—that I could be pure enough to be an instrument of his service. I said I don't want to be enlightened. I just want to be pure enough to do whatever work I'm supposed to do. He gave me a mango to eat, hit me on the head and said, 'You will be.' ''

Maharaji sent Ram Dass on a pilgrimage of temples in Southern India, and then Ram Dass arranged to spend the summer monsoon season in a remote mountain ashram meditating. "I saw that my mind was out of control. I was becoming wise in certain ways, but I felt I couldn't go further until I quieted my mind. So I arranged for the essence meditation teacher to come, and I put up money for a new water system, just to try to make it all beautiful. I told Maharaji about it, how I was going to go very deep, and then I looked at him, like, aren't I good? And he said, 'If you desire it.' That was the first inkling I had that my craving for meditation was one of my ego desires. Maharaji didn't say meditation was bad or good, but he said the way you're doing it is from ego. He kept showing me that my path, my dharma, is one of devotion and service.''

Ram Dass went to the mountains anyway, thinking, "At least he's still gonna let me do it." But a week later the teacher wrote that he couldn't come, and Maharaji sent thirty Americans to follow Ram Dass. "That ruined it. I gave up. I figured Maharaji's just stronger than I am. So I set up a place for the thirty of us and we had a beautiful summer." Each person had his own cell to meditate, they were silent at meals and Ram Dass worked with people individually. On Sundays they read the Bible, and on Tuesdays they fasted, worshiped Hanuman and read the Ramayana, the story of Ram. "Maharaji's presence was very strong. When we saw him later he told us everything that had happened. When I meditated I felt him so near me, he was like a shadow that I couldn't see no matter how fast I spun around. Then I started to feel this great loneliness, that he had gone away from me. It took a while to realize that we were merging, that I was just drunkenly falling into him through love, and ultimately there would be only one of us."

In the fall, he attended a nine-day holy fire ceremony, at the end of which people took a coconut shell, put whatever they wanted to get rid of into it and threw it to the fire. Ram Dass decided to throw sexuality in the fire. "My God, I'm forty years old, I'll give it up, I thought. And right afterwards I went through the most ferocious anger I'd ever experienced. One of the things that freed me to be angry was that I saw that every relationship I had was sexually toned. With women and men, young and old, there was always a slight, gentle titillation, and the minute I stopped seeing myself and others as sexual objects, that whole pull to get that little rush wasn't there."

Ram Dass and the group were now back with Maharaji, and Ram Dass resented the fact that he wasn't alone with the guru as he had been the first time. Maharaji made him "commander-in-chief of the Westerners," told him to love everyone and always tell the truth. "I figured I've never really told the truth that much," Ram Dass said, "and the truth is I hate all these people. This one's obsequious, that one's selfish, this one's too messy, that one's too neat. It got so that out of thirty-four people, there wasn't one I could stand. So I thought I'll be truthful about it."

He stopped speaking to them all, and for two weeks wouldn't allow anyone near him. One day at the temple, in front of Maharaji, a boy brought him a leaf of consecrated food and Ram Dass threw it at him. "Holy prasad—living grace! And I threw it at him because I hated his guts." Maharaji called him over and said, "Something troubling you?" Ram Dass said, "Yes, I'm angry. I hate everybody but you." Maharaji asked why, and Ram Dass said, "Because of the impurities which keep us in the illusion. I can't stand it anymore. I can't stand it in anybody including myself. I only love you." Then he broke into racking sobs. Maharaji sent for milk, and sat patting Ram Dass on the head, feeding him, crying with him, and saying over and over, "You shouldn't be angry. You should love everyone." Ram Dass said, "But you told me to tell the truth and the truth is I hate everyone." Maharaji said no. "A saint doesn't get angry. Tell the truth, and love everyone. There's only one. Love every one."

Recalling it, Ram Dass said, "Here was my guru telling me this is who you are: somebody who tells the truth and loves everyone. That's a beautiful box to be put in." He looked at the group and saw standing between him and them "this huge mountain—my pride. For me to give up the anger, I had to give up my whole rational position, my reasons for being angry, without sitting down first and talking it over and winning a few points for my side."

Maharaji sent him off to eat, and called the others over and said, "Ram Dass is a great saint. Go touch his feet." This made Ram Dass cringe and feel more furious. "I saw my predicament—I was going to have to do this all myself." He cut an apple into small pieces, went to each person and looked in his eyes "until I found the place in him I loved. Then I let all the rest wash away, silently. I fed them all, and when I was finished there was no more anger. Later I got angry again, but it went through very quickly because I relived that moment. I saw that anger is only because you're attached to what you were thinking a moment ago. It's not real, it's only a mind moment. Yes, I was angry then. Okay, now is now, and if you're right here, everything starts all over again."

It was still in the back room in Boston. Ram Dass had been talking for three hours. He showed no sign of weariness or impatience, so I put a new cassette in the machine, and asked what he feels are his impurities.

"I'm afraid of my desires. Like you being here, your desire to interview me—that comes out of desires I had which led to the book and the whole scene when I came back from India. When I went there, I had used up the psychedelic thing. I was sort of remotely known as a partner of Tim Leary's, and I could very easily have just disappeared into the background. But I didn't, because I had desires. When I saw those hippies in New Hampshire and said, 'I am not that kind of connnection'—there it was. All I had to say was, 'Gee, no, I don't have any acid,' get in the car and drive off. And I still would be that anonymous being."

He said when he tries to walk to Kenmore Square, students stop him and hang on him, and in the bookstore they give him free books and stare. "You can feel how caught I am in this issue—the landslide of fame and corruptibility. Instead of wanting fame I'm avoiding it, which is the same as wanting it, so I'm as stuck as ever."

Ram Dass refuses to appear on a public stage, but says he finds it "useful for my own consciousness to work with individuals." Maharaji instructed him not to have ashrams or students, and not to stay in any place longer than five days. But when people manage to slip through the net and find Ram Dass, he will sit down with them and ask questions designed to unleash the secret horrors they are keeping chained inside. All the while, Ram Dass is looking in their eyes repeating a mantra to himself. "Whatever they say gets completely neutralized the minute they bring it into my consciousness. Because I don't care. I know it's not real. And they feel this tremendous release."

I asked if one could bypass neurosis through spiritual work. What happens to a depressed person the day after he sees Ram Dass, or the hour after he does his meditation? Ram Dass said at the moment "when we're here together and not caught in any of that stuff—you can call it high—it's a very real feeling. Now the next moment you may go back to the old place, but the experience of the other moment we had loosens the hold just a bit."

He said spiritual work is everything that happens in your life. "Every neurotic hassle I've had was part of my awakening, which is why I tell people not to *do* anything about neurosis, just go to God and let neurosis worry about itself."

Ram Dass said he is at a point where he welcomes rather than tries to avoid pain, because he understands that suffering is purification. "And it's got to be real, not make-believe suffering, where your faith is gone and you're in despair. Suffering is the fire that burns away attachments. Despair is the prerequisite for the next level of consciousness.''

He said he has little interest in taking drugs because "when I'm down it's higher for me than when I'm up. When I'm up, I'm overriding the spots I have to work on, and I'm more interested in doing the work than in remembering how groovy it is. I know how groovy it is.''

He said drugs take people to one plane while excluding the others. The state of being happy or high is implicitly defined by its opposite—being miserable—and a truly conscious person is beyond all dualities. "That's why when Maharaji takes acid, nothing happens. When you meet a realized being, you see that there's nowhere he isn't, nor is there anywhere he is.''

It was late afternoon by now. Ram Dass wanted to rest, because he was recuperating from hepatitis, so we arranged to meet the next morning.

As I left, I turned impulsively to hug him. He laughed, held me and patted my hair. Then he said abruptly, "Maharaji told me not to touch people.''

SUNDAY, TEN A.M. Ram Dass was sitting in front of a window; because his face was backlit by sun, his features were difficult to distinguish and at times dissolved into blackness.

Several people close to Ram Dass had told me his weakest area was his understanding of women and sex. Ram Dass agreed. "Sex is one of the last ones you ever get conscious about." He said a number of couples come to him and say, " 'We're really concerned because our sex brings us down.' I say that's partly because of your habits about sex. To achieve oneness, you have to not get lost in the physical drive, but see your partner as Ram or the Divine Mother, so that every touch, every kiss, is an act of devotion to that sacred being.''

This is not easy, of course, he said. ''Most of the time, genital sex can only bring me down. I almost feel I've made it already with everyone I meet, because there's such an intimate connection and you've got to get caught in separateness to come together through sex. Maybe when I understand it clearly, I'll see it differently, but I'm beginnning to think Gandhi was absolutely right when he said if you're in harmony with the universe, the only time you have sex is to reproduce.''

On the subject of women, he was more insistent. ''Most women's major work is to understand why they were born a woman. It wasn't random. You take a woman's body because you have certain work to do, and it's my understanding that it's not a full incarnation if you don't honor your biological impulses—to reproduce and nurture children. The idea is not to end up more womanly, or restrict yourself to the house, but to understand what your incarnation is about. Just as I have to understand my incarnation, why I didn't come out a man in the full sense.''

He said his view does not preclude sympathy to the women's movement. ''I honor people's efforts to end inequality and relieve suffering, and if it's your dharma, your path, to be in women's lib and change things, change them. But don't get caught in thinking that's what it's all about.''

People involved in political efforts, he said, tend to confuse external and internal freedom. ''They're not the same thing. No matter how much another person suppresses you, even if he crucifies you, it has nothing to do with your internal freedom. These are the hardest things to accept—the relationship of the spirit to the external world. Political work is a noble way to spend your time here, so long as you do it without attachment, and with the understanding that it's not the whole game. Because there are people who have all the freedom, all the things these movements are designed to give everyone, and they're not fulfilled as human beings."

He said the highest thing anyone can do for society is to work on himself, because "every advancement in man's condition has come about by someone becoming a little more conscious. War is the result of lack of consciousness. So is hunger. There's enough food to feed every human being that exists, but the consciousness of man is such that he says, it's my food, not yours."

I asked Ram Dass what he does about money, and what has happened to the book royalties, which I estimate to be more than a hundred thousand dollars. He said the money is used by Lama Foundation to subsidize a "mishmash of spiritual projects." Lama gives Ram Dass living expenses, and his father is "always waiting at the post to give me money but I rarely take it. I could do lecture tours, you know, and make a thousand dollars a night, but I would like not to be connected with money in any way. Nothing I have is for sale."

He was starting to rock back and forth on his heels, and indicate, by sighs, that the interviewing had gone on long enough. Before I left, I had one more question. There had been contradictions in his theories, and some of his statements about India seemed jejune, but what troubled me was something I had learned the day before from a group of New Yorkers who had driven up in the rain—seven hours over flooded roads—to see Ram Dass. When they reached Boston, he said he couldn't see the group and there was no reason for them to have made the whole trip. Cathy, the woman who organized the caravan, said she felt disappointed because "nothing passed between us. He didn't even acknowledge the connection."

I wondered why he was giving me so much of his time. Why did he agree to see me and rebuff the others?

Ram Dass said, "Let's see if I can reconstruct this. I think the fact that you were doing an article had something to do with it, not because of publicity but because it was a collaborative effort that would push me to formulate things. When Cathy called up all gushing and emotional, I thought, Oh, why do we need this hysterical homecoming scene?"

He rested his chin on his hand. "Cathy's a beautiful being, but there's a place in me that doesn't like that kind of woman. When a woman is overbearing and smothering, I can't stand it." He made a sour face. "I want to shove her away. But I have to wrestle with that—that's where I haven't finished my work. I can't see the God in her."

I started gathering my things. Ram Dass said, "This has really been interesting. I can see from when you probe certain areas that there are subtle places where I'm not pure. I'm not all done with it."

"You never said you were."

He laughed, and stretched out his long legs. "Yeah, but I implied it."

Several weeks later, when I was back in New York, Marty called to tell me Ram Dass was in town and would be at the meditation group that night. Within six hours, word of mouth brought out more than two hundred and fifty people.

They prepared a special place for Ram Dass: a nest of cushions, with roses and gladiolas on one side and a mango on the floor in front. On a nearby table was a picture of Ram Dass, all in white, his eyes swooning, a garland of prickly flowers around his crown. At half-past seven, a man wearing a faded yellow polo shirt, brown pants and orange socks walked through the door. Hilda, who sat at the head of the room, asked Marty to bring Ram Dass up front. Ram Dass shook his head, and gave Marty a slight shove. Marty said, "This is like fighting for the check, man. Hilda wants you in front."

He would not take the seat of honor, but squeezed into the row facing Hilda. The group chanted *OM*, and ran through a repertoire of songs, from *"Hare Krishna"* to "Praise be to Jesus." Ram Dass closed his eyes and as he sang, his face gave off a contagious, pink-gold glow. He swayed, bobbed his head and clapped his hands on his knees. Hilda said, "I'm not going to ask Ram Dass to speak, so it's up to you kids. If you have enough will . . ."

"I give up!" Ram Dass laughed. He rose on his haunches, turned toward the crowd, picked up the mango and tossed it lightly between his hands. As the words began, the figure in faded clothing became something else—a perfect showman. He repeated stories he had told me during the interviews, but now they were polished little dramas, complete with sub-plots and comic relief. "I didn't really want to end up on the path I'm on," he said at the start. "I wanted something much more esoteric and exquisite. I wanted to know some secrets and give mysterious initiations, and have powers, and be able to do things *to* people, and just have a little shtick to go along with it. But all I know is to love my guru, love everyone and see God everywhere. You can't earn a living telling people that!''

He said he has been studying the concept of dharma, which is a person's particular path or method—the way of living that will bring him closest to the One. Each person has his own dharma, which could be meditating or raising children or selling shoes, and to know your dharma, "you listen quietly to hear the sat guru, the still small voice within.'' You don't need an external guru, he said, "that's only one method, and there are many methods.''

The trouble with dharma, he said, is that it changes. "That was a mind blower to me, because I figured once you get your dharma straight, you're cool. You say, well, I'm a Buddhist. You put a sign out in front of the house, 'Buddhist here,' and that's it. But our dharma is more like a floating crap game. At one stage, you follow a certain path, and later, you may discard everything you were doing.

"And don't worry if you feel like not doing any spiritual practices at all,'' he said. "Because doing one of them in a phony way—that will awaken you at the same rate as if you did nothing honestly.''

Ram Dass said he is not committed to any tradition. "I can study Buddhist meditation, I love Sufi dancing, I'm a Jew, and I love Christ—I get so far out on Christ it's unbelievable.'' But for the moment, Maharaji has said his dharma is devotion and service. "I asked Maharaji, 'How do you awaken kundalini?' and he said, 'Serve people.' That's a secret, by the way.'' The group burst into laughter. "I give that with initiations.''

He had been speaking more than an hour, and seemed, in the outflow of stories and ideas, to have lost his consciousness of self. For he sat back, finally, onto the tier of cushions that had been so carefully prepared for him.

"I know the day will come, and not too distant, when I'll walk into a room and nobody will say, 'There's Ram Dass.' Because it's, 'There's everyone.' It's all the light. Ultimately you will feel the light in yourself and you'll see it in everyone you look at, everyone. Then you'll realize there's nobody special. No heroes and no villains. It's just all of God's children.

"*Namasté*."

1973

7

What Do Women Want?

BIRTH PAINS

In the early days of women's liberation, in the spring of 1970, several hundred feminists gathered in New York for a Congress to Unite Women. Members of the press were barred and no account was made public. But as time passed, reports leaked out of violence, and the event became known in movement circles as the "Congress to Divide Women."

It was at this congress that lesbians wearing lavender T-shirts took over the microphone and accused their straight sisters of sexism—oppressing gay women. Members of a workshop on class spent three days drafting a resolution condemning two of the most committed workers, Lucy Komisar and Susan Brownmiller, for trying to "climb to personal fame on the backs of the women's movement." (This awkward image was to become a movement classic.) When Susan heard herself named, she jumped up and screamed, "That's *my name*, sister. Who the hell are you to say that?"

Then there was Anselma dell'Olio, founder of the Feminist Repertory Theatre, who read a paper called *Divisiveness and Self-Destruction in the Women's*

Movement. Her hands shaking, Anselma said she had been "destroyed and defeated" by her sisters:

"I learned three and a half years ago that women had always been divided against one another . . . and filled with impotent rage. I thought the movement would change all that. I never dreamed that I would see the day when this rage, masquerading as a pseudo-egalitarian radicalism under the 'pro-woman' banner, would turn into a frightening, anti-intellectual fascism of the left, and be used within the movement to strike down sisters . . . I am referring, of course, to the personal attacks . . . to which women in the movement who have painfully managed any degree of achievement have been subjected."

Every speech split the crowd into booing, catcalling factions. The tension reflected the paranoia which, for understandable reasons, was running unchecked through the movement.

After four years of developing issues in scattered local groups, with "no one noticing," women's liberation was going public. Toward the end of 1969, the big three— *Life, Time,* and *Newsweek*—had all started preparing major articles on the new feminism. Today, when terms like "sexism" and "male chauvinism" have been so diluted that they have lost their charge, it is difficult to remember that in the beginning, anyone who declared herself an advocate of women's lib met with abuse and ridicule. Members of women's groups were afraid that their ideas would be distorted by the press, and they would be labeled dykes, man-haters and lunatics.

But this was not the only cause for apprehension. There had developed within this movement an ideology that women on their own would act differently from men: they would be less competitive; more supportive, warm and compassionate; less selfish; more committed to the general good. There would be no leaders or stars in this movement. Labor would be divided evenly and fairly, because all women were capable of doing everything.

This ethos was so universally accepted that it prevented people from recognizing and coping with feelings of jealousy, insecurity and ambition. The reality in most groups was that if one woman showed talent, others felt threatened. Instead of dealing with this, women tended to use the movement code to knock the achiever down. She was accused of ego tripping, selfishness, ripping off her sisters. Marilyn Webb, who founded the Washington paper *Off Our Backs*, said, "It made people depressed if you did something well. The fear was that if one person made it, there would be no room for the others."

Curiously, despite this masked competitiveness, the movement was in many ways more humane and accepting than other political groups. The pro-woman line, developed in New York by Redstockings, had a powerful, seductive influence. The line was an inversion of women's prejudices about each other. Women were not untrustworthy, silly, catty or dumb; women were beautiful. Women were absolutely equal to men, not potentially equal. Women's feelings and perceptions were correct and to be trusted. The woman's position was always right. The policy of Redstockings was: "We will always take the woman's side." As Kathie Sarachild, one of the architects of the line, used to say, "The only problem with women is men."

"The line was so mind blowing," Anselma dell'Olio said, "that I *wanted* it to be true. I was meeting vast numbers of terrific women. Women were pure, women were wonderful. Women were IT. It was a naïve thing, and I soon came up against human nature. I didn't receive the same kind of acceptance from women that I was trying to give. I got slaughtered emotionally in a way I'd never been touched by men. Because I'd opened myself up to women. I was vulnerable."

By mid-1970, some of the strongest, most creative people had been purged from their groups. It was a period which one feminist writer has called one of "mass freak-outs all over the place. Everybody was demoralized. I stopped writing for a year because I was so upset and confused." Some left their husbands, left their sisters, went into therapy, turned to lesbianism, or sank into depression. Many had been made to feel so doubtful about their motives that they became paralyzed, unable to work.

Ironically, this was also the period when women's liberation had its major surge of growth. Consciousness-raising groups flourished in all parts of the country, and for new members, it was a time of exhilaration and hope. Over the next few years, the majority of those who had been casualties of the early purges found their way back. The climate softened; there evolved a spirit of tolerance and recognition of needs. The movement seemed, finally, to be in a strong enough position so that people could discuss internal problems, and look into the roots of the earlier paranoia.

I think it relevant, at this point, to make clear my own relationship to the movement. I have never been a member of any women's group, but I was a feminist before I knew the word. When I first learned about women's liberation in 1969, I decided to write an article about it, to promote ideas I believed in. Naïvely, I sold the piece to *Life* magazine, which had the largest audience—eight million. But when I tried to conduct interviews with feminists, I was subjected to attacks.

I was called a liar, an opportunist and a bourgeois capitalist dupe. In blatant contradiction to the prowoman line, women assumed the worst about me. When I refused to submit my writing to a group in Boston for their censorship, I was verbally battered for twelve hours, after which I went home wounded and enraged.

Four years later, *Esquire* asked me to write a piece for an issue on women. It occurred to me to look up some of the people I had met in those early days, suspecting that many had had changes in their thinking. The responses I received were completely different from four years before. The hostility was gone, and in its place was a blend of sadness, compassion and exhaustion. There was also humor—some of it unconscious—when people recounted the rise and fall of groups, the setting up and toppling of "correct political lines," the purges and counterpurges. As Kathie Sarachild said with a nervous laugh, "I had so many problems with women in women's liberation that I began to feel better about men."

I contacted twenty women, only two of whom refused to cooperate with *Esquire*. The majority were eager to be interviewed and have their contributions recognized. In the following interviews, four women describe their experiences in the movement and the events that have brought them to where they are presently, if tenuously, at rest.

REAL PROPERTY

1.

Kate Millett asked me to meet her at 11 P.M. at Phebe's restaurant on the Bowery. I had never seen her before, and was struck by her healthy-looking skin and hair—she was not at all the sallow creature suggested in news photographs.

Kate said she was completing work on a new book, *Flying*. "I wrote this book to regain my identity after being blood-sucked by the media," she said. Kate described how *Time* magazine had made her a culture hero by running her picture on its cover in 1970, only to discredit her five months later because she was bisexual. "The media tries to elect stars—me, Gloria Steinem, Germaine Greer—so they have puppets they can manipulate. They can say, 'Kate Millett is very smart,' and make me white sheik of the year. Then if I get too big for my britches, they can say, 'She's a queer, she can't think, her book's nonsense.' They blow up the balloon so they can puncture it. It had nothing to do with me, it had to do with the movement. The women's movement was getting too powerful, so the puppet had to be debunked.

"Of course I'm bisexual," she said. "We all are. This is the revolution. The women's movement has always had lesbians at its vanguard. Much of the running motor has been supplied by lesbians, even when they were in the closet. The lesbian is the archetypal feminist because she's not into men—she's the independent woman par excellence. The most important experience any woman, any feminist, can have is to love another woman."

Kate Millett was first called a lesbian at thirteen. For years, while struggling as a sculptor in New York and at the same time trying to earn a Ph.D. in literature, she lived in the gay subculture. "It was a very raunchy scene on the fringes of the art world. There was heavy role playing, and people looked upon you as lepers." In 1961, she met Fumio Yoshimura, a Japanese sculptor. While she had had affairs with men, "This was the first time I fell deeply in love with a person who happened to be male. Up to that point, tenderness and rapport were things I had only had with women." For eight years they lived together, and she felt no desire for relations with women. "Living with him was a wonderful relief. I could walk around without the leper bell." They got married when Fumio was threatened with deportation, she said, "but I kept my name."

During these years, Kate became involved in feminism. "I joined N.O.W. the first time I heard about it." She decided to write her Ph.D. thesis on "sexual politics." To test her ideas, she often traveled to New Haven and Boston to visit feminist theorists in those cities. She was at a party with women in New Haven, when the talk turned to experimenting with sensuality. The women were sprawled on a bed, "getting high on wine, caressing each other's hair, and there just grew such an understanding. I don't know at what point it happened, but almost accidentally, I slept with another woman."

A few days later, she went home, woke up Fumio and confessed: "This wild thing happened in New Haven. I slept with a woman." Kate recalled: "Fumio laughed and said, 'At least you won't get pregnant.' I thought, You sexist, you're not even threatened. Later, he was threatened, and it was very hard for us to work it all out."

Kate began to experience love again with women.

"During the years with Fumio," she said, "the lesbians around just weren't that tempting. Then when women in the movement started coming out, suddenly there were all these groovy people available. It wasn't the sad, desperate crew one met at the gay bars. It was different. We were friends, we loved and respected each other as equals. There was a great, high, utopian feeling at first. But then we came up against the same problems with each other that you have in any relationship: dominance-submission; how to deal with jealousy and insecurity; is it all right to just experience eroticism; how committed is each person?"

Many of the women felt ashamed. Kate said, "The media had always said we were dykes and suddenly by God we were becoming that. Part of the problem was that women get so close to each other it's really scary. There's always a marvelous, neutral, spacy meadow between a man and a woman, but with two women it's so close—you literally have the same body. Sometimes when you make love with a woman, you don't know if it's her body or yours."

In July 1970, when her thesis was published and became the best-selling book *Sexual Politics*, Kate Millett became a target in and out of the movement. Some feminists resented her lecturing and appearing on television, and suggested she should not have signed her book but published it anonymously, "so it would be from the whole women's movement." Kate said, "It was extremely traumatic. I felt guilty for ever having gotten my thesis together. I had to think a great deal about individualism and ego, and I concluded that it's vitally important for people to sign their work. That's my freedom—to express myself as an individual artist. That's what I want for everybody in the world."

She was under pressure from radical lesbians as well. An anonymous pamphlet was circulating accusing Kate of "exploiting lesbians on her media trip." In November, when she spoke at a forum on sexual liberation at Columbia, gay women in the audience asked her to state unequivocally whether she was a lesbian. Kate said, "What they did was very coercive. I was telling the truth when I said I was bisexual, because I'm in love with a man as well as women. But I said, if you want me to say I'm a lesbian I will, because I know you feel bisexuality is a cop-out."

The next morning, a reporter from *Time* was at her door. A few weeks later, *Time* printed a story stating that the disclosure of Kate's bisexuality cast doubt on all her theories, and was "bound to discredit her as a spokeswoman for her cause."

The women's movement in New York responded immediately. Representatives of every group held a joint press conference, declaring their solidarity with Kate and with the struggle for homosexual liberation. "It was the one time in the whole women's movement that we got everybody to agree on something, except Betty Friedan," Kate said. "Politically, it ended up being a wonderful thing. We showed the press they could not divide us by this tactic. But personally, it was a nightmare. I found I didn't have it together inside. I hadn't faced coming out in ninety-three languages before millions of readers. I hadn't settled things with my family or myself. I felt like I was standing on a platform, and suddenly this wind tore off all my clothes and multitudes were looking up at me and laughing."

It took her almost a year to "get my head straight." All the while, she was lecturing at universities and appearing on talk-shows, feeling frightened and isolated from her friends. "The most horrible thing was the loneliness, and being under the great glaring light of the camera. It's terribly complicated, because I knew I was reaching more people on television than I was with my book. But the price was intolerable."

She dropped out of the limelight in 1971, joined a gay women's consciousness-raising group, "and that saved me. I came back to the movement as a grassroots member, not a star." She began writing her autobiography on a farm in upstate New York, and when she visited the city, would stay with Fumio. "We both need more autonomy now. He's dedicated to his art, and doesn't want to know only feminists."

Periodically, Kate said, she grows disenchanted with the movement. "You always feel, hell, I'm losing the faith. You just have to give yourself a little space then. Go out to dinner and lose the faith a few nights. Doubt, doubt yourself, everything. If you let yourself doubt for a while, you may come up with what you really believe."

She said that after the wave of "bitching and savaging each other in the movement, I think we understand that people need air and freedom to develop. The revolution has to come from love, not hate. I want a society where we have goods, flowers, luxury, sexual ecstasy. It's something to work for, a better way to live."

It was 2 A.M. now, and as we walked down the Bowery, stepping over drunks, Kate gave me a pep talk about my own projects. Then, with a hug and a smile, she was gone, up the stairway to her loft, where she planned to stay up all night writing.

WHAT DO WOMEN WANT?

2.

A friend who has been active in the movement for years suggested I look up Marilyn Webb. "Marilyn's the clearest head I know of," she said. Marilyn worked in the student left before the women's movement, was married, tried bisexuality and now lives alone in the country. Her story is an illustration of what happened when women felt they were not getting all they needed from men, and turned to women in the hope of finding everything.

Marilyn and I spent an afternoon together in January. She is an open, easy person, with a mass of dark natural curls. Periodically, she would stop talking to put her face in her hands, or flop into a different position. She was wearing a navy sweater, red corduroy pants, aviator glasses and hiking boots, and because she had just given up smoking, held an unlit cigarette in her hand.

Marilyn said her first "feminist hit" came in 1965, at an S.D.S. conference at the University of Illinois. One of the papers circulated was written by women in the Student Non-violent Coordinating Committee, protesting their role in that organization. They said Stokely Carmichael, head of S.N.C.C., had been asked, "What is the proper position of women in the movement?" Carmichael had said: "Prone."

A large group of women attended a workshop to discuss the paper, but the men boycotted it as "counterrevolutionary." Left to themselves, the women talked about their grievances, but it was all considered "a little internal problem" of S.N.C.C. and S.D.S.

Marilyn was in graduate school at the time, and had

had experiences where professors feigned interest in her work to set up a situation where they could make sexual advances. "After reading that paper, it suddenly clicked that being a female grad student was different from being a male grad student. Before, I'd thought it was my fault that I wasn't treated with intellectual respect."

It was not until two years later, however, after she had married a radical leader, Lee Webb, and moved to Washington, that Marilyn began meeting with other women. "We did consciousness-raising, but it wasn't called that. We didn't use the term 'women's liberation.' We thought it was embarrassing to be called a women's group."

Marilyn and her friends soon learned that their "little problem" was being discussed by women in many parts of the country. In the spring of 1968, some of them gathered in Sandy Spring, Maryland, for a three-day marathon. Roxanne Dunbar and Dana Densmore, who had started Cell 16 in Boston, came bearing a copy of the S.C.U.M. (Society for Cutting up Men) manifesto by Valerie Solanas. Roxanne insisted on reading it aloud before discussion could continue. The issue which split the women was whether the enemy was capitalism or men. Marilyn took a position in the middle—but she was not to remain there for long.

In 1969, Marilyn and Shulamith Firestone, who was writing *The Dialectic of Sex,* were asked to speak for women's liberation at the counterinaugural staged during Nixon's Inauguration. When Marilyn took the microphone to address the crowd of ten thousand under a circus tent, she said, "I don't think I stammered more than two sentences, before fights broke out. I looked down and saw people hitting each other. They started yelling things like, 'Get her off the stage and fuck her!' and 'All women are good for is their cunts.'

"I was furious, grrrrr," Marilyn said. "It was a big shock for me—that movement men were no better than any others. That night I got a call from someone in S.D.S. who said, 'If you ever give a speech like that again, we will beat the shit out of you.' I stopped going to all S.D.S. meetings after that. I started organizing women alone."

In January of 1970, Marilyn and several friends founded a newspaper, *Off Our Backs*, to give women in Washington an independent voice. Marilyn was pregnant at the time. When her daughter, Jennifer, was born, her sisters taped a poster of the first issue opposite her hospital bed. She awoke from a cesarean operation and saw the newspaper and her baby— "Like the two greatest things in my life."

Three months later, she and Lee separated. Although he had not opposed her work, Marilyn said, "he didn't understand the enormity of it for me."

The newspaper was all absorbing. None of the women had had any experience in publishing, so they learned from scratch. Their ideal was to be a collective, with everybody doing everything, but from the outset, they could not fit the ideal into practice. "Everyone started from a different place, and that caused the trouble," Marilyn said. All the members tried to write something for every issue, but while it took Marilyn two days to knock off a piece, the others would struggle for weeks. They grew so frustrated that they asked her to stop writing and help them instead. "I agreed, but I felt very hostile. Our purpose was to create strong women, but it was being done at my expense."

To compensate, Marilyn gave speeches and acquired a reputation. When groups or colleges wanted someone to represent *Off Our Backs*, they asked for Marilyn. This led to scenes, tears, confrontations. "It was pretty gory." She was asked to stop speaking, and did in fact cut down on her appearances, "because I felt guilty. I'd helped create those values, and I believed the whole argument about collectivity. I still do. I just think we did it wrong."

The *Off* collective had other problems besides competition. Half the members started exploring homosexuality, which created such tension that the gay women split to found their own paper, *The Furies*. In August of 1970, Marilyn decided to accept a speaking invitation from the National Students' Association. She told the group, "I'm not going to be not speaking anymore, because I have things I want to say. If you want to speak, you should also." Shortly afterward, she was expelled from the collective. "They said I took up too much space."

I asked Marilyn why she didn't give up in disgust. She smiled. "Because I really believe in women. These things happen all the time with men. I get depressed to realize it happened with women. We just have to work harder. Besides, where was I going to go? Back to graduate school, where some pig professor could slobber on me?

She moved to Boston and lived in a commune for five months, and tried to work out her feelings about sex. While on the paper, she had slept with two women, "but it didn't really work. Politically, I wanted it to. I felt I was getting all my emotional support and love from women, but sex was something I went out and did with men.

"I wanted eroticism to be integrated with the people I loved in my everyday life. But I couldn't swing it with women. I would giggle. I mean, this was my *friend*, and her shoulders were so little. Some people told me it was because I'd been a cheerleader in high school. I was really upset, because I thought it would doom me forever to affairs.''

Most of the people in the Boston commune did not believe in monogamy and were having relationships with several people. "I was involved with a woman who had a lover, and with a man who was also involved with two other people. We struggled a lot, but I found having male and female affairs at the same time was not good. It was like two roles clashing. I finally decided I had to stabilize myself, fix a place of my own and pursue my own work.''

She moved to Vermont, where she set up a feminist-studies program at Goddard College. Both she and Lee began teaching there and could share caring for Jennifer. Marilyn bought a house, built a second story on it herself and began writing again.

The largest personal problem, Marilyn said, "is relations with men. I haven't been able, and I don't know anyone who has, to have a heterosexual relationship and still be independent. There's a point at which even the strongest women stop. Bit by bit, they relinquish their autonomy.''

She puffed on the unlit cigarette. "I'm doing all this independently—building a house, teaching, writing, learning survival. I just don't know how to fit sex in. If I could, it would be a completion.''

3.

Ti-Grace Atkinson has never operated in the mainstream of the women's movement. From the beginning, other feminists have seen her as extreme, a fanatic, even "sick." But her ideas and her presence have been a force. Dogged, relentless, she is always there, defining the outer edge.

When I interviewed her in her Manhattan apartment, Ti-Grace said she is used to "being alone ideologically. I've always been called crazy. If I wasn't, I would worry."

Ti-Grace joined N.O.W. in 1968. She was a graduate student in aesthetics, had grown up in Louisiana and had never been in a political group before. She became president of the New York chapter, but before a year was out she broke away and started her own group, The Feminists. Ti-Grace had attacked the N.O.W. leadership hierarchy because she felt women's liberation should create strong individuals, all capable of being leaders.

The Feminists took steps to create a situation of equality. The chairmanship was rotated. Tasks were assigned by lot. At meetings, women were given twenty chips and each time they spoke, they had to throw a chip in the pile. When their chips were gone, they couldn't talk anymore. "But there was still one little problem," Ti-Grace said. "How do you get people to be creative? To write, develop theory, conceive of actions? I found myself providing most of the ideas. I would write a paper, present it to the group and hammer it through. I was deceiving myself in thinking the ideas were coming from the group. You can't legislate initiative."

To deal with this problem, she set up a creative workshop where each woman would work on her own project. After a few meetings, the workshop changed into a class workshop. "They never defined what class meant, but they excluded me because they said I was upper class." At the same time, because she was lecturing and giving shocking quotes to reporters, Ti-Grace appeared in the media more frequently than all other members of The Feminists combined. "There was so much jealousy over this," she said. "I decided I should leave. Without me there, the group would have to face themselves."

The split was not bitter, Ti-Grace said. She kept in touch with The Feminists, and started work on a book, *Women and Oppression*, which she has yet to finish. Then, in the summer of 1970, she became intrigued by reports that Joseph Colombo, an alleged Mafia boss, was starting an Italian-American Civil Rights League. "I heard the League was organizing white working-class people. I told various leftist groups they should check it out, but nobody would go near it. They said, 'They're Mafia.' I said, 'Good! They've got some guts.'"

She stood up at this point to mix a "pep-up" drink. Her two Abyssinian cats, Simone and Ruthless, trotted after her. Ti-Grace said, "I'm on an Adelle Davis kick. We have a long fight ahead of us, and I'm getting my health back." She is tall, has very pale skin and wears her blond hair pulled back in a bun. She speaks softly, and tends to use pronouns like "they" and "it" without making clear what they refer to.

She talked about the first time she went to a League meeting: "I saw thousands of people who had very little education, people who are usually seen as hard hats and are ignored and spat upon by the left. They were ravenous for political talk and ideas. I ran back and told people, 'You gotta go out there.' A few women went and got upset because the Italian-American women had dyed hair. I said, 'That's where they are. Do you expect to find the working classes in the library, prepackaged by Marx? If you're interested in workers, you start where they are.' "

Ti-Grace decided the League represented "the only answer to Wallace." She checked into Colombo's background and became satisfied that he was not involved in prostitution or narcotics and was not a hawk on Vietnam. She began hanging out with him while he was picketing the FBI, and a most bizarre liaison began to develop. Ti-Grace had previously refused to appear in public with men. As she sat in coffee shops with Colombo, she thought, What am I doing here? I hate men. It's not my job to be here. But no one else is doing it, so I guess I'm going to have to act as the connection.

She said she "abused Colombo terribly." She called some of his acts "stupid," and told him, "I'm trying to overlook the fact that you're a man. Nobody's perfect." Colombo would tell her, "I don't try to boss you, why do you try to boss me?" Colombo started wearing a "Freedom for Women" button in his lapel, and Ti-Grace worked with League organizers on a case where a woman of Italian descent, Corky Willis, was protesting discrimination by a union. "When the League organizer and I walked in side by side, the union bosses just about fell over. They said, 'You're together?' "

In 1971, Colombo was shot and permanently incapacitated at a League rally. Ti-Grace was shaken. She declared to the press that Colombo was an "honorary woman." In August, she was invited to speak at a conference on "Violence in the Women's Movement," along with Gloria Steinem, Kate Millett, Robin Morgan and other feminist "heavies." The conference, held at P.S. 41, was closed to the press and men. When Ti-Grace got up to speak, she taped a blowup of Colombo, lying wounded on the street, in front of the podium. "That is violence," she said, adding that she was dedicating her remarks to "Sister Joseph Colombo."

She started reading a prepared speech, but women began booing and screaming insults. Several people who attended the conference said that Ti-Grace mumbled into the microphone and failed to get across her ideas about Colombo. Ti-Grace admitted, "I have never spoken 'well.' But when I put up the poster, people freaked out. At first I thought I must have it upside down. Women with hate on their faces were shouting, 'This has nothing to do with women. Take her off the stage if she won't shut up.' The people yelling loudest were the big champions of the working class. They were ready to do violence to me!

"I didn't finish the speech. I left. But I said, okay, I'm gonna remember this. I came home and for days just stared at the walls. I realized something terrible was happening. Women had been dumping on me as upper class. Now they were dumping on the working class. So I knew: they weren't here, they weren't there. Where were they? I realized we had nothing! I saw my sisters and I was repelled. They didn't care about the working class, that was just a gimmick to hit other women with. We got no movement. We got nothing but a bunch of big empty mouths."

She said the incident was a "terrible revelation. I had to sit down and rejudge everything, because lady, you've made some mistake." She stopped all speaking engagements, "because what could I say?" She turned much of her anger against herself. She decided her "mistake" was due partly to the influence of the pro-woman line. "The way I saw it, the pro-woman line meant: 'I do not have to examine myself at all. I am okay.' Well, if nothing is wrong with us, we don't have a chance. The problem is inside us too. Oppression isn't beautiful. Oppression is very profound, and the meaning of oppression is denial of individual identity. To have a revolution, you need strong individuals. Because they don't get you in a group. They get you one by one."

Although it had been two years since Colombo was shot, Ti-Grace said, "I still have trouble living privately with myself. I might have been able to prevent what happened to Colombo. If I had known what the women's movement and the left really were, I would have beat ass in the city, publicly denouncing people until they got over there."

Her voice grew hesitant and soft as a whisper. She said she felt remorseful "because I did nothing but abuse Colombo. There was somebody who as a revolutionary had terrific importance. He was under tremendous attack in his community, as I've always been in my movement. He had nobody but me. But because I made that distinction so sharply between men and women, I could not reach out with compassion to a man. I was saving myself for women, and then I saw what they were."

I asked if she felt sad. She nodded. "I don't know if I have the strength, the psychic energy, to do what has to be done. I don't know if change is possible and it literally breaks my heart. Because how many women have I gotten involved in something that's hopeless?" She picked up one of the cats. "C'mon, Ruthless, cheer us up." She sighed. "Sometimes I think Joseph is well out of it."

There was silence, broken only by the ticking of a

clock. "I guess I'm the leader of my own group," Ti-Grace said, her words coming slower and slower. "Women are the same. It was like Valerie Solanas, it was like everything . . . Nobody can be someone else's courage for them. I tried to be. You can't. How do you make people do that? I don't see . . . All of these evasion . . . How much can one person do . . . ?

4.

"The movement didn't defeat me," Susan Brownmiller said with a laugh. "I'd been around politics and was used to taking abuse. I had no illusions about groups. I knew the herd instinct operates against individuals and it was relatively easy to ride it out."

We were sitting in her apartment in Greenwich Village, just before midnight. Susan had spent the evening at Mother Courage, a restaurant run by and for feminists, where there had been rounds of wine to celebrate the Supreme Court decision on women's right to abortion.

Susan is thirty-eight, a journalist who enjoys planning political actions. She has brown eyes, short dark hair and an infectious laugh. Whenever I'd seen her on television or at meetings, I'd been struck by her ability to think fast and come back articulately, no matter how badly she was goaded.

When Susan joined the women's movement in 1968, she was writing news for television. She found it difficult at first to stay in women's groups. "At every meeting, people would say, 'Let's go around the room and talk about ourselves.' I think they invented consciousness-raising because they were obsessed with talking about themselves. One woman loved telling us about her lousy husband who was always cheating on her. That was not my style. I never talked personally or wrote personally. But my moment came."

One night at a meeting in Brooklyn, a girl began crying about a recent abortion. Susan started talking, she says, "out of competition. Here she was, wallowing in self-pity, and I'd had *three* abortions. As I talked, though, I cried. My best friend was in the room, and I realized I'd never mentioned any of it to her. I saw then that consciousness-raising was a valid technique for learning about women's experience."

Susan wrote an article about her c.r. group for the *New York Times Magazine,* an act for which she was denounced by other feminists. She thinks one of the reasons was that "every second woman in the movement wanted to be a writer. For most of them, it was a big mystery how you got published. They didn't know I'd been working at it for years."

Because of pressure in the movement, Susan turned down assignments for other magazines. She joined a group called Media Women, which came up with the idea of occupying the offices of *The Ladies' Home Journal* to protest the insipid content of the magazine. Susan took on the job of co-ordinator, and for three months did little else. She recruited Sally Kempton to help draw up an alternative magazine. They reconnoitered the office of the *Journal* editor, John Mack Carter, drew a map, set the date and alerted the press.

The action went off like a perfect movie caper. "It was the highlight of my life," Susan said. There were a hundred women in Carter's office and another hundred outside. They sang, shouted and read their article suggestions over and over. At midday, according to Susan's account, Shulie Firestone and Ti-Grace Atkinson demanded more militancy. "It got a little out of hand." Shulie, a small, wiry brunette, jumped on Carter's desk, cried, "We've had enough of this," and lunged for his throat. Carla Jay, who had been studying aikido, leaned over and flipped Shulie off the desk. "It was beautiful," Susan said. "She used Shulie's forward thrust to pitch her over the other side. It shook up Carter, though. He agreed to negotiate."

The agreement they reached was this: women's liberation would write an eight-page supplement and the *Journal* would pay them ten thousand dollars. Susan left feeling "heroic. It was the first money earned for the movement, and the first action to have immediate results." The next day, however, she knew she was in trouble when her name was the only one mentioned in news reports.

The following week, an underground paper called the *Rat* ran a story denouncing "the elitist Susan Brownmiller" for using the women's movement for personal gain. The *Rat* had been seized by women and renamed *LibeRATion*. It was later taken over by lesbian women, then by black lesbian women, then it went out of business. Susan called the author of the article and got "hysterical over the phone. I was so proud, I'd worked so hard and because of it hadn't earned any money for three months. What kind of personal gain was that?"

Around the same time, Susan appeared with Sally Kempton on "The Dick Cavett Show," where she tangled with Hugh Hefner. The segment was so successful that Cavett asked her back. But Susan was too spooked about elitism. "The movement was very important to me. If I'd done the Cavett show again, I would have been considered a star. So we arranged for two other women to go on, and *they* were promptly attacked in the *Rat*."

Susan was by now so embittered that she went into retreat on Fire Island for the summer. "I brooded, walked on the beach with my dog and took some hack assignments." When she returned to New York, still "wounded and shattered," she insisted on rejoining her c.r. group. Gradually her position in New York Radical Feminists grew stronger. "I think they admired my courage in sticking with it. Also, there came a time when the media had created real stars and I was not one of them. The elitist issue lost its steam. People realized personal recognition is important for everyone."

In 1971, Radical Feminists decided to hold a speakout on rape. Susan was appalled. "I thought they'd gone off the deep end. I'd never been raped, and I believed no woman could be raped against her will." After weeks of discussion, though, "I suddenly realized this movement had done it again. It occurred to me that rape was a conscious process of intimidation by which men keep all women in a state of fear. Rape is to women what lynching was to black men in the South. I formulated the phrase, 'Rape is a political crime against women.' It was the most exciting new idea that had ever entered my consciousness."

She started work on a book, which was to become the bestseller *Against Our Will*. Susan said this more than compensated for all the "guff" she had had to endure. "Feminism has been the most stimulating experience of my life. I've met great people. I've thought new thoughts. I've seen other people think new thoughts. And it's given me a book." She nodded vigorously. "It's given me rape."

Susan said she believes all advancements in the human condition grow out of movements. "I've studied political history long enough to know that new ideas are the product of groups of people who put their heads together and dare to conceptualize in new ways. People don't accomplish this sitting alone in vacuums."

She said the concept of organized movement is "the highest human value in the world, even though when it gets down to individuals, movements can be brutal.

"I've always been a movement person and will be until I die. At the same time I'm always a journalist, watching and observing. That's incompatible, but it's simply me." She smiled. "I've lived long enough to be able to accept that duality."

It was 3 A.M. when Susan finished stating, in a tone of certainty, why she believes in movements. She asked me to tell her some of the ideas of other women I'd interviewed. I said I had talked with Sally Kempton, who had become a disciple of the Hindu guru, Swami Muktananda. "Sally believes her involvement in feminism was personal, not political. Feminism was an attempt to solve her problems by blaming external conditions. I think Sally would say, now, that advancements in human evolution come about through individuals becoming more conscious."

Susan began to fidget. "I'm getting a terrible feeling. I'm saying I believe in movements, and Sally believes in individuals. I can see it appearing as if we're locked in separate boxes, obsessed with our own visions."

I had found Susan's argument about movements plausible. Why was she doubting it?

She laughed, and ran her hands through her hair. "It is three in the morning, after all."

There is a Zen koan about two monks who, on a windy day, were arguing about a flapping banner:

The first said, "I say the banner is moving, not the wind."

The second said, "I say the wind is moving, not the banner."

A third monk passed and said: "The wind is not moving. The banner is not moving. Your minds are moving."

1973

WHAT AM I
DOING HERE?

It is May in the Mojave Desert of California and I am
sitting by a pool with my ex-husband. We hear on
Radio K-DES that twenty Vietnamese refugees are
touring Palm Springs. In the bone-dry, noiseless, 102-
degree heat, in which no one ventures out except a
few elderly ladies wearing white socks and white sun-
bonnets, the Vietnamese will visit the Desert Museum
and see "Up with People" at the local high school.

"What are they doing here?" my husband says.
"It's ludicrous."

What am I doing here? It is 1975 and nobody is in
the right place. I am with a man I have not lived with
for three years, during which time I have moved
across the continent and he has fallen in love with
another woman, and yet we have not been able to let
go.

In the early evening we soak in the outdoor therapy
pool. A computer engineer in plaid trunks emerges
from behind the tamarisk trees and clunks cheerfully
into the hot water.

"How long you here for?" the engineer asks.

"Three weeks," my husband says.

"No kiddin'. What do you do here all that time?" He nods in my direction. "I argue with her."

There was a time, and not very long ago, when I could not bear to read a copy of *Ms*. I was obsessed with the notion that I had ruined my life by walking away from a marriage after five years. I had sailed without regrets, left everything behind, opened my lips to the new, to life, to liberation, and eight months later I was paralyzed with fear. I missed my husband, I even missed the routines that had made our life together seem stifling and impossible. I went to a dinner party, a reunion of friends from college, and found I was the only single person there. They had their families and marital tensions and I had my career, my own space, my own house. How hollow it was. I had possessed something special and thrown it away, and I believed I would not have another chance.

So I hated the Women's Movement, knowing in my heart that blaming the Movement or *Ms*. for my troubles was just as silly as blaming men or my mother or The Society. But feminism encouraged women to shed their skins and strike out on their own.

"I'm through being liberated," I told my friend Ron, who has a standing joke about "feminist thugs." "I'm needy, possessive and jealous, and I want to live with one man and have kids." He laughed gleefully and changed the subject, but the next morning he called. "I just wanted to tell you," he said, "I've been thinking that I'd like to get married myself and have kids in the next few years."

I am house-sitting for a friend in the Hollywood Hills. Every time I go to my car, there is a black and silver motorcycle parked alongside it. On the day I

348

move out, I walk to the car and meet the owner of the bike. His name is Tommy. He has tousled brown hair and the hard, straight-spined, supple body of a dancer. Underneath his Levi's and motorcycle boots he is wearing leotards for his evening class.

He offers me a ride and a week later we are lovers. He is six years younger than I am. In our first talk on the street, he tells me straight off that he is living with Laura, but things are confused. Laura is traveling in Europe for six weeks. Laura wants to get married and have children. Tommy wants to get married but can't deal with children. So Laura has told him to move out, she's looking for a husband, but if Tommy gets his life together before she finds a husband . . .

Tommy and I agree that we've picked each other because we're safe. He's too young and too small to be my mate, but he is honest, supportive, strong-willed yet soft, and I'm enchanted by his capacity to be startled and excited. We go camping in the desert and by the time Laura returns, things aren't safe anymore.

He tells Laura about me and she wants him back. She cries, she makes ultimatums. On an impulse, I call her up and go to visit her. We sit in her kitchen drinking tea. My voice is soft and shaky but hers is even softer. "I just wanted you to know," I fumble for words. "I don't want Tommy for a mate. He loves you and wants to make a life with you."

Her lips are set tightly. "I'm sorry," she says, "but I feel strongly about this. If he sleeps with you, Tommy and I are through." She tells me that sex is special to her, she wants a man who's mature enough to commit himself to her, to be faithful, "not because it's moral but because it works." I find myself agreeing. She says, "I've spent five years with Tommy, and I want to settle down and have kids. I want monogamy.''

She pours more tea. Her face has softened. We talk of other things—books, movies, *Scenes from a Marriage,* succulent plants—and I am warming to her. I want her to be happy.

Suddenly she asks, ''What do you want from Tommy?''

I feel myself blush. ''Truthfully? I've enjoyed the . . . relationship we've had, and I wouldn't like to have to give it up.''

Laura says, ''I wouldn't ask that of you, it's not my place.''

I tell her how I've been working on a book, a lonely, difficult project, and how important it is for me to have someone I care about that I can sleep with now and then. She understands. She wishes I could have what I want, but we are at cross-purposes.

As I leave we hug each other. ''I'm glad you called,'' she says. ''I feel relieved.''

Laura gives Tommy permission to see me from time to time. Tommy and I make a date for Sunday, but when Sunday arrives, Tommy's head is filled with Laura and I'm distracted by a recent call from my husband.

Oh, Lord, for a year I've been saying I don't want open relationships or multiple relationships, and yet I've created them again and again. Within the past month I've been involved in three triangles. With Tommy and Laura, I'm the new woman with less to lose. With my husband and his new woman, Rachelle, I'm the old mate who has the power of time on her side. I have also had an affair with two brothers. When the three of us spent the night together, they both slept deeply and had beautiful dreams while I, in the middle, had diarrhea and insomnia. "I'm not cut out for this," I told myself. "I'm a bourgeois Jewish girl."

So it is Sunday, and Tommy and I drive to Malibu for a party. The woman who is giving the party, Sharon, is now seeing Jerry, one of the brothers. But Jerry hasn't arrived yet, and Sharon introduces me to her ex-husband, Steve. "I just met your ex," Steve says.

I assume he means Jerry.

No, he means my husband.

"Oh, my original ex," I say. "How did that happen? He lives in New York."

"Right. I was just in New York. I went to visit an old lover of mine, Rachelle, and it turns out . . ."

"Oh, God, no," I say. Carly Simon begins to sing "Attitude Dancing" and everyone jumps up to dance the bump. I weave outside and crumple up in the sand. Tommy walks over quietly and puts his arms around me.

"Why are you crying?" he says.

"Because it's so confusing."

My younger sister Terry and her boyfriend Gary are getting married in Honolulu. Gary is the captain of a sport-fishing boat. He leaves the house at 5 A.M. and when he comes home at sundown, goes straight to the kitchen to cook up the mahimahi or aku he has caught that day. When Terry feels blue, he plays the ukulele, makes her laugh, or buys her a chartreuse parrot. "We're like two peas in a pod," she tells me, and when I visit them for a week, I see that she is right.

They plan a wedding at sea. Captain Choy will marry them, and their friends who have boats will form a flotilla. Around their necks they will wear the traditional Hawaiian wedding lei, made of fragrant green maile leaves.

But when I call Terry to congratulate her, her voice trembles. "I'm scared," she says, and breaks down. "All the other couples we know are splitting up. They keep saying, 'Why get married? Why ruin a good thing?' "

I fly to New York to ship my books to California. I let myself into the apartment where, for five years, I lived, slept, ate, worked, made love, cried, was sick and was high, and find there is not a trace of me remaining. On the bulletin board are pictures of Rachelle. The place looks shabby, gone to seed.

I meet my husband at a bar and we order champagne. He has an earache, a split lip and is suffering from hay fever. "I'm a sick man," he jokes. "Seeing you makes me tense."

As we have drifted back and forth like sea anemones, there have been new insights, revelations and greater intimacy. He opens toward me and I feel hope, perhaps it could work, then abruptly he withdraws and I flutter with rage. Hope-rage, that is the axis, the track on which I'm stuck.

After we finish the champagne, I tell him that I need money. He makes fifty thousand dollars a year and I'm having trouble paying the rent. When we married, I was earning more than he was and helped pay his debts. I would like him to help me out now.

He agrees. "But what about Women's Liberation?" he asks halfheartedly.

"Fuck Women's Liberation."

I visit a commune in northern California. Joe, a

bare-chested blond of twenty-four whom I've just met, is showing me the organic garden. We sit on the grass in the afternoon sun. "I have an idea," he says with a farm boy smile. "Let's tell each other exactly what we like done to us sexually, and then let's do it."

They're good at this, young ones. When they're older, it isn't as easy.

Take Jeffrey. We have known each other for several weeks, and when we speak there is a nervous pulse in my throat. We are the same age. I like what's on his mind. I like the way he looks. He seems available. I'm waiting for something to go wrong.

We make love for hours and I cannot come. The next time we meet, I tell him, with pauses and a voice barely audible, what might make it easier for me. Now he cannot stay hard.

"Christ, I don't believe it," he says. "For years I've wanted a woman to do what you've done. I've asked them to tell me what they like, but they haven't, and now I know why. I feel threatened, like I'm being asked to perform."

Jeffrey says that in his sexual fantasies, "there's always an element of conquest and domination." I tell him I have fantasies of being ravished. I like to be called "baby," I like being ordered: On your back, woman, spread your legs.

"And then when that's over," I tell him, "I like to come."

I often feel these days that I'm singing the reverse of what Rex Harrison sang in *My Fair Lady*. Why can't a man be more like a woman? I want men to be close to their feelings, intuitive, gentle, vulnerable and compassionate. I have known a few men who have been this way. There was only one problem. Sex with them was lousy.

"I don't think I should have to pay for your company," Jeffrey broods when the check arrives at Kenny's Delicatessen. "I mean, I like the feeling of paying for you, but I don't think I ought to."

He exasperates me, thinking he ought to feel this way or that. And I hate this business of splitting all the bills. "If I make dinner for you, I'm not going to ask you to pay for your share of the asparagus," I say. "Women as a class have far less money than men as a class. It's not fair to divide the financial burden fifty-fifty."

But these are rationalizations. I'm aware that I want the best of both worlds, and I'm aware that it's a luxury to spend this much thought on relationships.

A week before my divorce is set to be finalized, I walk home from the beach with a girlfriend and, to my shock, my husband is standing on my doorstep. "I give up," he says, arms hanging at his sides. "If you'll have me, I'm yours."

Without warning he has flown across the country on what we will later refer to as "Whim Airlines." I send my girlfriend home, take a shower and put on a long terry-cloth robe. I feel flattered, elated, wary, unusually pretty and confused.

"Do you laugh easier these days?" he asks. "You don't seem as down as when we lived together." Later he says with puzzlement, "Are your breasts larger?"

"No," I say, laughing.

"Yes, they are, they're enormous, they've grown." But they haven't. He has become accustomed to Rachelle, and he has forgotten.

WHAT DO WOMEN WANT?

After he has been in my house for twenty-four hours, I feel so heavyhearted I have difficulty crossing the room. All these months I've been obsessing about what I threw away. Suddenly he is back, and I remember what was so draining: his ambivalence, his rage, his insatiable need to get *his*. I cannot write or work; my head is a muddle.

"Why do you have to show up now. Just when I was beginning to get over it?"

He walks over and takes me by the shoulders. "Sara, I'm here because of you, too."

Tommy has broken up with Laura and taken his own apartment. I call him late at night from a pay phone in Hollywood. I cannot stop crying. I feel cut off from everyone. Tommy picks me up on his bike and drives me home.

"It's not true that you're completely alone," he says. "I love you. I can't say I want us to spend all our waking hours together, but we're connected, we're part of each other's lives."

The next morning, he is standing in my kitchen, washing dishes, when my mother drops by with a gift of a toaster she has purchased at a garage sale.

There was a time when my mother did not want to know certain things. But lately she has been studying Transactional Analysis and participating in a women's rap group. When Tommy leaves, she settles herself on the couch. "So? Tell me, what do you think of these young boys?"

I have to laugh. "It's not exactly what I want, but you can't always get what you want."

"That's true!" Her eyes light up with this perception. She has never heard the Rolling Stones.

*   *   *

It is May in the desert and the Vietnamese refugees drive deep into the Coachella Valley, to Mecca, where they have double-decker burgers and date milk shakes.

My husband and I sit beside the hot therapy pool. "I love you. I'll love you all my life," he says.

The next line is mine: "And I don't want to live with you."

We have a farewell dinner at Don the Beachcomber's. He orders two Zombies, his eyes are heavy. The waitress, a deeply suntanned blonde who is wearing dewy pink lipstick and dewy blue eye shadow, places the iced glasses on the table. My husband watches her walk away. "I hate women," he says. "No, I don't hate them. I just don't understand my relationship to them at all."

He looks sleepy. "What do you think will happen? I want to know what will happen."

"We never know."

He laughs, a wonderful, deep laugh, and slings his arm around my shoulders. "That's right. We sent a reporter up to God, but he said, 'No comment.' He doesn't give interviews."

1975

THE WEDDING DRESS

Danielle Laurent was about to be married, at the age of thirty-three. "Is this your first marriage?" people asked, as she drove around Jerusalem on her motor scooter, ordering flowers and cakes.

"Yes."

"Mazel tov!"

Danielle was a French Jew, raised in Paris, but for seven years she had been living in Jerusalem, teaching literature at the Hebrew University. Her fiancé was a professor of physics, thirty-six, also new to marriage. A week before the wedding, Danielle invited friends to come to the home of her aunt, Simone, to spend the evening sewing the wedding dress.

I happened to be visiting Jerusalem and was invited. "Please, make an effort," Danielle had said. "I need you."

Simone's small house in Abu Tor, overlooking King David's Tower, was filled with women, professional women, ranging from twenty-six to thirty-five. Four were American, one was Spanish, one was Romanian, two were French and three were native Israelis. None was legally married at the time, except Simone.

At seventy, Simone is still a beauty, tall and erect,

wearing her gray hair in a chignon. Simone has had two lengthy marriages, raised four children and enjoyed a career as a concert violinist. She lived in a villa outside Paris until her first husband died, at forty-two. Her children were away at school by then, so Simone, long a Zionist, immigrated to Israel, where she fell in love with her current husband, Moshe.

"I am someone who has lived by love, in love, all my life," she told me as she sat on the couch, her feet propped on pillows. "I have to be an example to the girls."

It had been Simone's idea to have the young women sew Danielle's dress by hand, from fabric Simone had bought in India: white silk, with delicate gold embroidery. As we came in, she made us wash our hands and cover our laps with sheets, so the fabric would not be soiled.

It was peaceful, sewing together, keeping a watchful circle around Danielle. But there was also a feeling of irony and self-mocking: we were not girls of sixteen, believing in the dress as a passport to the golden land.

Simone asked that we go around the circle and take turns telling stories and legends. Danielle, who was first, shook her head no. Her long dark hair covered her eyes as she bent over her sewing. For years, Danielle had been telling herself that what she wanted more than anything was to have a partner, a "permanent ally," and a house full of children. All through her twenties, she had given priority to her work, and assumed she would never have the patience to care for infants. But around the time she turned thirty, it became painful to walk past a children's store. She began to long, to ache for someone to share life with. For thirteen years she had been a waif, fend-ing for herself and traveling across three continents; now that was to change. But could she adjust? Would the love she felt abide?

"Sara, you must provide us with a story," Simone said. For a moment, I could think of nothing that seemed appropriate; then I remembered an Arthurian legend I had heard from a friend, Winifred Rosen, who was adapting the tale for a children's book.

I began to relate the story, as best I could, from memory. "In the time of King Arthur and the Round Table, the King was out riding in the forest when he was surprised by a strange knight in full battle dress. The knight drew his sword, but the King said, 'Wait. I'm not armed, you can't do this, it would violate our honor code.' So the knight, whose name was Sir Gromer Somer Joure, had to relent. He made the King promise that he would return to the same spot, alone and unarmed, one year later. The King's life would be spared only if he brought back the answer to this riddle: What do women want, more than anything?"

Danielle interrupted the story. "That's what Freud is supposed to have asked. 'What do women want, dear God?'" Simone laughed. "The question did not originate with Freud. It recurs through the ages." She turned to me. "What did King Arthur do?"

"He rode back to the palace and met his nephew, Sir Gawain, who was, you know, the most beautiful and perfect knight in all the kingdom. He told Sir Gawain his plight, and Sir Gawain said, 'Don't worry, I'll ride in one direction, you'll ride in the other, and we'll ask every man and woman we meet, what do women want?'

"So the two of them rode off, and for a year, they asked every person, high and low, wise and simple, what do women want? They were given hundreds of answers."

I stopped to ask the women in Simone's sitting room, "How would you answer if you had to, 'What do women want more than anything?' "

They paused in their stitching.

"Love."

"A child."

"Respect."

"To be worshiped."

The Romanian lady said, "I think women want to be men."

Simone smiled, as if she knew none of the above would have saved the King.

I continued: "At the end of the year, Sir Gawain and the King each had a book full of answers. But King Arthur knew he did not have the right answer, and he was prepared to meet his fate, when he saw a woman approaching. This woman was the ugliest hag in creation. She was fat and wrinkled; she had a big nose with snot dripping and hairs sprouting from her face. She gave off a terrible odor. Her teeth were like tusks. She had warts and pus oozing from her eyes. Her name was Dame Ragnell. She rode straight up to the King and said, 'Sir, I alone have the answer that will save you. I'll tell you on one condition: that you give me Sir Gawain as my husband.'

"The King was horrified. 'I can't give you Sir Gawain.' He would rather have died than commit his nephew to such a fate. But Sir Gawain insisted he would marry the hag, gladly, if it would save the King's life.

"So King Arthur accepted the terms. 'Now, tell me, what do women want more than anything?'

"Dame Ragnell said, 'Sovereignty.' "

I paused in my story. We looked at each other, silently, covered with yards of white silk. Everyone seemed to sense instantly how satisfying the answer was.

"When King Arthur returned to meet Sir Gromer Somer Joure, he told him the answer, and his life *was* spared. Overjoyed, he rode back to the palace, but he found Dame Ragnell waiting to be married. And she wanted a grand wedding, with all the royal court. After the ceremony, Dame Ragnell gave a little tug at Sir Gawain's sleeve and croaked, 'My lord, I'm your wife now, you have certain duties . . .' "

There were groans in the room.

"Sir Gawain could barely bring himself to look at her hairy snout, but he was bound by honor. He screwed up his courage, shut his eyes and turned to kiss her, and as he did, she was transformed into the most beautiful, delicate, sensuous creature he had ever dreamed of seeing. They spent the night making love, and as the sun was rising, Dame Ragnell said, 'My beauty will not hold all the time, so you must make a choice. Either have me beautiful by day, when the world can see, and ugly at night; or ugly by day and beautiful in your bed.' "

I said to the women, "Which would you choose, if you were Gawain?"

The Spanish woman said, "Beautiful by day." But she was quickly outvoted. Danielle said, "If he was a wise man, he would have her beautiful for him alone." Simone abstained, and asked me to continue.

"What Sir Gawain said was this: 'My lady, I leave it up to you.' And at that, she became beautiful all the time."

Cheers broke out; cakes were passed around. Danielle clapped her hands. "He was a very wise man."

Simone, quieting the group, said, "You know, sovereignty is not a problem when you rule alone in your kingdom, but when two sovereign people want to merge their domains . . ." She looked pointedly at her niece. "Ah, that is the riddle you have yet to answer."

1979